A Thousan Sleepless

A collection of tales from forty years in schools

By

Paul Henderson

Copyright © 2017 Paul Henderson

ISBN: 978-0-244-94956-3

All rights reserved, including the right to reproduce this book, or portions thereof in any form. No part of this text may be reproduced, transmitted, downloaded, decompiled, reverse engineered, or stored, in any form or introduced into any information storage and retrieval system, in any form or by any means, whether electronic or mechanical without the express written permission of the author.

Table of contents

Foreword
Part I – The Early Years, Norwich et al

1. Why….?   P.8

2. Echoes from Ancient Greece   P.13

3. Gettoni and Gelati – Italy   P.35

4. Turkish Delight, French Toast and "Jerusalem" P.52

5. Journey to the Underworld and back – Egypt   P.72

6. From "Mr Angry" to "Prince of Darkness"   P.90

7. Sports Tours – Holland, Canada and Greece   P.107

8. Close Encounters of the Third Man Kind   P.120

   Chronology I

Part II – The Eltham Years

9. Headship   P.138

10. *One thousand and one sleepless nights*

11. *The Dream*   P.152

12. Inspiration – Divine or otherwise   P.162

13. The Pilgrimage – China	P.176
14. *Always pay due reverence to the Gods*	P.188
15. The Fairy Godmothers – Tanzania	P.199
16. *The Grand Vizier*	P.215
17. Adventures in the Small Screen World	P.118
18. *The Hunchback*	P.232
19. A Tropical Adventure – Borneo	P.240
20. *The Poisoned Dwarf*	P.264
21. A Celebratory Year – 2012	P.272
22. *The Hobbit*	P.288
23. Large enough to excel, small enough to…	P.298
24. *The Genie*	P.309
25. Epilogue: The Black Hole	P.324

Chronology II

Foreword

Retirement gives you plenty of time to reflect on what you have done with your life and to decide on whether you have made a difference. However, writing an autobiography seems rather presumptuous and arrogant: my life has been full, but was it any different from many others? After all, I cannot claim to be a top academic: one should not be fooled by a degree in Classics – and many people are – it was a very modest degree from a good, but not outstanding, university. I have been a good club cricketer qualifying as a playing member of the MCC, but I cannot claim much more on the sporting front. I remain an enthusiastic amateur choral singer, and this has provided me with many opportunities to sing extraordinary works over the years, but I am a good "follower" rather than a leader, wishing I was a better sight-reader! So, what is there worth writing down for others to read?

Well, I feel privileged to have worked in schools: I have experienced a wealth of adventure within them. I had always wanted to work in education, having really enjoyed my own time at school: there seemed to be so many areas of interest and activity, and once I realized how rewarding it was to pass on one's knowledge and open the doors to opportunity and understanding for others, there was no alternative career. And that was before I realised how many opportunities my teaching career would give me to travel!

One might imagine that my memories will therefore focus mainly on experiences with children. That is probably right, although the sleepless nights that I still have relate far more to the problems associated with adults – teachers, parents, governors, inspectors. For the most part, the children have been a great source of joy and pride. Given the right encouragement, they have aspired to great things. Getting the critical mass moving in the right direction is crucial, and once this can be achieved, the rest will want to follow. Most children achieve success and handle failure in equal measure, and they can then pass on into the wider world with confidence and open eyes.

There have been so many joyful moments – ranging from the excitement of our early Classics Evenings at Norwich School to inventing the Board Game "Fuga" with Tim, which brought some fun into learning Latin; singing in Colin's twenty-four hour Singathon, and performing (the clown) on the stage with colleagues at all three schools, but particularly at St Albans in the "CWAC Cabaret" alongside one current star on Doctor Who; the Norwich U17 team reaching the national semi-finals of the Barclays Cricket Cup; members of the Eltham 1st XV singing and dancing in the School Musical, to the Eltham Trebles singing Mahler 8 in St Paul's Cathedral with the London Symphony Orchestra; the excellent quality and spirit of school sport played at every school, and specifically the successful introduction of hockey as a major sport at Eltham; improving academic standards, but getting staff and parents to recognise that securing a place at a "good university" does not have to mean "Oxbridge"; the outreach work in both the local community around Mottingham and abroad, especially in Tanzania; the construction and opening of an Art Gallery, and the uplifting experience of the fireworks finale at the ECCO Pops open-air concerts – I still cherish all these amazing moments; but I continue to have sleepless nights.

During the forty years I have spent in schools, it would be inevitable to have experienced the tragedy of loss. As King Priam realized when he was faced with the death of his son, Hector, one of the worst experiences for any parent is to have to bury their dead child. I have witnessed five families shattered by this experience and have seen how whole schools can be shaken by the loss of a pupil. I do not wish to tell the tales of Ben, Tim, Simon, Alex and Jack, but I feel it is appropriate here to honour their memories. Two died from unforeseen illness, two in tragic road accidents when everyone had seemingly done the right thing, and one experienced that sense of inadequacy that led him to consider taking his own life – no-one believed that he wanted to die but his actions most tragically led to his death. Five young lives snuffed out, and five families stricken with grief, which never goes away: the greatest hope is that you learn to cope with the loss better. I often wonder how those five lives would have flourished and how they would have gone on alongside their peers to make the most of their lives. However, they should know the impact their loss has on the community they left: there is a coming together, a feeling – particularly in a Christian community - that we can help each other deal in this by sharing the suffering. A strength emerges that is unexpected, and it should be acknowledged. A striking example of the community coming together to support grief an suffering occurred when I was at St Albans School: the father of one boy, Josh, had been given a blood transfusion in Canada with HIV-infected blood, and as a result the father, his wife and their daughter, conceived after the transfusion, were all overwhelmed with Aids. This left Josh - he set up a charity called Children With Aids Charity with the help and support of his friends at school. The "CWAC Cabaret" became an annual event raising thousands of pounds to help children like Josh, who were affected directly or indirectly by Aids. His determination to survive and the way the school community rallied around him was both unforgettable and very humbling.

I started collecting my memories some time ago, and I soon realised that they would be more interesting as individual stories or episodes. I hope that this makes them all the more readable, and it probably explains the large number of stories linked to trips I have led or been on (see the Chronology at the end of the book) – they tend to have a natural beginning, middle and end. It should also become apparent that many of the chapters are an amalgamation of events collected over a series of trips: which explains why in these accounts our son, Jozef seems to have been born before our daughter, Holly: which is definitely the wrong way round! I have also transferred one episode (a fall down some wet stairs) from a (language!) trip to Mexico into an expedition to Borneo – it just seemed to fit better there. To follow Eric Morecambe's philosophy, all the episodes I write about actually happened, but they appear not necessarily in the right order. To document the years as a Headmaster I have tried to continue with this structure, relating the events within the form of episodic stories. Inevitably I found it uncomfortable to relate some of the events surrounding particular personalities; so a number of those stories have been translated into an imaginary world discovered through "One Thousand and One Sleepless Nights"..

The idea of "One Thousand and One Sleepless Nights" came from an incident at the end of my first year as Head. I was asked by one of my mentors to deliver to fellow Heads an account of a problem that I had had to face in my first year as Head: I presented this in the form of a mythical story disguising the principal characters in a fantasy world. From then on I was nicknamed the 'Sultan of South-East London' by one distinguished colleague! So as I considered how to present my fourteen years at Eltham College, it felt appropriate to retell some of the tales in a similar fashion: a series of tales from an imaginary world. The episodes all had a real trigger in fact, but I must emphasise that the way the tales developed owe more to my imagination than to anything which corresponds to actual fact. Indeed there is a greater comfort in having them cloaked in a world of 'costume and drama' that encouraged my imagination to fly, and perhaps for my brain to conceal any offence that may be caused. I confess to have enjoyed recreating these events in this guise, and I apologise if sometimes they seem both contrived and unnatural. I once read somewhere that "Independent Schools are the breeding grounds of surrealism": I hope that these stories are not too surreal because of the manner in which I have dressed them! These seven tales form alternative chapters in the second half of the book.

I suppose that the episodic nature of my memories has meant that large sections of my life have been omitted – my family, my friends and colleagues, the Governors and the former pupils particularly of St Albans and then Eltham College, have all played a huge part in my life, but they hardly feature within this collection of memories. I wish to acknowledge how important they have all been in my life and career, and I hope that they will realise why they play a limited role in these stories. I am deeply grateful to Viv and Ian (The Leys School), Geoff and Linda (Ipswich School), Tim and Dot, Claire and Martin (all 4 from Norfolk), none of whom feature greatly in these tales, if at all, but all of whom have played a huge part in supporting Maryta and me throughout our years at different schools. In addition, I owe a great deal to Geoff (Adelaide), Chris (Norwich) and Andrew (St Albans), three excellent Heads for whom I worked, and Robert (St Albans) and the two Davids (Eltham) who were hugely supportive Chairs of Governors; at Eltham I am grateful to the Senior Team, particularly Simon, Les, Edmund, and John, as well as Lorraine, my PA. I count all as good friends who have helped and guided me through many difficult situations.

Finally, and most importantly, my family – Maryta, Holly and Jozef – have all had to put up with my commitment and enthusiasm for life at these schools, which kept them in second place. I wish to dedicate these stories to them, as an apology for my apparent lack of interest in them and as an explanation for my passion for school life.

My gratitude goes to Tim and Holly for their advice on the construction of the text and to Mark for his proof-reading skills.

Part I – The early years, Norwich et al

At midnight my thoughts went out
To the dark reaches of space; no shining thought
Brought me comfort at midnight
Friedrich Rückert (Trans. Richard Stokes)

1 – Why...?

Why did I end up being a teacher? I completed the obligatory Careers Questionnaire at school, and it indicated that I should be an architect because of my strong sense of "special awareness"! But my Housemaster, "Tex", dismissed this with his broad Scottish drawl, saying "Ach, we all know that you're going to be a teacher, laddie! So I shall cross this nonsense out." My parents – well, my mother actually – wanted me to be a solicitor. She obviously thought that the Law had more social status than education, and being a parvenu herself, rising from being a butcher's daughter to being the GP's wife, she had an appreciation of status. To appease her I spent a very boring two weeks at the Law Firm of a family friend in Darlington – divorces and house conveyancing was not exciting!

In a Gap Year (before they were properly invented), I spent one term at my old Prep School in Sunderland, teaching some Latin, coaching rugby and helping produce *The Royal Hunt of the Sun* with another Student Teacher. Then from January to September, I flew to Australia to take up a temporary post as a House Tutor in one of the Boarding Houses at Prince Alfred College, Adelaide (PAC). A former teacher of mine at The Leys School in Cambridge had just taken up the appointment of Head at PAC, and he came from Sunderland – so we had a common bond. Coaching (and playing) cricket and rugby, teaching English (in a foreign language!), and accompanying camping trips into the outback, still left me time to play golf once or twice a month with the Head while he off-loaded his problems away from school to someone without any agenda. If I had a mentor, Geoff Bean, would be at the top of the list. He used to stand outside the College (Methodist) Chapel on

Sundays, and greet all the boys by name – I know that my Head at the Leys could not have done this, and it was a clear indication that Geoff not only knew but wanted to know all his pupils! To me, that seemed very important.

At University, only one other fellow Classicist (and there were 16 in my year at Nottingham) considered teaching. My application to the BBC to become a producer went nowhere, because they were apparently cutting back on their own production work? So, the easiest option seemed to apply for a PGCE. Doing it at Cambridge, pleased my mother, and gave me a good insight into the philosophy behind the Cambridge Latin Course, since our Tutor was one of the designers – we all thought that she did this job because she would have been a poor teacher! Applying for jobs came in the Spring and I had my first bit of luck in this process: one of my fellow students had applied in December, but been rejected by Colchester Royal Grammar School (CRGS), who were looking for someone to teach Latin and German. By March, they had changed their minds and were looking for a straight Classicist, able to teach Latin Greek, Ancient History and possibly Classical Civilisation, a new course recently designed by the retiring Head of Department. My other interests, particularly sport, suited CRGS and I took up my post as teacher and House Tutor in a small Boarding House in September 1977.

I suppose if I analyse why I went into teaching, I would have to confess that self-interest played a big part – it enabled me to maintain my fascination with the Classical World while also allowing me to keep active in sport and music. CRGS was a great place to start my full-time teaching career with the strength of the Classics Department enabling me to learn from the best, including the new course in Classical Civilisation. In addition I became heavily involved in coaching cricket both in school and for North-East Essex, as well as rugby. What of course I had already learnt during my Gap year was that I enjoyed working with children and passing on my enthusiasm and knowledge to them: it seemed to work as well!

The next stroke of luck came during the second half of my second year at Colchester. I applied for the post of Head of Classics at Norwich School. What I did not know was the man leaving Norwich had been Master i/c Cricket, and although they had interviewed other candidates, by May they had not found anyone suitable to fill both roles – until my application landed on the Head's desk. I was interviewed more by the Deputy than the Head, and he wanted to know that I could cope with the Classics, but suggested that I could secure the job because of the Cricket!

So, why did I want to be Head of Classics? I suppose I had discovered that I enjoyed trying out new ideas, and even though my subjects were some of the oldest and potentially most traditional, there was always room for a new approach. Taking charge of a department seemed a natural step forward, and I hoped to be able to make the subjects I had enjoyed at school come alive even more for the pupils at Norwich. The added attraction of being in charge of cricket meant that I had found the best step-up possible. I suppose my ambition to take charge has been with me since school days, and being in control should ensure it was easier to make a difference. But, of course, with this responsibility came greater demands and almost inevitably sleepless nights.

That came later, but on my interview day the cherry blossom was in full bloom in the Cathedral Close and I knew that my luck was in. I also knew that I had one more thing to do – ask Maryta to marry me and join me in Norwich. So it happened at a cricket match and I had to ask the captain permission to go and buy an engagement ring after I had batted!

Naturally one of the first principles to establish was to make clear to one and all how important and valuable the Classical subjects are in modern educational world. The Cambridge Latin Course had made the language much more accessible to pupils of most abilities, and the language's value to understanding English and many other Indo-European languages should never be under-estimated. The debt that we owe to Roman and Greek civilizations is considerable and making sure that young people today appreciate this is one of the roles that we can play as teachers. One of the more surprising aspects of learning Latin is that the logical structure of the ancient language is a skill that complements computer language, and one of the brightest pupils I ever taught went on to study Computing and became a programmer. But I tried never to forget that I had really enjoyed studying Latin and Greek because of the stories in their history and passed down through their literature.

With this philosophy I aimed to breathe new life into The Classics Department. Latin plays and the invention of a board game (FUGA!), the introduction of Classical Civilisation (a great subject for those with weaker linguistic skills), Classics Open Evenings (with boys acting as slaves once parents had bought them at the "slave market"), and Roman food available for all to taste etc), all made a difference over the years: the appointment of two teachers who contrasted but complemented each other were the final pieces in the jigsaw – one the intellectual who could promote Oxbridge at the top end, and the other the all-rounder who could attract the rest. The new Deputy Head had announced on his arrival that he intended to "wipe out the Classics Department", but he soon had to admit that his arguments to do so were groundless and that he should let us carry on with the good job that we were already doing. Perhaps one other thing made a huge difference to the popularity of the subjects – the trips abroad which allowed us to immerse the boys and girls in the world that had so excited us before them.

2 – Echoes from Ancient Greece

It had seemed most appropriate that one of the first boys to sign up for our trip to Greece was called Jason. However, the omens were not good as we gathered before the coach arrived to take us to the airport. Jason had always been the most enthusiastic about the trip, so I was more than a little surprised when Jason was the first to cause a headache. In fact, I was convinced on that first day that Jason would be the one person not to make it to Greece.

I had expected that you could never quite prepare for every eventuality, and that our pupil companions would be just as unpredictable as the weather: but that just sounded like another one of those platitudes. Looking back on it I could have predicted disasters at almost every corner. But when Jason posed the first problem, I began to realise how unreliable many of our charges were likely to be. It was just like taking fledgling birds on their first flight from the nest. I had been on a trip to Greece as a pupil myself and had enjoyed it but perhaps not fully appreciated the demands placed on staff. I saw from day one that there were going to be unexpected challenges, and the success of the trip was not going to be judged on the weather, nor what the food was going to be like: it was how we were going to handle the problems that arose.

Dick from Ipswich School, my mentor from teaching practice, was in charge: familiar from his yellow shirt and purple tie, Dick was very experienced in these trips – he knew the best way 'to do Delphi' which was of course to start at the top in the Stadium and then work down. He was also the only man I know to have actually seen the model of Ancient Rome in E.U.R., Mussolini's pseudo-neo-Classical suburb. I had learnt a lot from Dick on teaching practice, and when he had suggested joining forces to take a party to Greece, I leapt at the opportunity to observe the great man at close quarters.

As the coach from Ipswich arrived in Colchester, our group from CRGS had all gathered ready to get on board; there was a general buzz of expectation. They were mostly pupils from the middle and senior years, and I hoped to identify any future leaders who might make prefects in future. After a final check to see that everyone had their documents I discovered that one of the Sixth Formers, Jason, had arrived but had no idea where his passport was. We had no time to wait: Dick was eager to keep to a timetable and the coach was ready to leave for the airport. I had to make a decision and quickly:

"Jason, you will just have to go home and hope that you can find your passport somewhere there. If you do find it, then your parents are going to have to drive you to the airport and meet us there."

As Jason disconsolately headed back home with his parents, he could see his friends' disappointed faces looking out of the back of the coach as we headed south towards Gatwick Airport and eventually our flight to Greece with all that it promised. I tried not to see it as an omen, that all would not go well. Dick had clearly approved of my prompt decision, although I was not convinced that the rest of my group did; but I hoped they would see that I meant business and that they had to accept responsibility for their actions - there was no room for sentimentality. But it was not a good start!

The journey to the airport took approximately three hours. I did not expect Jason to re-join the group, and had dismissed him from his mind; but much to our surprise just as we were going through passport control, Jason arrived. His father had driven like the wind to catch us in time. Jason himself was somewhat embarrassed –

"My passport was in my luggage all along. My over-efficient mother had packed the documents, but perhaps she had forgotten to tell me!"

It was a lesson for us all: the real problem had been a lack of communication from mother to son (not the other way round as it often can be!). The mood which had sagged upon our departure from Colchester had picked up significantly and, despite this false alarm, we all now felt sure that the trip would go well.

The total party numbered 35 youngsters, with 20 pupils from Colchester; Dick had a few outsiders from different Suffolk schools as well as his dozen from Ipswich. As far as the staff were concerned, I had recruited two of my most trusted companions to aid me on the journey, Roy, and my wife, Maryta, while Dick had brought along Andrew. Andrew was essentially a "renaissance man": he had apparently flopped out of school, lived in a barn at the age of 25 writing essays to become a mature student at the University of Essex; his passion was Byron, which suggested that he might have something to contribute when we got to Cape Sounion and Pylos, where he was expected to sing the praises of his "heroic lord". The other thing to know about Andrew was that he was a vegetarian, but one who did not like cheese! Greek salads "οχι φεττα" (no cheese) would be the order of the day!

I was more than sure that we were going to have sleepless nights during the trip, but I was also confident that with Dick's experience we should be able to deal with almost anything. However, throughout the outward journey I remained concerned about a young woman called Katy who kept herself to herself and rarely joined in the discussions or activities on the flight. The others in the group tended to ignore her, and she seemed content with this. When I mentioned her to Dick, he just replied:

"Her background is a bit of a mystery to me. She has come from Stowmarket and I am told that she is interested in studying the Classics at university."

"She doesn't look as though she wants to get to know any of the others on the trip." I said. "No, she is definitely one to keep an eye on." agreed Dick.

When we finally disembarked at Athens Airport, we made our way up by coach to our hotel in the city itself. I was beginning to have a good feeling about the youngsters - they had been no trouble so far and were beginning to enjoy each other's company – except for Katy! After dropping our bags in the Hotel Euripides, I suggested to Dick that we should take a quick walk up Mount Lycabettos to help everyone get their bearings. He agreed but decided to stay at the Hotel to sort out some paperwork. As we were setting off from our Hotel, I said clearly to the assembled group:

"Everyone, keep close together! Remember the name of the Hotel and how to retrace your steps in case you get lost in the streets of modern Athens. It's a short uphill walk, but it will be worth it."

Athens' city streets were essentially unimpressive, and not very memorable, full of flats and parked cars. However, it did not take us too long before we started to climb and very soon we found ourselves emerging from the undergrowth on the top of the hill (hardly a Mount!), which gives a spectacular view out over the markets of the Plaka towards the Acropolis, and the route back down to the harbour, where the line of Pericles' Long Walls, built to protect the city against the invading Spartans in the 5th Century BC, can be seen in the route of the main road down to the harbour.

I had enjoyed this view on my previous visit, and I sensed that my enthusiasm was apparent to all of the group as I picked out those sites familiar to me. I was really looking forward to taking this group through the Agora up onto the Pnyx, the birthplace of democracy, as well as round to the theatre of Dionysus, where I hoped to explain the origins of drama as we know it. I was not sure we would manage a trip to the Kerameikos which Dick intended to offer instead of a trip around the Archaeological museum: the former enjoyed the calm and charm typical of burial grounds in the middle of a city, while the latter was undoubtedly important with the treasures from Mycenae and the fabled statue of Poseidon (or is it Zeus?). In contrast, modern Athens has little grace or charm - and I was relieved to see that the "νεφος" or cloud of smog that often rested over the modern city did not obscure their first view of this fascinating city. I also knew that Dick wanted to make an early start on the following morning in order to get up on the Acropolis before the hordes of tourists arrived flocking to visit the Parthenon and its companion temples, (without really understanding them!).

"Right! Let's all head back to the Hotel. Don't forget to stick together, and when we get back they should have got our supper ready".

So I led the group back down the slopes. As we retraced our steps I enjoyed hearing the youngsters talking about what they had seen and how they were looking forward to getting to grips with the sites tomorrow. I hoped that the evening meal would help them settle down, and then enable everyone to retire early and re-charge their batteries ready for the exertions of the following morning. The instructions upon arriving back at the Hotel were to have a quick wash and then come straight down for the evening meal - no doubt a traditional Greek welcome of moussaka and chips! The dining room was big enough to accommodate us on five tables, but when we had all sat down, Andrew, who had been detailed to check that everyone was there, reported that one of ours was missing: Smiler! His room-mates had no idea where he was - he had not come back to the room at all; in fact, no-one remembered seeing him on the walk back. This was not good, and after Roy had made further enquiries he learnt that Smiler had been one of the few who had not been an enthusiastic volunteer for the trip in the first place: his parents had made matters worse by taking their younger son to Disneyland – which is probably where Smiler would have preferred to go. Known only for his sour face (hence the 'affectionate' nickname) and not for his endless chatter, he was definitely the dark horse who was the first to introduce the idea of a sleepless night!

After a fruitless retracing of our steps back to Lycabettos, and a long conversation with the Hotel Owner, Dick decided that the Police should be contacted - Athens has a group rather intriguingly called the "99", whose sole purpose seems to have been to find lost tourists within their metropolis. After giving out a description of the lost boy to the "99" – a boy of medium build with mousey brown hair wearing casual clothes with no distinctive marks! - I decided that I could not just sit and wait for Smiler to turn up; so, Dick, Andrew and Roy stayed to keep a close eye on the rest of the group, while I set out with Maryta into the darker corners of Athens' central districts. It was a good job that I had Maryta with me, as on more than one occasion I found myself in an area where women were happy to draw my attention to what they were or were not wearing under their very short skirts!

"What would Smiler have done, confronted with that?" asked Maryta. "I have no idea." I replied.

I felt a bit like Heracles searching for his lost squire, Hylas, who went missing on their journey with the Argonauts. Calling out at regular intervals, we hoped that Smiler might just hear us searching for him. We checked back at the Hotel every hour in case any sign of him had been found. Dick joined us in the lobby of the Hotel wearing the most immaculate purple silk dressing gown, and tried to keep me calm. But by midnight, I was becoming more and more worried.....

Shortly after 1am there was a phone call to the Hotel, and we were given some hope. A young man had been spotted by a taxi driver sitting outside the Railway Station, and he had seen him again over a period of three hours in the same place. The "99" were on the case and if he answered to the name of Mark, Smiler's real name, they were going to bring him in for questioning. Shortly after 1.30am I was escorted to a flat near to the Hotel, where I was introduced to a well-fed middle-aged Athenian called Janis, who was apparently the Police Interpreter. He had just started to reassure me that all would be well, when there was a knock on the door and Smiler was brought in. He wore no expression on his face, except one of exhaustion, and I realised that the poor boy was obviously shattered. The last thing he needed now was a lengthy enquiry into what he had been doing. I wanted to suggest that the boy would prefer to go through the story on the following morning rather than stay up even longer. However, this was not the method expected by the Athenian Police, and Janis started to get out food - a hard-boiled egg and anchovies - and a drink of Ouzo for our long lost boy! I tried to intercede on Smiler's behalf, apologised for all the trouble he had caused, and gradually edged our way to the door. Janis, however, was not to be deprived of his moment of glory - he hardly asked Smiler any questions about how he had spent the evening, but he did insist on showing Smiler his photographs of himself, Janis, with Antony Quinn during the rehearsals for the film, Zorba the Greek.

"I am not sure what Smiler made of all this" I confessed to all the teachers when I eventually got back to the Hotel Euripedes with my rescued charge. "It's an old film which had been made many years ago, and shown mainly in Greece!"

Anyway Smiler did eventually confess to Janis that he had wanted to find a way home, and that he was angry with his parents for going to Disneyland without him. He had quickly realised that he could not succeed in his plan and by chance ended up at the railway station where he sat down and waited….! By 3am, our group were all back in the hotel and some of them were able to enjoy a good half night's sleep before the wonders of the next day. I resolved not to let Smiler out of my sight for the rest of the trip, wherever we were!

In many ways the days spent in Athens restored some calm to the group and particularly to me: the chance to talk about 'entasis and the golden mean' when looking at the Parthenon, and Andrew led a great debate on what democracy really meant on the Pnyx, bringing an intellectual distraction and academic challenge which lifted everyone's spirits. The visit to Cape Sounion had some value, if only to debunk Lord Byron for being a graffiti artist on the temple of Poseidon, much to Andrew's annoyance! Dick had not come with us on this outing, but instead got on a No. 46 bus which after an hour took him and four of his A level students to a site which was allegedly the quarry for all the Pentelic marble used on the Acropolis: one of his lads confessed that any hole in the rocks could have been a quarry!

After a couple of full days in Athens, our itinerary took us into the Peloponnese. There I was able to wax lyrically about the "cyclopean" walls of Tiryns and how this reflected the power of rulers like Agamemnon at Mycenae. At Epidaurus, following Dick's encouragement to making the most of the 'experience', Roy seized the opportunity to demonstrate the extraordinary acoustics and the power of its setting in the great auditorium, hand in hand: reciting in English and Greek from Aeschylus's Oresteia as well as Aristophanes' Frogs was one of his party pieces, and it was not just his own students who appreciated the demonstration with a standing ovation, although some Japanese tourists looked somewhat bemused!

The biggest issue we experienced here was what to do with our guide: in Greece groups are required to be accompanied by a Greek Guide. The problem we faced was that Nana, our guide, spoke very poor English and much of what she said was incorrect. She also wore leather trousers which squeaked whenever she walked. We had put up with her in Athens, by one of us talking after her to keep our group informed of the right information. At Epidaurus, we decided to ask her to allow us to wander about the site on our own, so that we could just "absorb the spirit of the place". However, it was always difficult to convey the idea of the whole site with its hippodrome as well as hospital facilities - in ancient times more visitors came here to be cured than to hear the poetry of the great playwrights. The votive offerings displayed in the Museum certainly gave a clearer picture of the ailments from which the patients suffered. It was really important to make sure that all our party heard the story of the patients, huddled in underground tunnels, being visited during the night by the God's serpents to bring them a cure (a positive side of a sleepless night?), accompanied by the whispered chanting of the priests from above. Unfortunately another Greek Guide objected to Dick giving this talk and despite our assurance that we had a Greek Guide resting in our coach, the other Guide was threatening us with all sorts of penalties. We made a swift retreat deciding to keep Nana on hand in future in case of further discontent.

The journey over the Central Peloponnese was a relatively peaceful day. On the fourth day we arrived in the coastal settlement of Pylos: now a calm fishing village, while previously it had been another of the great Mycenean City States ruled by the legendary Nestor. As was Dick's custom, he instructed our party to spend the late afternoon exploring the village's charming harbour and market area, while I arranged a boat for the next day's adventures to the island of Sphacteria. Smiler was instructed to remain as a shadow close to me and

Maryta, while Andrew and Roy kept an eye on the rest of the group. Dick again retired for completing the paperwork.

Dick had told me that it was easy to book a local fishing boat to take us out into the bay on the next day – "Just ask for Janis!" he said. Well, unfortunately everyone I approached claimed to be called Janis. Eventually I just plumped for the one whose boat looked most sea-worthy. I was blissfully unaware of what was going on in the village: I suppose I should have expected another incident soon, but I was not prepared for the gravity of it when it actually happened. Roy revealed that Andrew had disappeared to the local Museum which had items relating to his beloved Byron's campaign at Messalonghi: we learnt that these items were actually only two letters and three cannonballs associated with this battle. Roy was worried that he had not been able to keep a close eye on all of our group by himself. I tried to reassure him that nothing much could go wrong in this small village.

After the evening meal at a small but very friendly restaurant on the side of the harbour, most of the party decided to enjoy the "Volta" performed by the locals in the market square - an opportunity to allow our food to settle while enjoying the company of friends and relatives while parading up and down the square arm in arm. I felt that this was one of those cultural experiences the modern youngsters should learn from, and was happy to see most of the group throwing themselves into it, when my arm was grappled by a very agitated Roy. "You have to come back to the Hotel - Philip is very ill and we can't get him to talk to us".

I quickly followed my side-kick and once back at the Hotel went straight up to Philip's room. Philip, a boy of fourteen years, was flat out on the bed, unconscious, sweating and very pale. It did not take long to discover the bottle of 'Metaxa' brandy hidden in the bathroom, and Roy was able to get some more details of Philip's pre and post-prandial activities from other members of the group, who were all trying to press into the room to find out what was going on. Philip was a young man who probably did not have too many friends – he was still growing into his body, but was rather inclined to giggle at almost everything in an immature way; His actions this evening had probably been an attempt to gain some street-cred within the group. He had decided to sample the local hooch, which he had secretly bought from a back-street trader. I had heard about the different strengths of Greek brandy, and knew that only the locals could normally handle the quantity he had drunk.

"We need to act quickly." Dick said "First of all, let's put him under a cold shower to wake him from his slumbers, and then we shall try to get black coffee or just water into him."

After about twenty minutes there was little sign of progress, and we agreed that more experienced medical help was needed. The Hotel Manager broke the shocking news that there was no doctor or hospital in the village, as the clocks struck 11pm. However, the Hotelier's son was prepared to drive me and Philip over the mountains to Kalamata, where there was a good hospital. As Roy helped me lower Philip into the back of the car, the storm clouds started depositing their rain onto us. The other adults would stay behind to keep an eye on the rest of the group. Georgiou, the driver, was entertained by the whole episode until he realised that the heavily drunk young man behind him might leave his mark on the back seat at the very least! It was not as if the road up over the mountain was helping, hair-pin bends abounded and the weather was not helping either - the thunder and lightning only increased the drama. I tried to talk cheerfully to Georgiou, if only to take his mind off the sick boy and to keep his attention on the road. In turn, Georgiou was just hoping that Philip was distracted by the storm to think about his delicate stomach. Meanwhile Philip kept pleading with me that his behaviour would not have an adverse effect on his GCSEs – it is really strange what passes through a boy's mind when it has been led astray by drink!

After a journey that seemed to last forever, but probably only lasted 90 minutes, we eventually emerged from the mountain pass and arrived in the outskirts of Kalamata. Even the rain decided to stop and a calmness began to settle over everyone in the car. However, as they approached the first crossroads of the town, I could make out something, or someone, lying in the middle of the road. It soon became clear that the squirming body was that of a man whose motorbike was lying on the other side of the road. After Georgiou had stopped the car, I got out to investigate: there was a lot of blood everywhere and the man obviously had a broken leg as well as whatever internal injuries had been inflicted upon him. I realised that we should not move him themselves for fear of doing further damage. So I tried to calm the injured man in pigeon-Ancient Greek, covered him with his coat and told him that we would send a doctor as soon as we got to the hospital. Perhaps one of us should have stayed with him but Georgiou was keen not to get involved. I certainly had less sympathy for Philip moaning in the back of the car, as we hurried to find the hospital. As we caught sight of the hospital an ambulance with two men visible in it passed us going in the opposite direction. "Someone has already summoned the ambulance" said Georgiou, as he found a space to park near the hospital entrance.

I helped Philip get out of the car and stumble up to the main entrance of the hospital; I knew that Philip would not be the priority in the emergency room and reconciled myself to have a long wait until the injured man had been dealt with. It was not long before the ambulance returned and the paramedics came out to help bring the victim into the hospital. Bizarrely the main entrance into the hospital was on the first floor and there was a lift which enabled those arriving at the hospital on a trolley to be taken upstairs. However, the old man was lying awkwardly with his broken leg sticking out to one side as he was brought out of the ambulance. The attendants clearly did not care what happened to him, and they pushed the trolley feet first into the swing doors into the lift. Not surprisingly the agonised cry that the old man let out at this point probably woke most of the town. This tragi-comical scene was repeated as the trolley was wheeled out through more swing doors on the first floor and the "victim" was taken into the theatre.

It was only at this moment that I spotted two figures keeping themselves hidden in the shadows of the hospital entrance. One was a younger man and the other a smartly dressed woman of "indeterminate" years: He was obviously much shaken and seemed to have a slight limp, but there were no signs of recent injury. She was just upset. I could make out some of the words that the younger man kept repeating to the woman, as they were trying to comfort each other –

"I didn't…… to kill him - …… in the way and …..wouldn't let me through".

"He must have been involved in the accident that left the older man injured, and left to get help from the hospital" I thought to myself, and I was about to reassure the younger man that I didn't think the other man was going to die, when we heard the siren of a police car. At once the younger man disappeared from sight. In contrast, and to my surprise, the woman stepped forward and into the hospital.

There was little to do but wait for the doctors to give their attention to the old man from the road accident, and the more Philip sat in the fresh air of Kalamata, the more his mind returned to normal and his nausea abated. Eventually after at least an hour, a doctor emerged from the operating room and came to have a look at Philip. I wanted to know what had happened to the old man, but no-one was prepared to tell me. The smartly-dressed woman came out with the Police, but I found it difficult to gauge what her emotions were: what was her connection to the young man (perhaps her lover?), or to the older man (perhaps her betrayed husband?). What had I witnessing? Was this a re-enactment of Oedipus killing his father, Laius, at the crossroads and then going on unwittingly to marry his mother, Jocasta? Surely not....it was just my imagination getting carried away with Ancient Greece!

After all this waiting, the doctor eventually decided that Philip's demeanour was returning to normal and there was no need for any medicine. While this may have been good news, I was not sure how well Georgiou would take the news that we had had a wasted journey over the mountains, but he charmingly accepted the news with good cheer, saying: "Well, at least the journey home will be less dramatic!" Indeed, the road back lacked all the excitement of thunder, lightning and road accidents, but I spent much of the time trying to work out what had really happened at the crossroads just as we arrived in Kalamata. Philip continued to mutter on about his GCSEs! We were all delighted to draw into the narrow streets of Pylos by 6am, just in time to enjoy a shower and shave before an early breakfast.

Philip was given prime position at the back of the Janis' small sailing boat which took the whole party to Sphacteria, so that he could enjoy the rocking of the boat as it ploughed its way through the choppy seas. It seemed that he had not enjoyed a shower before breakfast, but he was keen to take advantage of the swaying of the boat and wash his hair by leaning over the side as I lectured the rest of the amused group on the siege of the Spartans by the Athenians on the island. Perhaps Metaxa brandy would be kept off the menu for the whole group from now on and certainly would not be forgotten by me.

Not surprisingly Andrew spent a lot of the time on our boat with his flame kindled for his hero Byron, while Dick was at pains to point out the twists and turns of the siege carried out by the Athenians against the Spartans on the island of Sphacteria. In many ways it was intriguing to see how this modern day battle was developing.

Olympia was next on the itinerary north after Pylos, and despite the underwhelming aspect of the ancient site, a race along the stadion is always popular especially with boys. By way of calming their enthusiasm, I pointed out just at the entrance tunnel to the stadion those bases of the statues which had been paid for by those who had been caught cheating - a salutary lesson to modern-day cheats perhaps?

It remains difficult to imagine that Olympia held one of the Wonders of the Ancient World - the statue of Olympian Zeus created by Pheidias within the main temple. Today, one can only gauge the impressiveness of the temple by the piles of huge block that made up the columns as they lie on the ground following one of the many earthquakes in this area – resembling a pile of pancakes fallen from the great god's plate?

It came as no surprise that expectations were high as the party moved on in our clockwise route up towards Delphi - the so-called "ομφαλος", the navel of the earth in the eyes of the Ancient Greeks. I was confident that the group would be impressed by the ancient sanctuary's setting, high on the hillside, and Dick reminded us that the best time to visit the site would again be early in the morning before the other crowds arrived in their buses from Athens.

However, as we checked into our Delphi hotel for the next two nights, a small problem arose. As the party were allocated their rooms, many quickly returned to the Reception area with stories of incomplete facilities. Some doors were not yet fitted and if they were, no locks were to be found; one bathroom had no pipes connecting the sink, or more importantly the toilet with the drains; another room was good on air-conditioning but low on window panes; and finally, one room had only one bed, a double which the three occupants were reluctant to share!

The hotelier who was trying to help sort us out was suitably embarrassed, and kept muttering her apologies. The owner it seemed had been abroad for a number of years, and the job of keeping the hotel functioning had been left to his wife. Madame Konstantides, and her hotel, was seen as quite a catch in the modern town of Delphi, and as a result she was being hounded by all the local business men with offers she tried hard to refuse. Her main tactic it seemed was to keep delaying any work on completing the rebuilding work on the hotel, so that any decision about it and her future had to wait.

I remembered how impressive a lady she was and her demeanour triggered another echo from Homer and Ancient Greece. She attempted to calm our anxiety by presenting Dick and myself with charming bags which she had made herself by way of compensation: I could hardly contain myself when I realised that they were made from woollen tapestry: she had to be called Penelope, like Odysseus' wife. We quickly put aside any qualms we might have had about being "wary of Greeks bearing gifts", and accepted them graciously! To add to my curiosity, an older gentleman had arrived shortly after our group; he had been given one of the incomplete rooms, until our group had left. He appeared to have fallen on hard times, but beneath the traveller's grime he had a surprisingly fit set of muscles, and he displayed far too much knowledge about the town, and indeed the hotel, to be just another stranger. Could this be Odysseus returning in disguise to reclaim his wife, Penelope? All that I needed now was to find the twenty year old dog, Argus, who would recognise his former master before dying!

As predicted the party thoroughly enjoyed the ancient site, and despite the loss of so many fine artefacts from each of the ruined buildings (many of which ended up in Roman

Constantinople), everyone was capable of appreciating why the ancients felt the mystic qualities of this setting. Apollo's temple and the cavea of the Pythia, with its advice "Know thyself" and "Everything in moderation" provoked much thought and discussion while they gathered in the steep sided seats of the theatre: even Katy tried to join in the debate expressing scorn on most of this philosophy, but the rest of the group seemed to be more open to the wisdom of the ancients.

"At least," I said to Dick, "she is beginning to get involved." Dick stressed how easily any number of ambitious rulers had too quickly assumed that the Pythia's prophecies meant a positive outcome for them. Instead the temple's guardians or priests nearly always translated the priestess' mutterings into a suitably ambiguous response, thus ensuring that their reputation was safe, while those rash tyrants might rush headlong into a trap. I was glad that he had no prophecy for the final leg of their trip as we eventually departed back to Athens. However, the maxim "Know thyself" remained stubbornly in my mind, and I wondered if it might be pertinent to some drama that was about to be enacted back at the hotel in Delphi between the old guest, the lady hotelier, and her suitors.

We returned to the Hotel Euripedes on the outskirts of the Plaka district of Athens; then a number of the group approached me with a concerned look. Both Andrew and Roy had picked up the same story about Katy: she was still not anyone's friend and had apparently kept herself to herself during most of the trip around the Peloponnese. However, that was not quite the whole story – it seems that she had spent every night leaving the hotel room she shared with other girl students, and eventually we were told that she was spending a lot of time with the driver of their coach. Her nocturnal adventures were a huge surprise to everyone: she was eighteen but we were still responsible for her well-being. Dick quickly challenged the coach driver who denied any impropriety, and

Katy just said she had been lonely and enjoyed talking to the older man. One of her room mates had revealed Katy's absences, and she suggested that Katy had a distinct plan for the group's final night in Athens.

Dick had arranged for the whole party to spend the evening at a small restaurant in the Plaka district so that they could enjoy local food and entertainment (music and dance). It transpired that Katy had decided that she was going to go off with the driver and enjoy a final night of her entertainment! Dick and I were determined to put a stop to this.

"I know what you have been up to throughout the trip, and it has got to stop. If you think that you can go with someone else tonight, you're wrong!" Dick made his intentions quite clear – but what sanction do you have on the last night of the trip?

Katy just shrugged her shoulders: she obviously thought that she was still going to be able to escape from the restaurant. There was nothing for it. Dick instructed all the adults to take up strategic points throughout the restaurant to prevent Katy making a run for it: unfortunately a convenient road ran straight past the front of the restaurant, and I had an image of a fast car being driven up and Katy jumping into it. So Roy and I took up position on the front door, Maryta on the door into the kitchen, and Andrew at the back of the restaurant which opened onto a garden area, while Dick remained in the centre with the rest of our group. Unexpectedly, the weakness in the building was in the toilet department. What actually happened was that Katy went to the 'Γυναικες', but timed it badly since Maryta needed to "powder her nose" at the same time, and she had the presence of mind to grab Katy as she was trying to out the back window. Dick had no choice but to summon our coach, move the whole group out of the restaurant, go to the airport, and wait for our plane home early - no music or dancing, but instead another night without sleep, guarding the whole group safe together, even Jason, Smiler, Philip and Katy!

As we sat on the marble floor waiting for our flight call (not until 4am!), we had time to reflect on the pluses and minuses of the trip. Everyone agreed that the Ancient Greek World was worth revisiting, but there were far more concerns about the members of the trip. Roy was keen not to have any girls from other schools on future trips, having been more put out by Katy's behaviour than most. Andrew went further and argued strongly to have only pupils that we knew personally to avoid the problems that Smiler had created. We all felt that we had learnt a great deal about supervision of the pupils – it has to be 100% all the time – and we recognised the importance of good communication: Jason's mother had highlighted this problem. The one thing that none of us felt confident about was the fact that when in a foreign country we were left in the hands of local agents or hoteliers: if a hotel was not finished yet, one had to hope that a solution could be found as at Penelope's Delphic Inn!

When we eventually got back to Colchester I was determined to explain to Smiler's parents what had happened in Athens; perhaps I should not have been too surprised when they did not turn up to collect him at the appointed time. Mark eventually revealed that they had told him that they had booked to go to the Mercury Theatre in Colchester (after getting back from the Disney the day before), and that he would just have to wait for them. I was not very impressed when they turned up two hours after the appointed time, with no apology, but instead with an expression of surprise that I had waited with Mark. They greeted my account of their son being lost on his own in the Greek capital city for over six hours with the comments "Oh, that's typical of Mark!" - they didn't seem too disturbed at all. I was not impressed by their attempts, or rather absence of them, at parenting!

I left Philip to tell his own parents first the story of his alcoholic adventure to Kalamata – what he could remember of it. Meanwhile I wondered how Dick's conversation would go with Katy's parents.

We had all agreed with Dick that despite all the issues we should not be put off organising more trips as part of our promotion of the Classics: there were so many places to go (Italy obviously, Turkey, Southern France, and even Egypt) and such a lot to discover.

Lessons to be learnt:
Never trust any of the children to do what you expect, and never let your guard down!

Try not to let your imagination run riot, even if the temptation to relive the myths from Ancient Greece is too tempting!

Post eventum
Smiler left school a couple of years later, not progressing into the Sixth Form, and my friends from Colchester reported that he had last been seen wandering around the town sporting a very impressive rainbow-coloured Mohican hairstyle! Philip became a tea-totaller who ended as Director of a Museum. We never heard of Katy again, but suspect she will have pursued a successful career in the Media.

The theatre at Epidaurus.

The theatre at Delphi.

3 – Gettoni and Gelati

There is no doubt that my first trip abroad had had as many challenges as triumphs, but it had generally been deemed a success. So when I was appointed as Head of Classics in Norwich, I was determined to organise more trips that would further promote an interest in the Classical World. Within a year I had established that there was definite interest in the school for such trips: the obvious one to take was to Italy, with Rome and Pompeii, being the star attractions. I had spent time discussing my proposals with Tim, a young member of the Norwich Classics Department who seemed keen to be part of the trip.

"By making Italy our next destination we should attract younger pupils, who have studied the Cambridge Latin Course and want to make that 'pilgrimage' to Caecilius' house. If they get hooked, we should have plenty of interest for future trips." Tim suggested.

"Our trips should not just be about wanting answers - we need to show our pupils that the questions are just as important, if not more so. I hope that the trip is not going to be based around long lectures at every site." Tim was making a good point, and we agreed to prepare some brochures with relevant material to help the pupils guide themselves around the sites we were going to visit.

"It is a great idea to allow the kids to feel as though they are discovering these sites for themselves. Our trips should be built around a sense of discovery about the Ancient and Modern World. Maybe we will even discover more about ourselves in the process." I agreed.

Italy

I had made the decision to restrict all our future trips to pupils from Norwich School only: after the episode of Katy, I hoped to avoid any such problems by keeping the group to pupils we actually knew. Many parents were impressed by the way we had promoted this opportunity to enhance their son's study of Latin, and so it was not difficult to find the numbers suitable to make up a party just from Norwich School to go to Italy. Maryta was sure that the absence of female pupils was not necessarily the solution to all problems – indeed, she was sometimes heard expressing the view that the presence of females raised the intellectual capabilities of the whole party. I was not prepared to open the matter to debate!

I had recruited John from the Art Department to help construct the Tour brochures with Tim, and it seemed a good idea to have him along for the trip since we were going to visit the centre of the Renaissance revival in Art: it was going to be helpful to have someone who could answer with authority any questions we might be asked in that area. John's artwork has a very distinctive style, and he produced an excellent cover for most of our future trips. He was also a most affable companion, and I was confident that he would add a lot to our trip. What I had not anticipated was how unlucky he was going to be in Italian cities full of pick-pockets and corrupt officials. Naivety balances nicely against hindsight: John and Tim appreciated that every trip would have its issues, but we were all sure that we could face whatever challenges were thrown our way.

Maryta was not able to pursue the question about females on the trip as our departure date fell almost exactly when she was due to give birth to our son. Just to complicate matters, Jozef was born on the day before we left for Italy: he had been due to be delivered by caesarean section two days earlier but it was decided that Maryta needed a couple of days to recover from a slight cold. My anxiety to be present at the birth was never quite appreciated by all, but it did lead to a sleepless night! The trip to Italy had been planned over a year before and I felt that the trip still needed my presence despite the urge to withdraw to support my wife and child. Maryta was due to stay in hospital because of the caesarean for nearly a week, and her mother had agreed to come to help Maryta when she was discharged with Jozef. Although I had some misgivings about this plan, I had decided that I could remain in touch with Maryta throughout the trip by telephone, and my colleagues knew that I might have to depart quickly if anything unexpected happened.

Anyway, I was able to kiss both my wife and new-born son "arrivederci" on the evening before we set off to Gatwick again for the flight to Italy. To provide that extra cover necessary when taking a party of 40+ younger boys, I had asked Carol, the school nurse to step in as a member of the adult team for this trip. There may not have been girls on the trip, but Carol would fulfil the role of "Aunty" especially for those boys who may not have even been outside Norfolk!

Typical of Travel Agents who organise these sorts of trips, one can never rely on them for accurate details of the itinerary until the last minute. Just to add to my anxiety during Jozef's birth, I realised that we had not received any airline tickets by the Saturday for our Monday flight. My phone call to resolve this matter was countered with the comment – "Don't worry, our courier will sort you out at the airport. See her at 9am."

"But we are supposed to fly at 8am, as your latest corrected version of the itinerary says." I said in despair.

"No. I'm, sorry but the time of the flight has now been changed to 10am."

This led to frantic phone calls to all members of the trip and the bus company to delay the start by 2 hours. When we finally arrived at Gatwick, we were met by a hopping-mad courier from the travel agent: no-one had told her that the flight was 2 hours later and she had been waiting for us since 6am! As we are going on a chartered flight, and the person responsible is busy writing out tickets by hand – I was beginning to smell a rat at this point – he is pretty angry too because he would prefer to be selling some stand-by tickets for this flight, which is now going to be at least one hour late in taking off. And finally just to add to the complications, we are told that our flight will take us to Verona instead of Rome. From there we shall board a coach which will drive us all the way to Positano, a small fishing village south of the bay of Naples. The original plan was to fly to Rome, but school travel agents were always looking at ways to cut the costs. The only issue for us was that the coach journey lasted eight hours! I was not convinced that this would be the best preparation for the boys before going out to visit the sites around the Bay of Naples, but what can you do when presented with these alterations at the last minute – and all so that the costs are reduced for the travel agent.

After we had all settled into our charming hotel, I asked Tim to take all the kids down to the place where he had seen a sign for a "Disco", in an attempt to burn off a little energy within the group as well as perhaps get to know some of the locals. I should not have been too surprised when Tim arrived back after one hour with the party of boys following him rather like the Pied Piper. Either this was a monastic town or there were no females in sight: the Disco sign had not attracted the company that the boys might have hoped for - but at least they had spent time getting to know each other better. Tim was not very impressed by this start to the trip. So the Italian agents who were handling our trip agreed that on the following day, after our visit to Paestum, we would be moved from Positano to Sorrento, which would certainly be a better location from which to start our visits to Pompeii and Herculaneum.

Paestum has some extraordinary Greek temples (it was a Greek colony initially) as well as a very strange swimming pool with the foundations of a kind of pavilion or diving board built within the pool itself: that always provokes good discussion as to its purpose. We had time to visit the beach where many of the boys went for a paddle – much to the surprise of our courier, Genaro, who was happy wrapped up in his very smart woollen suit! On the coach journey back to Sorrento, John reminded us that it was Good Friday, and he wondered whether the holy processions in the evening might stimulate a different level of interest amongst our party. At our new Sorrento hotel another English school group had checked in before us, and we were somewhat surprised to discover that they had not shown any interest in going out during the day to visit any of the ancient sites. As both parties sat down for the early evening meal, I was again surprised to see how enlivened the other group became when the food was brought out. Just at that moment a commotion was heard outside, and John returned from checking it out with the news that the Good Friday Procession was just starting. I never wanted to let food get in the way of genuine experiences, and so instructed our party to follow John out onto the pavement to absorb the 'local colour' of this Catholic Procession. Despite a few boys who muttered that they would be missing their food, the whole group quickly followed John out of the dining hall. As I passed the leader of the other group, I quietly leant over and encouraged him to do likewise with his party so that they too could discover something new. The other leader ignored me completely and when I looked over the tables where this group were eating, I was struck by how absorbed they were in eating, and seemed to have no awareness of anything but the food. Thinking nothing more of it, I joined our group out onto the pavement where we watched the procession as it passed down the street. All the participants, except those in the band, were wearing black hoods rather strangely similar to those worn by groups like the Klu Klux Klan. The focus of the procession was the items used on Good Friday to crucify Christ; nails, a hammer, a crown of thorns, a sponge of vinegar along with a cross and ladder were carried through the streets on purple cushions or over the shoulders of the priests. The band and local choir chanted as they went, making a wholesome noise, not like anything our group had ever heard before and I could see how struck by the whole event they all were.

Just as the procession was coming to an end, a local man approached Tim and asked whether we were staying at Circe's place - by which he meant our hotel. Tim nodded and the man quickly told me how there were strange stories about groups staying in the hotel for weeks; one question he kept asking "Are you there on an Italian cuisine trip?" Tim said that we were not and confirmed that we had not yet eaten any food. We all reflected on the stultified look on the faces of the other group, who had been completely absorbed in the food! It seemed all rather reminiscent of a tale from Homer! So, after quickly gathering John, Tim and Carol together we agreed that our group would miss their meal at the Hotel tonight:

"Instead we shall all go out to have a pizza each, as that is also part of the foreign experience we deserve."

We politely thanked the local who had warned us: almost inevitably he was able to direct us to a restaurant where we could get good pizzas "at a very good price"! I did wonder whether there was anything wrong at all with Circe's place – was the pizza restaurant owned by our informant's cousin? Who knows, but we decided to check out of Circe's place the next morning, even before breakfast was served, to be given our third new hotel in three days!

Trying to put all this awkwardness behind us, that day's coach journey took us up to the Bay of Naples and for a day's sight-seeing in Pompeii. The first target was the pilgrimage to

Caecilius' house; all the boys had read the stories about him and his family in the Cambridge Latin Course, and many had gone on to study what it was like being a man with Caecilius' status living in a town like Pompeii. In order to reach the house, I suspected that we might have to face some problems.

Once we arrived on the vast archaeological site of Pompeii, I confidently led them on to the road where I knew Caecilius' house was to be found. I was not expecting to see just around the corner two large barriers blocking our way with signs saying "Danger! No Entry!" painted on the barriers. I was, however, not put off by such signs - I had been to Italy before, and even though Caecilius' house had been destroyed by the volcanic eruption, I was confident that there would no repeat today.

As we pondered what strategy to adopt, Tim noticed that some people were beyond the barriers – "They look as though they are very important. One of the men looks like he is carrying a very large movie camera!" On hearing this, I quickly instructed our group to climb over or under the barriers - they were not indicating any real threat but had probably been put up by some custodians who were making a handsome profit by charging others to be given exclusive rights to see Caecilius' house. Having come all this way, we were not going to be outdone by such under-hand tactics, and we quickly followed the "important people" into the next street and from there into Caecilius' house. The custodian was furious at the sight of our party arriving, but it turned out that the Director of the film crew (which is what they were) was delighted – once he heard our story of the need for a pilgrimage to the house of such a significant 'father figure' from our studies, he wanted to interview and record for posterity the boys' enthusiasm as they recalled those stories which had inspired them from the start: how Caecilius and his wife Metella had argued over his purchase of the slave-girl Melissa, how Grumio the cook had fallen asleep in the kitchen and Cerberus the dog had nearly eaten all the food (including that peacock!) for Caecilius' party, and finally how Cerberus had remained behind loyally guarding Caecilius, who had been crushed by falling masonry during the eruption of the volcano, Mt. Vesuvius. Mr. Da Parma, the Director, was delighted with the boys' input and he promised to send us a copy of his film as soon as he had managed to complete it. (Needless to say, we never saw a copy of it, but at least it enabled us to get into Caecilius' House without bribing anyone!)

The rest of the day was spent enjoying the wealth of sites around Pompeii – the baths, the forum, the theatres, the amphitheatre and the many shops and houses that give you a real image of what it was like to live there nearly two thousand years ago. This was where our Tour booklet came into its own, with various tasks set, and a check list to complete as they moved around in smaller groups – we saw plenty of other groups being forced to listen to lectures at every corner, with the tourists looking very bored! What was really important was for the boys to enjoy that sense of discovery.

One of the pupils, Timothy, stood out in this respect – from the outset I knew he would. One hopes for as many 'Timothys' as possible on these trips. He had spent most of his holidays finding ways to raise the money for such trips. He was an avid archaeologist and by his 15th birthday was an expert on Venta Icenorum (Caistor Roman town near Norwich); after he had gained the confidence of the local farmer by saving a cow from being mown down by the 4pm Norwich to London Inter-City train, he had easy access to the fields around the site. He hit the headlines with the discovery of the first "defixio" (Roman curse) in East Anglia – which is now in the Castle Museum. In Pompeii, he was not dismayed by the fact that millions had walked over the site before him – he was sure he would find something: his head down on the look-out for anything interesting, his main problem was what to leave behind. At the end of the day he had a large pile of potsherds which were interesting but not spectacular, but his passion for discovery had been set alight, and my only dilemma was to convince him that the Italian authorities might not let him take all his 'finds' back home!

As we waited by the coach for all the groups to re-join us at the end of the day, Tim (the teacher) and I began to explore the idea of having a game, back at school, where the players had to get out of Pompeii, by answering questions on life in this town, before Vesuvius erupted; and so was born the kernel of the idea that became Fuga!, our Latin Board Game.

That evening I decided that it was about time I tried to contact Maryta to see how she and Jozef were coping in hospital. The hotel operated a system whereby one had to put "gettoni" (tokens) into the telephone booth to secure a call: having collected the limited supply of tokens from the hotel staff, I dialled the number I had been given by the hospital staff. Inevitably I had to deal with the switch board operator first and when I eventually was put through to the right ward, I could see that my gettoni were running low. The Duty Nurse greeted me cheerfully and was clearly aware of who I was and where I was.

"How was your trip out there and what is the weather like? Are the boys all behaving themselves? What are the locals like? Have you been to Pompeii yet?"

She seemed oblivious of my anxiety to speak to Maryta but kept pressing me for news of our trip. Eventually she realised that I was more interested in talking to Maryta, and rushed off to get her from her bed. Just as Maryta reached the telephone and said "Hello, darling" the final gettoni ran out and I was cut off! The Hotel had no more to hand. I was forced to return to my room and try to imagine how Maryta might be reacting to that experience at the end of her telephone. I cursed the garrulous Nurse, and lay down to enjoy yet another sleepless night, worrying about Maryta and Jozef. I subsequently learnt that the Head, Chris, had very conscientiously visited Maryta regularly in hospital while I was away taking this school trip. He was such a regular visitor in fact that many nurses assumed that he was Maryta's husband and therefore the father of the baby!

Time can be spent doing various trips around the Bay of Naples – Herculaneum is a smaller site than Pompeii and perhaps a little easier to visit – as long as the custodians are not on strike, which seems to be a regular occurrence! You can also drive up to the crater of Vesuvius and be told by the local guide that an eruption is due soon. It is perhaps more dramatic to visit Solfatara within the Phlegrean Fields: the whole area was littered with craters and fumaroles, and the smell of sulphur (as the name suggests) is almost unbearable. If you bend down to touch the ground you soon realized that it was important to tread lightly and quickly before the soles of your shoes might melt. We visited this site on April 1st, and I am afraid that the adults had decided to play a little April Fool's joke on the children. We told the coach driver to park very carefully. The boys were all beginning to get the whiff of sulphur, and they looked somewhat anxious. The driver, who was in on the joke, made it obvious that he had parked in such a way that we could get away quickly in case of an eruption.

"Now, lads. You have got to be very careful here. You heard the man yesterday talking about how an eruption is due at any time. So you have to tread very lightly in case your boots might provoke a violent response. We need to be ready to spring to the edge of the crater in case an eruption is triggered. The coach driver has given us the best chance of getting away by parking facing the exit."

Fortunately nothing happened, although the boys did tread warily across the first section of the crater; but when Tim started jumping up and down on one hump to show how hollow it all sounded, the boys quickly worked out the joke, especially when someone realised what day it was!

That evening as the sun began to set, the whole party shared our experiences around the Bay of Naples over the evening meal with a sense of merriment. The adults decided that, to help remind themselves of our time here, we should all wear a bow-tie on a Tuesday for as long as possible: why a bow tie? Why Tuesday? I am not sure we had any proper reasons, but we agreed that it was wonderfully eccentric, and easy to do!

The rest of the trip focussed on Rome: it remains a wonderful place. Although I have been to the Eternal City innumerable times, I always find something new to see. The Forum was the "centre of the Roman world" and despite its confusing collection of partially collapsed buildings, it is still possible to conjure up a scene with Caesar, Cicero and Octavian passing amongst other luminaries from the time of the Republic in those grounds. The Colosseum and the Circus Maximus are impressive, but I think that we convinced the group that the Pantheon is the most striking of all Roman buildings – it helps that the Christians turned the second building on this site (a repair by Hadrian of Augustus' original building) into a church and helped preserve it in an almost faultless condition. If you are lucky the sun will shine through the circular hole in the ceiling and light up a cross in the concrete of the dome. After our visits to these amazing sites, we took an afternoon break in the Piazza Navona.

"OK, everyone. It is time for you to have a wander around this area; buy some souvenirs, if you want – just make sure you stay in groups of at least 4 and if anything happens you will be able to find us back here sitting in the shade of this café. You all need to be back here in one hour." I felt that my instructions were pretty clear, and the groups began to form. Shopping always seemed to be a major preoccupation of the kids on our trips. In one group, Simon was trying to convince some others to follow him to a cheese shop he had seen on the way back to the Trevi Fountain. Simon was certainly not a Classicist, and one might have been forgiven for thinking that he was actually working for his mother who owned a rather exclusive Cheese Shop: every foreign country that Simon visited had a collection of cheeses, and some free time had to be aside for Simon to vet the local shops to take a new variety back home. The fringe benefit for the Trip Leader was a 'thank-you' slab of Brie waiting on return to Norwich.

Another group was being orchestrated by Adrian: his main aim throughout the trip, like many others, was to have a good record of the sites visited, and so he spent most of his spending money on guide books. His enthusiasm was such that he inadvertently picked up two the same, and even one in German. I was determined to find a guide Book of Rome in Japanese to make his collection suitably idiosyncratic. Meanwhile Tom was a boy who wanted to buy everyone at home a gift: this included an onyx chess set, a tea set. and a dress for his mother. The difficulty with the last item was the size, but this was solved by an approach to Carol, the school nurse – "You look about the right size: could you try this dress on, please?"

As these groups moved off to enjoy a few minutes of freedom, the staff moved into the shade of a parasol to enjoy some freedom of our own at one of the many cafés....only to find a collection of boys doing exactly the same thing. For some, 'freedom' is not what they wanted at this stage of the trip. So we enjoyed our soft drinks and gelati together, whilst enjoying the views of Bernini's amazing fountain in the middle of what had been the site of a Roman Circus for chariot-racing.

What is often missed on a trip to Rome is the ancient site of Ostia – you need to take a brief local train out to the coast. Here you can really experience that sense of archaeological discovery, by walking through the grounds almost on your own, finding mosaics, hypocausts for bath-houses, blocks of flats, and market-places where the goods brought in by boat to Rome were sold on. Our boys really enjoyed this site, possibly more than Pompeii, especially Tim who was lost in wonder at the experience of turning a corner to discover the remains of a block of flats, or a fish-market, or the largest suite of toilets to be found on the Roman mainland.

The down-side of Rome can include pick-pockets – on the way to the railway, our art expert, John, was surrounded by street urchins who were trying to sell him a newspaper, but they were actually distracting him while his wallet was being lifted. The Carabinieri were not very sympathetic and blamed the whole incident on Yugoslav refugees! The Hotel where we stayed was close to the main railway station, Termini, which was good for getting on the Metropolitana underground railway, but you sometimes had to climb up stairs past a number of druggies injecting themselves just to get to the Hotel Reception! Getting on local buses with 40+ children meant being ready to put to good use scrummage training from the rugby field, especially in the rush hour: heads down and push together!

Our final day included a visit to St Peter's Basilica and the Vatican: being a school party with a letter identifying our school, pupil names and authorised by the Headteacher, enabled us to get to the front of the queue – a very useful tip to know: I learnt it from Dick at Ipswich. John was in his element describing the rich art in both the Basilica and the Sistine Chapel, even if he had to run the gauntlet of the Vatican Guards who made more noise telling all the tourists to be quiet in the Chapel than all the tourists did together. Unfortunately, somehow on that day John managed to lose his remaining travellers' cheques: but God was obviously looking after him as they were found by two nuns and they returned them to our Hotel before our departure. Another prophetic experience (as it turned out) was that Tim wanted us to visit the Crypt in St Peter's because he knew that was where the only English Pope was buried. Sure enough we found the tomb to Pope Adrian IV, whose English name was Nicholas Breakspeare and who attended the Abbey School, St Albans for his education. Little did I realise that I would get to know more about him later in my own career!

The most bizarre, but ultimately amusing, incident happened just as we were waiting for our coach to take us to the Airport for our flight home. One could have predicted that the coach would be late, given Roman traffic, but the boys were getting bored in the Hotel lobby. One youngster, Mat, decided to take the weight off his feet by sitting down but the only space left was on a glass-topped table: suddenly there was a crash and the top disintegrated into a pile of fine crystals. The Hotel Manager was furious, as only an Italian could be. I decided to let him aim his wild gesticulations and shouting at me rather than Mat. I asked him in my pigeon Latin/Italian to calm down and told him that we would be prepared to compensate him for the loss. However, when he quoted four hundred thousand Lira he expected to replace the broken table, I decided that he was just trying to take us for a ride. After a brief discussion with the rest of the staff we were happy that given the right paperwork we would be able to claim the money back from the School Insurers; however, we also agreed that the Hotelier was charging for the whole table and not just the top. Therefore we felt totally justified in taking the legs, which were still in good condition, with us back to England: especially after Mat, who had broken the glass, let us know that his father worked at a well-known D-I-Y store in Norwich, and so would be well-placed to find a replacement sheet of glass "dirt cheap"! Mat said that he hadn't seen anything else nice for his dad on the trip and was sure that he would like this sort of thing. That clinched it – we tied the legs around a suitably-sized case, and walked out with a very pleasant (if incomplete) gift from Rome! For once, the Hotelier was lost for words. History does not relate what Mat's dad said!

Finally, we reached the airport for our flight home - four hours early (presumably so that the driver could get home to his wife or girl-friend) – just imagine how early we would have been if we had left the hotel on time! Anyway the boys enjoyed watching how Italian drivers seemed to be blissfully unaware of the rules of the road – I think they counted at least five or six crashes in only two hours! Norwich was a calm place when we eventually arrived there and I could not wait to see Maryta and our eight-day old son, Jozef.

Lessons learnt:

Italian Agents and Hoteliers can rarely be trusted, but don't be afraid to take them on at their own game! Also try to arrange the date of your children's birth to avoid important events like school trips!

John's wonderful design for our Italy Brochure.

Quarantasei gelati!

Paul, Tim and John interpreting mosaics at Ostia.

4 - Turkish Delight, French Toast, and 'Jerusalem'

So, after the success of our Italy trip, Tim, John and I began to plan a series of trips for the next few years: Turkey looked like an attractive venue for Classical sites; quite apart from Istanbul with Hagia Sophia, and the artefacts taken from Rome, there was Troy, Pergamum and the other Hellenistic sites down the West Coast. Southern France with Nimes, Arles and Orange had some of the best large Roman buildings in Europe, and finally, although it had never been done before, Egypt had to be on the list for serious students of Ancient History. How we thought the United Soviet Socialist Republics would fit into a collection of Classical Tours is another story altogether!

Turkey

Our ambition rose for our next trip by choosing to go to Turkey, a country which none of us had visited before, but it was full of archaeological potential. As usual the first problem would be getting the travel agents to agree with the proposed itinerary. Sure enough when they responded in writing their itinerary had us visiting 4 sites spread over a distance of 200kms in one day, but leaving us with a day free after that. My final comment in the itinerary that I had sent to them, had read "and then back to Istanbul via Bursa", but I had failed to include the words "as in your brochure", where they had expected us to stay the night in Bursa. I had expected to stay the night in Bursa too, but my slip led them to send us back to

Istanbul overnight without a stop in Bursa. Fortunately these problems were easily corrected before we departed.

The next issue was the airline: the agents decided to use the Yugoslavian JAT – there was a rumour that this stands for "Joke About the Time" – the price increased substantially before we departed, but I was able to convince all members of the group that this was outside my control but still good value for money.

The trip was very popular with the children and their parents understood that a visit to Turkey really meant further study of the Ancient Worlds of Greece and Rome. Two parents even asked if they could join our party, Norman and Trevor; both were good company throughout, even after Trevor was stopped at the security check at the airport – the x-ray revealed that his hand-luggage had a small pair of scissors concealed within its lining. Poor Trevor had no idea that this item had existed, but after we eventually cleared security he became known as Trevor the Terrorist amongst the party!

I had not expected too many problems with the flight to get there, and only once did I have to resort to a tried and tested tactic of speaking very formally and forcefully to a crowd of Italians who did not understand the basic principle of queueing to board our plane. My secret was to speak confidently in Latin! "Ego sum rhetor notissimus: ego multos discipulos optimos educo. Vobis interest cedere. Exspectate huc et sequimini nos!" (*I am a very well-known teacher: I am teaching many excellent pupils. You should give way. Wait here and follow us!*). The use of an ancient language in a commanding voice nearly always had the desired effect, and sure enough the Italian crowd stopped pushing and parted, making way for our party.

Istanbul is the city where East meets West, and is dominated by Hagia Sophia (Holy Wisdom) the largest Christian Church in its day, now turned into a museum, after spending a long period as a Mosque. I suggest that it is one of the modern wonders of world, and architecturally even a rival to the Pantheon in Rome. One of the secrets of Istanbul is the underground water cisterns, accessible by a small hut next to a bus stop in the main square, which in turn had been the Circus for horse-racing in Roman times.

I was determined to take the boys to what has to be one of the experiences in Turkey, a genuine Turkish Bath, or Hamam. On our second night in Istanbul we found one locally to our Hotel. Above the entrance there was a sign which read "For only men" – nothing could be more suitable for this party, although this meant that Maryta would have to forgo the delights of this place. She reluctantly trudged off to a café with one of the younger boys who had decided not to join us along with our guide, Yilmaz. As our group trooped through the entrance, I wondered whether this was a good idea, but I knew that Maryta of all people could look after herself.

Inside the Hamam, we could initially see no-one, so I took the opportunity to warn everyone to keep their wits about them. We found what we identified to be a changing-room by the clothes lying abandoned on the floor, and, although the whole place smelt of lemons, there was little other evidence of civilisation. Eventually a huge man appeared. The most striking thing about him was that he had a patch over one eye, which gave him a rather daunting appearance. Without introducing himself he immediately demanded to know who we were and what we wanted. I quickly replied that we were hoping to have a true Turkish experience at this Hamam. The huge monster of a man laughed knowingly at my words, but then he quickly moved past me and shut the door behind us.

"I'll show you what happens in this place".

He instructed everyone to follow him and he herded them into the next room which had small alcoves. "Now, off with your clothes!" Much consternation followed as everyone reluctantly did as we were told – and we covered our embarrassment with the tiny tea-towels the giant had brought in for everyone to use. I led the way by showing that even I could wrap one successfully around my midriff. Then the giant directed us into the next room which was warm due to some form of underfloor heating. I tried to remain calm in the face of what was happening, but I was very conscious of the younger boys in my care and was anxious that they should not be overawed by this experience. I anticipated that the next room would be very hot and that some physical ordeal might be being prepared for them all. In anticipation of this, Tim stepped forward and offered himself as a "sacrificial lamb" when a volunteer was called for. I accepted Tim's offer readily – he was the youngest and lithest of the adults and he was likely to be the most able to 'survive' the treatment handed out.

Once we moved into the cavernous central room, we were all shocked by the heat. Tim stepped forward before the one-eyed man could call for a volunteer, and he was immediately picked up and deposited face down on the circular stone platform in the middle of the room. This platform was directly above the furnace and the stones were extremely hot. Tim lay there expecting the worst. The giant approached him wearing an intriguing pair of gloves – they were rough and looked more like a pair of oven pads. He also carried a bottle of oil and a bar of soap. He then proceeded to rub the oil vigorously into Tim's back and as he did so he manipulated Tim's legs and arms, contorting them into impossible positions. Tim's face was equally contorted as he accepted the manipulation, but tried not to show any pain. Eventually he could not refrain from grunting and groaning as he was pushed and pulled into different shapes, shapes that I knew would have been impossible for me. After the oil had been applied, the soap was then rubbed all over his body – this was the source of the smell of lemons: it was amazing.

The boys watched somewhat anxiously as Tim went through this torture. It was clear that not many of them would cope with such treatment, but after Tim was doused with warm water to rinse off the soap, the giant encouraged Tim to move away from the circular plinth. It became clear that the big man had taken the opportunity to test Tim to see what stuff he was made of and he had clearly passed the test! At that moment, some other local men appeared from behind concealed doors, and under the instruction of the giant they led the boys off to have a similar 'rub down'. I nodded my encouragement to all and was relieved to see that none were being placed on the hottest part of the platform, and only soap was being used with hardly any manipulation of limbs taking place. The one-eyed giant then came over to me and insisted that I followed him – he was taking Philip, the youngest boy, into a side chamber and it was clear that he did not want to remove him from the rest of the group without me being aware of it. I was happy to chaperone Philip, as he was given a gentle massage and wash with the lemon-scented soap. Philip enjoyed the experience and was even slightly disappointed that he had to be watched over, wanting to be seen as one of the big boys rather than needing special care!

The process for all took approximately half an hour and then we made our way into a room, where a cold circular pool awaited us. A quick splash and everyone was blowing the air out of our cheeks as the cold water provided that necessary shock to the system. Needless to say the tea-towels were highly inadequate in terms of drying our wet bodies, but we were shown into the area were the furnace was burning, and the warmth of the fire helped dry off our damp bodies. Finally, an extra set of towels were brought in, and everyone was able sit on couches and relax before getting dressed. To complete the whole experience our gigantic host then brought in a tray laden with glasses: he proceeded to pour a rich pungent liquor into each glass for everyone, and invited us all to drink it all in one.

Although there was a level of consternation of amongst the boys, I raised my glass and after saluting the giant I drained it down in one. It was the most glorious mint tea and everyone laughed as they realised that they had been afraid of such a harmless potion! The other local men then came in to join the party and a good time was spent comparing notes on the ups and downs of various teams in the Premier Football League.

We eventually caught up with Maryta and the guide back at our Hotel. She had had some difficulty making sense of what had happened to us inside the Hamam: she had seen the door closed on her by the giant, and she said that she had heard many strange noises, which "sounded as though someone was being tortured"; and then she heard the splashes as if the boys were being drowned in gallons of water. She was pleased to hear their reassuring accounts of the adventures inside the Turkish Baths, but she was not so impressed by their time wasted over discussions of football. Furthermore she was not very sympathetic to Tim who was having difficulty making his limbs go where they normally should have gone, but she was impressed by the way he smelt of lemons - wonderful! When asked how she had got on with Yilmaz, she produced a red rose which he had bought her at the café. He had wanted to make her feel welcome in his country!

Before heading out on our coach tour to the rest of Ionian coast, we decided to take a boat ride up the Bosphorus. Despite Yilmaz deciding not to come with us, this turned out to be more straightforward than one might imagine. The ferry was boarded by the chain bridge and it cost hardly anything. The problem came when we decided that the journey had reached the limits of our interest – after two hours we disembarked on the north side and walked en masse to a taxi rank in order to return to central Istanbul. As soon as they saw us coming – or so it seemed – all the taxis drove off! Not too worried, I led everyone to a bus stop which looked like it was going to have buses heading in the right direction. Relatively quickly a bus arrived and I bought the whole party's tickets from the somewhat surprised bus driver. Buses had priority over other transport in the Istanbul area so progress was relatively quick. As we sped along, I found myself talking to a well-dressed gentleman who had expressed an interest in what we were doing. After I had briefly explained the purpose of our whole trip, he said:

"But you are on the wrong bus to get you back into central Istanbul – you need that one behind us!"

At which point I passed the message to the rest of the team "Get off at the next stop and get on the bus immediately behind us." No sooner had I said this, we pulled up at a stop. I quickly thanked the gentleman for his help and led our group off one bus and onto the next one, waving the tickets from the first bus at the driver of the next bus, who looked even more surprised than his colleague, but nodded and let us all on. We eventually reached the spot where we had caught the ferry in the first place, and I confidently headed up the hill towards the direction where our hotel was. Maryta was amazed that I knew where I was going, especially as it was now getting dark. In truth, while my sense of direction has always been good, on this occasion it was more by luck that we found ourselves back at the hotel in time for our evening meal.

At Troy we were full of doubt that the rather naff construction resembling a horse was the type of thing the Greeks following Odysseus' cunning plan would have used to get inside the walls of ancient Ilium. Yilmaz just wanted Maryta to have a memento of our visit there and so bought her a souvenir copy of the wooden horse. At Pergamum, we saw the largest open-air theatre in Turkey and were impressed by its extraordinary acoustics. I realised that our bus driver, Umit, was planning in collusion with Yilmaz to take us to his cousin's alabaster shop after our tour before driving south to Ephesus, and I encouraged the boys to 'get lost' for a while to delay our departure. As a result we found a genuine alabaster factory near where our coach was waiting for us, and this proved much more interesting and had no feelings of compulsion to buy! A similar issue arose when choosing restaurants to eat in: Yilmaz or Umit always seemed to know someone in the restaurants – not surprising since they did these trips frequently, but I was not convinced that the entertainment was always appropriate for a school party. In one of the more remote restaurants the owner challenged adults to drinking competitions, and then donated head-dresses to married couples whose lips he had forced into an uncomfortable kiss! Goodness knows what the boys made of this, especially when they were then serenaded onto the bus by the owner's henchman on a ukulele!

Ephesus is a huge site spread over acres and in some ways rather difficult to appreciate, but at that stage it was still able to absorb the large crowds disgorging from coaches which have collected the tourists from the cruise ships docking at Bodrum. In contrast, Kusadasi, the small town designated to host visitors struggles to deal with such numbers and our hotel that night failed to have any water until after 9pm – a real shock for the delicate visitors from Norfolk. I feared that Turkey was in danger of "prostituting" itself in an attempt to attract visitors, while failing to create the infra-structure to support mass tourism yet. However, back on the ancient site one could not fail to be impressed: in addition to the famous Library, the theatre where St Paul is said to have lectured the locals on the birth of Christianity was most impressive. The other area to explore was the Harbour Road which is flanked by shops, and one can even find slots in the pavement where street lights would have been placed every evening in ancient times.

Our tour then headed back inland and northwards towards Bursa; the countryside is dominated by the simplicity of the countryside. If you are lucky you might spot the young shepherd boys wearing their cloaks made from felt which act like a firm tent around them in wet weather. When we reached Aphrodisias, and as it was April 1st, we adults agreed to play the customary pranks on the pupils. After parking our coach, I instructed everyone about the dangers around the site.

"First of all, you have to avoid the poisonous spiders that lie in wait on the fields that surround the ruins. So I advise you all to tuck your trousers into your socks to make sure that the spiders can't get to your flesh. Secondly, you must not tread on the wild anemones that decorate the meadows at this time of year – the Turks consider this brings bad luck, and I don't think Umit will let us travel on his bus ever again!" At least this made them all walk very carefully over the site which at this time of the year was truly wonderful to behold.

Aphrodisias, like Ephesus, is another huge site, but it was not as easy to understand; it looked as though it was still being excavated, but we saw very few workers on site. My stand-out memories are twofold: one was the sound of the frogs in the flooded orchestra of the smaller of the two theatres – it made me realise what Aristophanes was imitating when he had his Chorus of Frogs call out "Brekeke-kex-koax-koax" in his satiric comedy of the same name. The second powerful memory was that of the whole group walking across the flat meadow area which led to a sharp drop: it was not until we were on top of it that we saw the jaw-dropping size of the 30,000 seater Stadium used for both athletics (popular with the Greeks) and gladiatorial and wild beast fights (popular with the Romans). Almost everyone had a sharp intake of breath on seeing it.

The pupils were all delighted that Umit would let us back onto his bus after our careful avoidance of the anemones: I had prepared a bag of genuine Turkish Delight for everyone as a reward for their care and attention during this site visit. From Aphrodisias we drove to Pammukale, a site with hot springs and lime deposits from the pools overflowing down the mountainside. It was quite an experience to swim in open-air pools, admiring spiral-carved Hellenistic columns lying below us in the deeper parts of the pools. Our last stop took us to Bursa, where at last Maryta was able to sample the Turkish Bath experience along with the rest of the group. The hotel had hot springs in the basement and we were reassured that this was for both sexes with everyone having to wear swimming costumes. She was not so impressed by Yilmaz, our guide, who seemed to think that his tea-towel (again!) was an adequate covering with or without his swimwear. Yilmaz, however, was still trying to impress her, and because he had discovered that she was a journalist, he produced the largest pile of newspapers "for her scrap-book". I am not sure that many of therse made it back to Norfolk!

As we boarded our JAT flight back to the UK our minds were full of the extraordinary images which we had seen during this wonderful trip, but most of all the smell of lemon soap from the Hamam lingered in everyone's memories. However, our adventure was not over yet: much to our surprise we had an unscheduled extra touch-down at Zagreb Airport. No-one got off, but one new passenger boarded the plane, carrying an elephant's foot (which occupied one seat) and wearing the largest gold bracelet. It almost seemed as though he had stuck his arm out and requested the plane to stop like a local bus! At least it alleviated the boredom.

Lessons learnt:

Try to take as few parents as possible on trips, in case they turn out to be terrorists! Turkey is a male-dominated country where it is not wise to abandon one's wife, even in the company of the courier.

Always try to remember the direction from where you have come, in order to find the way back home.

Provence

Rather surprisingly the attractions of Southern France are many for the Classicist: Nimes and Arles with their amphitheatres still in use as either bull-rings or open-air cinemas, but don't miss out on the Maison Carree in Nimes which is one of the best preserved Roman temples in the world; Orange has the most complete Roman theatre that I have ever been to, which is also still in use – when a young boy I attended a Jazz concert by Duke Ellington and his Band there. The other well-known site has to be the Pont du Gard, a Roman aqueduct which stands proud over the Gard, a tributary of the river Rhone. But there is much more worth looking out for – the small town of Vaison la Romaine as its name suggests is home to a simple Roman town lay-out; Glanum is also a good site revealing an interesting mix of Gallo-Greek-Roman styles in its town buildings; and finally Barbegal, the site of a flour mill powered by 16 water-wheels – a place which Time Team would have loved!

But if you go to Provence, it would be a mistake to miss out on the Art; this is where Van Gogh, Gauguin, Cezanne, Renoir, Picasso and Chagall all spent time in or around Aix-en-Provence, Arles and Avignon, so we decided to combine our trip with John from the Art Department. Since we were not sure how many pupils would sign up for this trip, we adopted two other ideas which might keep the trip affordable with manageable numbers: firstly, we decided to reduce the cost by going by coach, and secondly, we invited the Girls' High School to join us.

Coach travel is never the most comfortable especially as it involved driving over-night to the South of France, but it did mean that we had our own drivers throughout the trip and they were staying at the same accommodation in the Youth Holiday

Park in Vaison la Romaine. One thing that has happened since the arrival of Mobile Phones is the inability of young people to either observe the world around them and the reduction in their preparedness to talk face to face to each other. In those pre-Social Media days, we were quite hopeful that by traveling by coach the members of this trip would at least talk to each other and possibly look at the countryside as we progressed through France. Of course that was a forlorn hope and instead the use of the coach's cassette radio was in demand: as no-one could agree on what type of music was acceptable, Maryta solved the problem by playing Roald Dahl's The Giraffe, the Pelly and Me to the whole coach – we had both Holly and Jozef with us on this particular trip and they became particularly popular members of the group, providing welcome distractions at both the Holiday Park or on the coach.

In many ways the trip was extremely successful with very few hiccoughs along the way. This may have been because Elizabeth from the Girls' High School had been required by the Girls Public Day School Trust (their governing body) to produce extensive documentation about what the girls could and could not do. Risk assessments were produced before they became a requirement in all schools and although they seemed very 'over the top' at the time, they probably made good sense. There was only one site which caused me a particular concern: the medieval hill-fortress of Les Baux is very impressive to visit, but the concept of Health and Safety clearly did not exist with the slightest of low metal railings keeping visitors away from a 200 foot drop. All the adults were quite relieved when we managed to get everyone back on the coach safely.

The other issue I remember causing a major concern was surprisingly the food. The Holiday Park served good French breakfasts, but eventually gave in to the demand to have toast for the 'poor English kids'. You might think that in France you would enjoy good food, and I have fond memories of our own family holiday where lunch was just bread cheese and tomatoes – but what bread, cheese and tomatoes! So we were expecting to have packed lunches for our group along a similar style. The hosts at our Holiday Park decided that we should experience at more robust lunch, and our coach drivers opened the boxes to reveal slices of cold beef – but beef that had probably only just been shown the oven, never mind cooked in one for any length of time. I am ashamed to say that none of us, not even the staff, managed to eat any of this rare meat, and we had to prevail upon our drivers to find us a suitable place to buy bread, cheese and tomatoes. The other image I have is of the pupils enjoying a version of "Pooh Sticks" with the un-ripened oranges, we had been given, down a hilly road near Avignon: not very clever, but quite entertaining!

It was quite interesting to see how some of our boys reacted to having girls as companions on this trip. One young man, Alec seemed completely oblivious to them. Alec had been a regular on our trips. This year he had returned from the German Exchange the day before our departure to France and so he just transferred his bags from one coach to the next one. Unfortunately Alec was not very hygienically aware either. It soon became apparent that he was always wearing the same T-shirt, with two pullovers on top finished off with an anorak. We began to fear that he had probably worn exactly these items throughout his visit to Germany as well. Maryta boldly raised the subject with him – he was completely unaware of his behaviour and immediately changed his clothes to a new set, which he then wore non-stop for the rest of the trip!

John, our Art specialist, was invaluable on this trip as expected, and the visit to the galleries in Aix-en-Provence enabled him to reveal his passion for Cezanne in particular. I think all the children appreciated his description of how the artist used geometrical forms to reproduce his images of the countryside. I am not so sure that they were as interested in his talk about Van Gogh and Picasso in Avignon, because of the distractions provided by the hawkers on the "Pont"! Children always seemed to want to buy something even if it is clearly tat! At least we did not have the problem that another group had which was that some of their party had bought fireworks and a large "hunting knife" – fortunately these were revealed before their coach reached customs and were disposed of before an explanation was required at the Border!

Lessons learnt:
Health and Safety rules are not consistent throughout the European Community, so beware long drops! Be prepared for the paperwork associated with schools from the Girls' Public Day School Trust.

Moscow and Leningrad

Singing Parry's "Jerusalem" may not have been the most tactful thing to do in the USSR, but part of the Itinerary included a visit to one of Moscow's People Palaces where we were going to be entertained by the talented young people being educated there, and we had been warned that we would be expected to perform something in return. This sort of activity had not featured on any of my Classics trips, so it had not been high on my list of priorities before setting off to Moscow. So Parry's Jerusalem, the one hymn that the whole school actually joined in singing was going to be our fallback solution at the People Palace!

What we were doing in the USSR proved that we had to sometimes think outside the box: there had been a regular series of trips to the obvious Classical sites (Italy, Greece, Turkey and France), and after one of these a child had suggested that we might consider somewhere beyond the boundaries of the Classics. The USSR came to mind – although the Iron Curtain still existed in 1984, the Olympics had been held in Moscow in 1980 and Travel Agents did a good business in taking school parties to Moscow and Leningrad. So we sold the trip on an experience beyond the norm: there were a good number of takers, and David and Mary joined Maryta and me as staff helpers.

The first challenge was negotiating passport control on arrival in Moscow: there were a couple of other school parties on our chartered flight and when some of the pupils were presented with a metal-detecting arch guarded by a soldier armed with a Kalishnikov they collapsed in a fit of hysteria. No staff from the other schools seemed to rush to the rescue, so Maryta just told them to calm down and walk through the arch without causing a scene – "It's no big deal. The soldier is just doing his job, providing security here."

Meanwhile I spotted the one young man in our party who was likely to keep me awake at night: Chuck was an American – he had had to get a different Visa to all the Brits, so he was going to stand out in the first place – but to add to his uniqueness, he had decided to wear a couple of lapel badges, one for the Stars and Stripes flag and the other for "Solidarnosc!" (the Polish Revolutionaries) on disembarking the plane. I intercepted him as he approached the booth where his passport and visa were about to be checked, and removed the two badges before the Immigration Officers got the wrong (or right) impression of Chuck! He was going to be trouble!

Our accommodation in Moscow was in the Olympic village, which was quite pleasant: a block of high-rise flats with a large communal dining-room. Each floor had a "Guardian" sitting outside the lift, keeping an eye on all the comings and goings. This did create an image of "Big Brother" (or Sister), and David was quite convinced that his room was bugged by the KGB, but as Maryta tactfully pointed out to him "What are you going to talk about that they would want to hear?" The last thing I wanted was the staff spreading anxiety amongst the kids.

During the time of the USSR, Moscow did not seem to have anything worth seeing that existed before 1917. At least that was the impression we got from Irena, our official guide. The Lenin Museum, the Space Park and the shopping Mall Gum were interesting without being really special. We did not join the queue to see the mummified corpse of Lenin but wandered around St Basil's in Red Square and cathedrals inside the Kremlin, surprised by their preservation during the Communist regime. Just to prove that there was some Classical experiences to be had even on this trip, I was delighted by the irony of the iron railing s around the Kremlin: they were decorated with the "fasces" (bundles of rods and axes) of Ancient Rome, as well as the symbols of the 20th Century Fascist States!

Irena was very polite and tried very hard to make sure that we saw everything that we wanted. One evening I had led a small group of kids back into the centre of Moscow from our Hotel using the underground: this is one of the secret delights of Moscow, majestically decorated with Art Deco reliefs and with piped classical music (mainly Tchaikovsky and Rachmaninov) being played in between the arrival of the trains. Another feature seemed to be the large number of down-and-out Muscovites who resorted to drinking floor polish as a means of forgetting their lot: presumably alcohol was too expensive. When we reached the centre, I led our party to the Bolshoi Opera House. We arrived just as an interval had started – a performance of Boris Godunov was being sung to a packed audience. As we were standing observing members of the audience as they emerged for the break, a large Caribbean man came over to me and offered Maryta and me his two tickets – he and his friend were from the Cuban delegation visiting Moscow and they clearly did not enjoy Mussorgsky's music. I would have leapt at this opportunity, but with the small party of boys with us we had to decline his kind offer. Just to add an extra disappointment, and concern, at the end of the evening when we returned to the Hotel, I found Chuck sitting at the bar negotiating the sale of his extensive collection of lapel badges (how I wish I had searched his bag before departure) with the barman in return for a regular supply of vodka! I quickly put the barman straight about "none of our pupils drinking vodka or any other alcohol", and then I disposed of Chuck's badges discreetly.

We told Irena of our experience on the following day, and she decided that she would do what she could to get us into the Bolshoi before we left by train to Leningrad. That evening as our coach drove towards the railway station, Irena told us of her plan: Maryta was to walk and talk as if she was a 'prima ballerina', and I was to accompany her saying that we were from the London Festival Ballet - in fact, my cousin was the Ballet Master with this company, so I knew the role! The coach just pulled up by the Stage Door of the Bolshoi and we were ushered via some back stairs into a box. It was quite something to see the inside of the famous theatre – which clearly dated from before 1917! – and it transpired that we were being offered the box for the evening's performance of Swan Lake: if only we had not got a train to catch!

Leningrad was a much more cultured city: the Hermitage Museum stands out in my memory as being full of amazing works of art, particularly the Rodin sculptures and the Room of Mirrors. The Itinerary had included a trip to the Russian State Circus, which was full of acrobats and animals which had been "trained" to perform for the delights of the Russian audience – not really to our taste, I'm afraid. Therefore, after my experience with the Bolshoi in Moscow, I was determined to see if we could get tickets for the Kirov Theatre while we were in Leningrad. It transpired that on the one evening when we could get tickets for the ballet "La Sylphide", Leningrad were playing ice-hockey against Moscow: probably the biggest match of the season. David and Mary were keen to go to this and so we offered the pupils a choice of which event they would prefer to attend. Much to my surprise 24 out of the 26 opted for the ballet. We had a wonderful night, even joining in the 'Volta' sipping a glass of cheap champagne as we processed around the Green Room during the interval. David and Mary, with the two remaining boys (including Chuck!), equally enjoyed the ice-hockey, which I believe Moscow won. Chuck was particularly pleased as he had managed to sell an old pair of denim jeans for $30 to one of the Muscovite supporters who had been sitting next to him – was this the 'black market' or the 'blue market'?

I was always determined not to miss out on anything interesting in these cities, and on one occasion as the coach was driving along one of the wide avenues after our visit to the St Peter and St Paul Cathedral, I knew that we were going to pass the Natural History Museum, in which there was the frozen remains of a baby mammoth. I insisted that the driver should stop the coach, and I led our whole group without any tickets through the museum to see the mammoth and then led them all the way back onto the coach, thanking everyone profusely.

The most embarrassing moment we had on this trip was upon leaving our hotel in Leningrad on the way to the airport. Everyone was on the coach, but there seemed to be a delay. Eventually one of the "Guardians" from our floor in the Hotel appeared and it was explained that one of the Hotel towels was missing. I was furious – I deplore this custom of stealing such items as a memento. I suspected that Chuck was likely to be the thief, but I was more disappointed to discover that one of the other senior boys had put a towel from his room into his case. I would have to deal with him when we got back to Norwich, but for the time being the towel was returned with as many apologies one can muster under the circumstances. It was almost as embarrassing as singing "Jerusalem" at the People Palace – which we did not actually do, because one of the other British schools came to the rescue by volunteering to sing "I'd like to teach the world to sing in perfect harmony!" – much more appropriate for the occasion, and probably more tuneful than our all male rendition of Parry!

The final excitement came at the Airport: one of the girls from another school had lost her ticket for the return flight and had been presented at the check-in with a document that indicated that she was liable to pay 3 million roubles (with 40 roubles to the £Sterling, that was quite a sum!) if she was conducting an act of fraud. I am fairly sure that she was the girl who had over-reacted to the metal-detecting arch on arrival, and once again she was being ignored by her school's staff. I reassured her that all would be well – it was a chartered flight booked to carry all the pupils and staff from our schools, so she was not conducting any fraud – her roubles would be safe. It is extraordinary to me how some staff seem to forget, or avoid, accepting responsibility for their charges on such trips. I am always amazed that more problems do not hit the news.

Lessons learnt:
Despite worries about visits to a totalitarian state, the main problem will remain with those individual pupils who go outside the box: so be prepared to keep a very close eye on everyone at all times. However, don't be too surprised by the willingness of your charges to experience new cultural challenges.

The theatre at Ephesus.

The stadion at Aphrodisias.

5 - The Journey to the Underworld and back

Any voyage to Egypt would need proper planning, and I approached a schools' travel agency to talk through the itinerary and they assured me that their advice would prove to be invaluable. What they had not admitted at first was that they had never taken a group to Egypt before. So their advice might be invaluable, but based on no experience whatsoever!

I was sure that, despite the travel company's lack of knowledge, our own experience and confidence would enable us to create an itinerary taking in the most extraordinary sights. I wanted the best team to support me but Tim, an obvious choice, was unavailable. However, Rev. Robin had volunteered to come along – a good idea to have someone with a religious background! Given that we were going into the unknown, I decided not to take any risks with someone who might lack the confidence to face this challenge. Therefore I turned to John Jake, a Senior Housemaster and Geology teacher whose knowledge of the terrain might prove useful: and most importantly, he had been grown up in Egypt.

At a planning meeting some six months before we set off, I had discussed the proposed itinerary with the Travel Agent's Representative, Cassandra, who was encouraging and yet unable to answer all of my questions, having never been to Egypt herself – she was from Greece! The final question I posed Cassandra left her speechless for a while. "What will happen if Sadat, the President of Egypt, is assassinated?" Eventually she replied "Then you should forget your trip to Egypt. There will be no stability and you cannot rely on the support of those whose help you will need to get you home."

"Well, let's hope that I am worrying over nothing!" I said. Cassandra rather melodramatically gave me the impression that she believed our trip might be cursed. I just laughed and tried to wipe that idea out of mind.

However, I confess that I found it difficult to settle that night and spent most of my time tossing and turning in my bed. When I awoke from a fitful final hour of light sleep, I was greeted by Maryta who had just heard on the radio the dreadful news – "President Sadat has been assassinated – last night at a State Celebration he was killed by one of the soldiers on the parade ground." My first thoughts turned to Cassandra's words "You can forget your trip". But I was not going to be put off quite so readily, and instructed all the staff to keep the preparations on track – after all there were still six months before we intended setting off, and I remained confident that Egypt would have returned to some form of equilibrium by then. What I was really worried about was whether I should expect a visit from the Egyptian Secret Service: after all I seemed to have extraordinary foreknowledge of the President's assassination. And if they ever did hear about this, how would I explain myself? Fortunately, they had other things to worry about and they never came calling.

The Travel Agents agreed that after six months we could still run the trip, and the parents of the children on the trip all seemed comfortable with our reassurances that all would be well. To add an extra complication, Maryta wanted to accompany me on this trip, but she was seven months pregnant when we set off. However, she is a determined woman and I was happy to have her with me, especially over this time. Our plane touched down in Cairo just after midnight. We were greeted by Moufid, our courier for the trip, at the airport and were taken straight to our hotel. Moufid seemed somewhat anxious as we approached the Hotel and I thought that he was merely concerned that we should not be exposed to any dangers. However, when we stepped inside the Hotel, it became clear that Moufid's anxiety related to the availability of beds at this early hour. Whatever I had agreed about the itinerary with Cassandra back in Norfolk was irrelevant in Egypt: another group (a party of Germans) had checked into the Hotel one hour earlier and had been allocated the rooms which were originally reserved for our group. Despite my protests it seemed that nothing could be done. There was only one room available, which I was about to offer to Maryta – a bed for the rest of the night was the least I could offer in her condition. However, John Jake had already made his move and taken up occupation, seemingly claiming "Age before Beauty"! I was furious, but Maryta calmed me and said that she was happy just to be with the rest of us.

Meanwhile Moufid had decided that the best way to overcome the "lack of beds" issue was to provide us all with a three-hour lecture on the history and customs to be found within Egypt, and had directed our group into the spacious Hotel Lounge where most of the party could find a chair or sofa to occupy. By design or accident, Moufid's languorous talk allowed 'Morpheus' to cast his spell over the party and most of them managed at least an hour of sleep: they would not have been able to score too highly in any test on Egypt's customs, but I was confident that they would have plenty of opportunity to discover those throughout the rest of the journey. After what seemed like no more than three hours the sun appeared to lift the gloom outside, and the whole party were ready to enjoy a hearty breakfast – that was until the waiters pulled back the heavy curtains, which were laden with clouds of flies! No-one's appetite was particularly healthy, while the flies swarmed about the dining-room and eventually settled back on the curtains.

Over breakfast I was informed that rooms would not be available for us until much later in the morning, so I decided to get everyone out of their lethargic state by a good brisk walk in the sunlight. Although I had never been to this city before I adopted my usual approach which was to appear confident and to keep my wits about me. I had asked the Hotel staff in which direction the main Museum was and by following the basic directions I felt comfortable as I led the party of twenty-six down a broad public street. We all noticed the sandbags surrounding what turned out to be the Post Office building with armed soldiers looking out suspicious of anything unusual: this was probably the only real sign we saw indicating that the last President had been assassinated, and that the country was still in a "State of Emergency" – ironically, given his eventual demise the newly elected President Mubarak was very popular with the Egyptians!

Anyway I reiterated my instructions to keep together as a group and to maintain an air of confidence. "Keep your eyes on me and my panama hat – that way we can keep close together!" I said. Not everyone felt so confident, especially without a reasonable amount of sleep, but I wanted to send out a positive message. However, I was particularly concerned as to how Maryta would cope with the 'forced march'.

After a short while I found that there was an Arab-looking gentleman walking right next to me, keeping exact pace with me: when I slowed down for the group to catch up, so did the man, and when I hurried to cross the roads, the man did the same. Eventually I decided to catch his eye and challenge him, but the man beat me to it. "Welcome to our city. Where are you from? Where are you going?" I tried to keep my responses simple for I saw little benefit at this stage in engaging in a full blown conversation: "We are from England and we are heading towards the Museum". "Oh, England! I sell crocuses to a firm in a place called Yorkshire: do you know them?" and he mentioned the name of a company, which I had not heard of. "England has many people in it and we do not come from that area" I explained. "But where are you going with all these boys following you?" the man pressed. "We are just going to the main square where the Museum is." "What an excellent idea. I have a perfume factory just next to the Museum, and you must bring your boys to see what we do there – it is free of charge and I would like to help make your visit to our country most memorable."

My mind was not as sharp as I would have liked after the previous sleepless night, and I could think of no good reason for refusing the man's offer; and so the group headed off towards Mansoor's Perfume Factory opposite the Museum. Of course, I realised as soon as we entered the "Factory" that this was just a euphemism for "shop", but I was able to warn the group once we were shown into an anteroom with soft cushioned benches around the four walls. "They are going to show you some perfumes and tell you how they make them, and don't be surprised if you are then urged to buy some. My advice is to politely refuse – it is just the start of our trip and I suspect that we may come across many more such "factories" on our voyage, and you may want to delay until you have seen what else is available." Mansoor had gone into the back room while I was talking, and he shortly emerged with a servant carrying a large tray with drinks poured in glasses: this turned out to be peppermint tea which everyone accepted politely.

The talk about the making of perfumes was probably very interesting, but I was not sure that many of the group actually took much of it on board – they could not be described as being mentally alert at this stage either. Only Maryta seemed to be absorbing all the technical details outlined by Mansoor. Eventually after a second glass of peppermint tea, the sales pitch was put to them. Mansoor assured everyone that he had the best price in town and he was sure that the boys' mothers or sisters would appreciate them returning with a bottle of his perfume which he normally sold on for packaging (and selling at increased prices!) by the great perfume companies in Paris and London. The party all remained pretty nonplussed at the invitation to buy, and I felt happy that they all were taking my advice not to buy anything. However, I then became aware of someone near me becoming restless and then her voice broke forth asking if she could have a bottle of the golden perfume. Maryta's enthusiasm had got the better of her, and sure enough it opened the flood gates with boys from all corners of the room piping up that they wanted one or two bottles for their family back home. Mansoor's smile grew broader and broader as almost everyone took a parcel from his "Factory". In fact, he was so happy that he took me into the backroom and presented me with a complimentary bottle of the finest perfume in his possession. What could I do but accept it gracefully? I emerged from the Factory to see Maryta congratulating the group on securing their "special prices" from Mansoor, and so I led them all back to the Hotel (and their freshly prepared rooms!) in buoyant mood. What I was not to know at the time was that Mansoor's perfume was all "concentrate liquid" and needed to be mixed with specific proportions of alcohol to achieve the form that normally appeared on the open market – perhaps those who were fully awake during the talk on the manufacturing of the product would be able to present their mothers and sisters with the final product, but I suspect that many of those bottles remained unused once they had returned to England!

The remaining days' visit in the capital city was most memorable for the right reasons: the ancient sites were full of wonder, particularly the huge pyramids, lying like huge cakes (which is what the word 'pyramid' means in ancient Greek) outside the city limits: walking inside an almost solid building, bent double down the narrow passage to gain entrance to the Pharaoh's tomb is a unique experience – you can feel the weight of all that stone around you. Outside, hawkers tried to tempt our group into buying papyrus paintings, carpets, or even taking a ride into the desert on wild horses. The most adventurous of our group went for a camel ride around the base of the Great Pyramid. I had been reassured by the fact that I had seen members of the police force on their own camels - these animals rather comically had perfected a siren call through their large nostrils to announce their arrival.

Then our itinerary took us south overnight by train: I remember the porters at the station having a challenge between themselves to see which of them could carry the largest number of cases onto the train at one go. They threaded a leather cable through the case handles so that they could carry as many as possible. They were clearly hoping to win a larger tip commensurate with their efforts. The champion of them all disappeared under the mountain of cases he was carrying, so that one was confronted with the sight of a mound of cases making their own way down the platform, moving as if on their own.

One incident that I had not expected occurred on the overnight journey. Rev. Robin knocked on my cabin at around ten o'clock: he had discovered that some of the other travellers had been particularly attracted to one of our party – Helena, the sister of one of the boys, had been allowed to join the trip at the last minute. My memory shot back to the problems of that earlier trip to Greece, but Rev. Robin quickly disabused me of this concern. In fact, the problem was potentially greater, in that one of the local men had taken such a shine to this pure and innocent girl that he wanted to buy her! He had offered three camels and five oxen for her. Robin had interceded and made it clear that no-one was for sale; we agreed that Helena should be removed from the eyes of the locals on the train. She was to spend the rest of the journey sharing the cabin with Maryta, while I took up occupation of her cabin, ready to fend off any interested parties! Another sleepless night!

Once we had arrived early at Luxor, our party was shown to our hotel and given rooms. I was eager to transport them soon after a light breakfast, and before the sun rose too high, across the great river Nile to visit the Valley of the Kings with its Royal burial tombs. While waiting for the last table to finish their fruit and tea breakfast the rest of the group were treated to a display by a boy whose job was to keep the Reception tidy and clean. He arrived carrying a large bottle of water and a broom. He positioned himself firmly in the centre of the open floor area near the counter, took a large swig of water out his bottle and then proceeded to spray it back out of his mouth around the floor area in front of him. The whole party were stunned by what appeared to them to be a display of uncouth behaviour – until he then picked up his broom and his tactic then became clear. His mouth-watered spray had dampened the dust sitting on the floor, so that when he swept it to a pile it did not fly away on the wind, but collected neatly in solid pile for him to collect in a pan. It took him several more sprays of water to complete his task, but the party left the lobby impressed by his skill which had been acquired over a number of years.

At length, the group followed me out of the Hotel to the river jetty, and discovered that the ferry which we had hoped to get had already departed to the other side of the river. A second boat was moving into place, but I could see that this was going to be very full of locals on their way across the river and there would be little room for our party. Nevertheless I urged the boys to pack together and be ready to squeeze themselves onto the boat as soon as they could. Rugby training has its uses, and without too much difficulty the group managed to be some of the first on board. Unfortunately when the ferry was fully loaded, it became clear that we would now be some of the last to get off on the other side. Despite it being a short journey across, the delay of missing the first boat and then disembarking from the second boat last was potentially disastrous. As I came down the gang-plank, I was greeted by Moufid, who had gone on ahead: "Our coach has been stolen – the Germans have got here before us and have taken it." I was lost for words, but Moufid knew that it was his responsibility to solve the problem. He left me to find the local Tourist Police, known locally as the "Furies". They were absolutely clear in their action. At the long blast of a whistle, five taxi cabs were summoned, and their drivers were given strict instruction to take our group to all the places we requested. The last comment that I heard was the "Furies" telling Moufid that the bus driver would lose his licence for his actions, and that they would watch out for those Germans who were proving to be the bane of our journey.

The taxi drivers were obviously scared stiff of these Police, who had clearly earned their name "Furies" over the years. The drivers did exactly what they had been told and the visits to the various sites passed very well. At one stop we suddenly saw one of the drivers chasing after us as we walked up to the entrances of tombs dug into the pale orange rocks. He was waiving something in his hands, and eventually when the driver reached us, we worked out that one of boys had dropped his wallet on the back seat of the taxi, and the driver was anxious not to be seen as a potential thief. Nothing could have been further from the truth as they gave us an excellent tour of the various valleys that contained tombs on that side of the river.

The pharaohs' tombs are extraordinary works of art, with all the passageways lined with exquisite art leading us down to the main tomb chambers. However, my most abiding memory was that of Moufid demonstrating to the boys how the artists lit the tombs deeply buried in the earth as they painted such amazing scenes of the Gods and the human passage to the "next world". He produced a number of metal trays which had been finely polished, and one was held at the entrance of the tomb catching the sunlight and directing it down the straight line of the tunnel; at a bend another tray was held to redirect the shaft of light down the next tunnel and the final tray was used to shine the continuing beam onto the wall where the painters were working. It was such a simple method and yet it was an excellent example of the craftsmen using the resources to hand (ie the sun) and understanding what we today would have called the physics of light! The look of amazement at something so simple yet effective on the younger boys' faces was the picture that I have always remembered.

On the following day our party travelled to the huge temples in Karnack and Luxor built by the Pharaohs nearly two thousand years ago. I had lined up a treat for the party: as they emerged from the Hotel in the morning expecting to see a coach, instead they saw a line of caleches – pony driven carriages. The journey took about half an hour and everyone thoroughly enjoyed it, even some of the carriage drivers who seemed to believe that it should be treated as a race. The Temples were truly amazing and even the younger boys enjoyed them after I instructed them to seek out various cartouches belonging to the key Pharaohs, as if they were following an orienteering course.

The final leg south brought us to Aswan, famed for its power-generation created via a dam across the Nile cataracts. As we approached the outskirts of the city, the sight of fluorescent lighting tubes attached to the outside of mud huts or TV aerials sticking out of the reed roofs caused much mirth amongst the group. The Hotel we were staying at was called the Cleopatra, and I had decided that I would take no risks on the first afternoon. So I instructed everyone to remain within their rooms until the call for dinner: I was determined not to lose occupation to those Germans who had plagued our group so far on the trip. "Keep the doors locked and save your energy for tomorrow's exertions" I advised them all. The biggest irony, however, was that after everyone had come down for dinner, there was a power cut in the Hotel Cleopatra! Fortunately it was short-lived and the most of the food had already been cooked. At last I was able to look forward to a night full of sleep, especially after I had learnt that the Germans had been allocated to another hotel.

Perhaps I was over-confident, but halfway through the night I was awoken by the knocking on my door. One of the boys had come to report that two other boys in his room were being violently sick. At least I was sure that this was not alcohol-related – hopefully it was just something that they had eaten which had not agreed with them. By the following morning the sickness had moved on to being diarrhoea. The two boys were clearly not fit to go on the day's venture and Rev. Robin volunteered to stay behind with them while the rest of the party took a sail boat trip to one of the islands in the middle of the Nile to see an ancient temple and a quarry where various building materials had been sourced. I did become somewhat concerned when I had gathered all the party together in order to return to the mainland, only to find that we were missing one member of the party – John Jake whose main interest, and purpose for coming on the trip, was to explore the geology of this quarry. The boys said that they had last seen him disappearing over the brow of a hill armed with his geology hammer. Eventually – nearly half an hour late - he returned with a broad grin on his face and carrying a large sack full of granite rock samples: not the best of examples for the boys! I did also wonder how he was going to get these samples past Egyptian Customs.

The guide for the day had been a strikingly tall lady who spoke English with an American accent, but she was dressed all in black and definitely not from this part of Egypt. I had been impressed by the guides so far and had expected the same quality from this lady, who went by the name Electra. I was bitterly disappointed: Electra seemed distracted and not interested in our group at all. She gave limited information and when the boys pressed her for more she responded in a curt manner. By the end of the day, Moufid approached me about the usual process of tipping the guide. He had already sensed that I was not impressed, and he was fearful that Electra would be insulted should little or nothing be given to her. Probably because he feared that he would be reported to the "Furies" for failing to instruct me in Egypt's customs, Moufid even offered me some of his own money to be given to Electra, and thus avoid any insult. I stood my ground "No! She has not done her job and she does not deserve any reward."

As we returned to the Hotel Cleopatra, I decided not to ignore Electra but went up to her to explain why I was not going to give her a tip. Electra anticipated my approach and acknowledged that she had not carried out her role as guide at the level she normally performed: she did not expect a tip from school children. I appreciated her honesty, even if I still felt that our party had been short-changed by her performance throughout the day. Over dinner Moufid explained that Electra was related to the President Sadat's family and she was still in mourning for his death, hence her black clothes. I felt more sympathetic at this news, but I sensed that Electra's lack of enthusiasm for her job on that day reflected her preoccupation with the turmoil within her family; was it too fanciful to suggest that her distraction was due to the possibility that she was part of a group planning revenge for Sadat's assassination? Perhaps I had read too many Greek tragedies!

The journey back to the capital city was another overnight train journey. The two sick boys were seen by a doctor before they boarded the train, and they diagnosed amoebic dysentery. The only treatment recommended was to put them on a saline drip throughout the night. Moufid had somehow negotiated with the doctors to allow him to change the drips during the journey, which would enable the party to keep to our timetable. He had apparently informed the doctors that he was a trained dentist, which was news to me - I remembered an earlier conversation with Moufid where he had described himself as an out-of-work engineer! Not surprisingly I spent most of the overnight journey awake keeping a check on the sick boys and Moufid's attempts to change the drips. It was a good job that I had stayed awake with them, as not only did the "dentist" proved less than competent in finding a vein when trying to re-attach the drip, but once he even allowed some air to get into the tube feeding the needle! My father was a doctor, and I was at least aware of the fatal consequences of pockets of air flowing around the body via the blood system, and so I stopped Moufid from reconnecting the drip with the air in the tube. I wondered how much of these experiences I could pass on to our parents, or even to other groups wishing to travel around Egypt, the Land of the Dead. Nonetheless Moufid tried to maintain that he knew what he was doing. I was utterly relieved when we reached Cairo, and a local doctor was summoned to check over the boys for this last day.

The main focus of the last day was a visit to the Museum in order to see the world famous Death Mask of Tut Ank Amun, whose tomb we had visited in the Valley of the Kings. Maryta was determined to make sure that the two sick boys would be able to tell their parents that despite their illness they still managed to see this Death Mask. She undertook to escort the boys by taxi to the Museum – the rest of the party went again by foot: after all we knew the way, via the Perfume factory! Once at the Museum, Maryta sat the two boys down at the foot of the main staircase while she sent a couple of others as scouts to find the quickest and most direct route to the Mask. Once this had been established she marched the two up to the cabinet that held the Mask, ensured they stayed there for at least five minutes to take it in and then marched them back via the toilets, and finally back to the hotel.

For our final coach journey back to the airport, Moufid had decided to take our group via the parade ground where President Sadat had been assassinated – was this just to remind us all, as if we needed reminding, that we had been in the 'Land of the Dead', I wondered? Our visits to the tombs of the pharaohs had all taken us to an Underworld where the ancients believed that their rulers would continue to live beyond death. I did not feel that this was the belief in modern Egypt about its recently assassinated ruler. I was relieved to get out of Egypt with all the party together and, while they might not all be in the rudest of health, in a few days I would be able to reflect positively on our experiences as the first group ever to have travelled to Egypt and survive to tell the tale! I even took the opportunity to doze lightly as the aeroplane took off.

There was still one issue to confront us as we touched down at Gatwick – John Jake, who had not travelled light, could not find his two suitcases on the carousel from our flight. After the routine search, he had to complete the appropriate forms at the Lost Property counter and we headed back by coach to Norwich. Two weeks later one of his cases was returned to him – it had been found in Iceland! The second case, which had included his rock samples, he never retrieved: perhaps Egyptian Customs were more efficient than he had thought?

On our arrival back home, I was surprised to find a message from my sister awaiting me, asking me to phone home. This was a surprise, since she had been abroad when we had set out for Egypt and was not due to return for another two months. When I contacted her, I realised that there was a real problem. "Paul! Thank goodness, you are back! Our father has died" announced my sister, "He had a heart attack five days ago, was taken into hospital; he seemed to be recovering, but then had another fatal attack yesterday." I was left to wonder whether the voyage to Egypt had carried a curse after all.

Lessons learnt:
Life is about when will it end, and death is about what you did before it to make a difference.

Remember the courier, whatever he claims, is always just a courier and not a multi-talented and hyper-qualified professional! And always get there before the Germans!

Post eventum: After travelling north to Sunderland and my father's funeral, I had to seek medical advice for Maryta who was showing real signs of illness: given her advanced state of pregnancy it was essential to maintain a close eye on her health. The local doctors were concerned that she might have contracted malaria in Egypt, and they admitted her into hospital so that they could keep a closer eye on her. I sensed that they probably wanted to keep her away from the inevitably emotional experience of my father's funeral. They took repeated blood samples during sleepless nights, to monitor her condition: when Maryta asked for an explanation of this, the doctor on duty replied, with a level of dry humour, that this was how they "made the black pudding in the North-East"! The tests did reveal that her illness was most likely to have been pneumonia or Legionnaire's Disease, caught on the return flight. There was one bizarre incident which suggested that communication in the hospital was not brilliant – a nurse began her shift by wandering in to check up on Maryta for the first time, and she was startled by Maryta's shape "You are not pregnant, are you?" she asked, and then was embarrassed when Maryta's reply did indeed confirm her condition.

My father's funeral was a memorable event. Because he had been the local GP for nearly 40 years, many families wanted to recognise the care and support he had shown all of them: not only was the Church was full, but so was the Health Centre where a wall newly-covered in images of the village's history was unveiled in my father's memory. Maryta was discharged from hospital a few days later. Eight weeks later Maryta gave birth to a healthy daughter, Holly, in whom her grandfather would have delighted. I felt the loss of my father deeply, but I never fully appreciated how much my mother suffered at losing her husband when she was still only 56 years old. The arrival of a grand-daughter was a welcome distraction for my mother at this time, and I only wish my father had been able to play the role of granddad – he would have been a natural! One week later I took the Norwich School Senior Cricket side on a tour to Durham; my sense of timing seemed to be impeccable! But at least it meant that I could pop in to visit my mother again.

Maryta seven months pregnant with Paul at Giza.

Outside the Hotel Cleopatra, Aswan.

6 – From "Mr Angry" to the "Prince of Darkness"

While I was appointed as Head of Classics, I know that being a cricket coach had something to do with my selection, and the cricket at Norwich had also needed attention, requiring a lot of my time and energy.

I had always been an enthusiastic sportsman: I may not have been outstandingly talented but I had always played hard and enjoyed team sports most. I had always considered that, despite the generally accepted maxim which said that sport was "character building", I rather tended to believe that sport was "character revealing". How did an individual or the whole team cope with defeat? How did a player respond to victory? Within team-sports natural leaders would emerge while others preferred to be led.

My favourite sport was cricket – a sport that I had played successfully at school and university, when I qualified as a playing member of the MCC, and then coached at school and county level in Essex. I was a good all-rounder, being an entertaining batsman as well as not a bad bowler especially making excellent use of grassy pitches. In my youth I had enjoyed captaining sides, adopting the view that it was worth risking losing a game if it gave you a chance to win instead – a maxim promoted by the great Richie Benaud. This was particularly true against sides who just wanted to play for a draw. Captains often need such confidence as well as a shrewd tactical use of one's forces.

As part of my professional development, I had enjoyed being a coach of junior teams. I tried to pass on my knowledge and I found that I could communicate well the techniques of both batting and bowling – because I was not naturally gifted I could understand the problems faced by others who did not have a natural talent for the game. I had attended an Advanced English Cricket Board Coaching Course with some International players like Gordon Greenidge from the West Indies, of whom I have more to say later! I always tried to emphasise that the game should be fun, whilst stressing that determination would help even the average player to achieve well.

After two years coaching a young side for a couple of years in Essex, I was keen to accept the challenge of taking forward Norwich's senior side whilst overseeing the other coaches of the school's younger teams. I took a serious approach to the pre-season training and hoped that the senior players would respond, but it was clear that they had not been used too as much formal coaching before and while some of the players had skill, many of them were there to make up the numbers in the side. When the first match came round I was most anxious about the outcome: not only did I feel that my reputation was on the line, but I was not sure that the side cared enough about their own performance to make a difference. I had organised extra practice sessions in the weeks leading up to the match, and while the batsmen seemed to be accepting the need for a more serious approach to the game I was not convinced that they would reproduce this in the match. If they did play seriously, then all would be well; at the same time I feared that the bowlers were too inexperienced and naïve.

The main school pitch is in the Cathedral Close and one could not have a more picturesque setting for the sport. All that was needed was the quality of the play to reflect the same class. However, it came as no surprise to me when the first match ended three hours before it should have done. Our team showed considerable ineptitude when batting – none of the team managed to hit the ball with any sense of timing or technique, and they only managed to amass a grand total of 12 runs in their innings. Not surprisingly the bowlers were not able to defend such a low total and the match was over within an hour. As the opposition were celebrating their easy victory, I discovered from one of the younger members of our team that many of the batsmen had spent the previous night out partying and so were in no fit state to show what they had learnt. I wondered whether this was their way of gaining more confidence before the match. It was normal for the opposition side to depart once the match was over, but I left instructions to my team to stay behind while I saw the opposition off. When I returned I remained silent while the members of the team gathered for a dressing down. In a quiet voice I merely instructed them to get ready for another match. I then took them out onto the field for another practice session, lasting three more hours. I was determined to make it clear that their performance had been unacceptable. I believed that they had more ability, but that they did not need a great deal of technical coaching to bring out the best in them: it was far more in their minds and their approach to the game. Inside I was so angry at the way the team had let me down in the first match, but I was equally determined not to let them see this. By the end of the session I felt that I had made my point and everyone departed slightly chastened, exhausted but hopefully having learnt a lesson. That episode earned me the nickname "Mr Angry", but I did not object to it: gradually it became apparent that it was well meant and possibly even an affectionate title.

Fortunately there were plenty of opportunities to show a more light-hearted approach to life. I helped coach a rugby side every year, and found a real joy in taking charge of an U13 squad, mainly because of the colleagues with whom I worked. Colin, the Director of Music, always kept me on my toes, especially when he was trying to name his U13b side after I had chosen the U13a team – Colin was never very good at remembering the names of the players and I frequently had to fill in the gaps or correct his selection. On one infamous occasion we arrived at the playing fields, at Beeston Hyrne, to be confronted by a serious fog. It was always our custom to warm up the squad with running exercises. On this day our usual relay race meant that the first group of boys set off from one set of goal posts to the touchline at half-way, and handed over to the next group who ran to the furthest goal posts and then the third group would set off back to the opposite touchline at half way for the final group to head back to the first set of goal posts. Because the weather was so dreadful we quickly realised that this might have some difficulties on that day. However, we were not deterred and sent the boys off to their starting positions, only for them all to disappear from sight within 25 yards. The relay took place with Colin and me standing in the middle of the pitch blissfully unaware whether the boys were actually completing the exercise as we had instructed. We had to summon all the boys back with a sharp blast of the whistle – it was the only way to get them back to us out of the fog!

Not long after the cricket match when I earned the title of Mr Angry, I unwittingly advanced my reputation forward as a guardian of honesty when I carried out a simple honourable act. While looking out from the Staff Common Room at the front of the Cathedral, I observed someone acting suspiciously: he was looking furtively around before examining some bags and satchels that had been left between the School gates and the West Door of the Cathedral. He was a young man still in his teens, but his clothes were rather tattered and this suggested that he was looking for an opportunity to 'improve his situation by whatever means'. As soon as he was confident that no-one was watching him – I was standing back from the window to conceal my interest in him - this young man picked up one of the larger bags and ran off to the Cathedral Cloisters. I realised that I had just witnessed a blatant theft. Without thinking I ran quickly down from the Staff Common Room and over to the Cloisters, where I found the thief. He was emptying out the contents of the bag, and was stuffing the best items – anything that looked valuable, even books and a pencil case – into another bag which he had obviously concealed in the far end of the Cloisters in advance of stealing the bag from the West Door. Not waiting to think too much about how I would tackle the situation, I rushed up to the thief and grabbed him by the arm.

"You can put all those belongings back! They are not yours."

The young man was completely surprised and just looked in amazement at me, and after a few seconds he started putting the stolen items back into its rightful bag; he said nothing but kept staring at me.

When everything had been returned, I said "Right! Come on! We are going to the Police." Not having arrested anyone before, I was not really sure what would happen next: I was not convinced that the thief would just follow him meekly, so I grabbed hold of one of his arms while carrying the bag with the stolen goods in my other hand. All went well as we progressed back through the Cathedral until we got to the Main Door out into the Cathedral Close. The young thief clearly sensed my grip relax and took his chance to make a run for it. However, I quickly shouted to some members of the Ist XV Rugby team who fortuitously happened to be on their way to lunch. They took delight in grabbing the runaway thief! We then led him to the School Office and summoned the Police. Meanwhile I waited for a short while outside the Cathedral until I discovered the owner of the bag looking for it in vain. I explained what had happened and handed over the recovered property, asking the boy to confirm that nothing was missing. The boy who was only aged 12 or 13 was extremely grateful, and agreed that in future he would not leave his bag in such an obvious place for potential thieves.

News of my exploits in catching the thief eventually reached the ears of the press and thus more reputation was enhanced. I even received in the post a rather strange document, praising me for me "Celeritas" ('speed of action' in Latin!) congratulating me on my prompt action and determination to catch the thief! It was seemingly anonymous but actually signed by "The Bagman of Cantley". I never really understood why I was sent it but somehow I did feel proud on receiving this accolade, and have kept the certificate ever since.

Following the appointment of a new Head (Chris, who by chance had taught me English at The Leys School), I was soon offered another challenge as Head of General Studies, and then eventually as Director of Studies, designing the timetable and contributing to curriculum development. I learnt from Keith who had done the timetable for a number of years that when he started on it the tradition at Norwich for creating the timetable was for all the boys to line up in the main playground during the whole of the first week of the academic year. Then staff went out and collected those they wanted to teach for each period. This process was continued throughout the first week, and in this way the timetable was created! Keith had advanced the process by using paper, pencil and rubber before the term started, and I was able to gradually move towards the use of computers to plan the timetable before the end of the previous summer term. However, following my own experience, I would always advise timetablers to start working through many of the basic structures on paper before allowing a computer to plan the whole timetable.

I welcomed my advancement up the 'greasy pole' which gave me the opportunity to cut my teeth of man-management and planning for the whole school. Most of all it showed me how to step away from the minutiae of daily school life and consider the bigger picture. The only problem with the increased responsibility was that when I sought to arrange a year's exchange in Australia, it was deemed that there would be too many 'plates to be kept spinning' during my absence.

I suppose it became obvious to most people that my ambition would lead me up and away from Norwich eventually. As well as leading an academic department and being in charge of a major sport, I had always been a Tutor within the pastoral system at Norwich and even a Head of House – in many ways, pastoral work was the area where I wanted to take on more responsibility. Getting to know the children really well and having to work with a team of other Tutors, dealing with disciplinary problems and particularly issues relating to the whole family, tests one's ability to remain calm and look at a variety of situations as dispassionately as possible. Even in independent schools, children can be difficult and dysfunctional families frequently contribute to the unacceptable behaviour of children. I could not believe one year the problems that a couple of divorced parents caused for their own son by putting themselves first with no thought for him: he was a young lad keen to play rugby and I was happy to select him for the Under 13 side. The only problem was that he never had any kit to play in when it came to the matches. After some investigation I discovered that his mother looked after the boy during the week, and then the father had him from Friday evening. The animosity between the parents was so strong that they refused to meet each other to hand over his rugby kit for him to play. In the end, Maryta and I found him some kit from the second hand store at the school and shamed the parents by insisting that the boy played because we provided him with the kit he needed.

Later in my career I was confronted with a father who decided after separating from his son's mother to object to him being educated at the Independent School the boy had been at for the past four years. As a solicitor the father felt confident that he could convince the courts that his preference was right. However, supportive statements from the school countered his claims and the boy was allowed to stay where his mother wanted him. It was all the more galling then to witness the father turning up and singing his son's praises on both the rugby pitch and on the stage at the Independent School from which he had tried to remove him. It was just another example of one or other parents using the potential unhappiness of the boy to get at the other parent! Solving problems like this for children encouraged me to believe that it was important for the children to have someone on their side.

Eventually, the time came to risk leaving the safe world of Norfolk and seeking further promotion. When the Deputy, Alan, was granted a sabbatical I was given the chance to be Acting Deputy Head for nearly a term. This helped me develop the confidence to know that I could make this step up, and convince others I was worth taking a risk on. The timing seemed good, when I sat down with the newly appointed Head at St Albans, Andrew. He was seeking to build a new Senior Team and he specifically wanted a "Second Master" to help introduce a firm regime of discipline. The second interview with the Governors went well, particularly when one of them announced that he was "bowling me a googly". Two problems remained when I had been offered the job: well, one really – Maryta. I remember having a conversation with her about the next stage of our respective careers. My line was that she would always be able to get a job as a journalist, especially as a sub-editor; whereas I was not so easily employed as a Classics teacher. I suspect her memory of this conversation will be slightly different! So having got the job at St Albans, would Maryta come as well? Initially I had my doubts, especially when the sale of our house in Saxlingham Nethergate fell through at the eleventh hour. The issues to be addressed were -

where would Maryta work, and could we afford to move from Norfolk to Hertfordshire? The school solved the latter problem by finding us a house to rent. The former took longer to solve: initially the local (Watford) weekly newspaper filled a gap, but then she decided that getting up at 5am to reach the London's Evening Standard would fit the bill.

I saw the role of Second Master as the ideal opportunity to establish my credentials as a potential Headmaster. Approach to discipline at St Albans School had been relaxed under the previous regimes and Andrew was keen to re-establish a firm line on how the pupils should behave; he wanted his Second Master to take the lead. One thing became apparent very soon: too many children were allowed into the city centre at lunchtimes and the school's reputation had slipped thanks to the lax behaviour being witnessed by the general public. So my first move was to reduce the numbers going into the city – only Sixth Formers would be allowed out and I introduced patrols to show the students and the public that we were taking a stronger line on discipline. It did not take too long to catch a few older boys smoking in the local park – they were gated and made to pay a fine which went to Cancer Research! Some younger boys were then caught shop-lifting sweets from Woolworths: I made sure that these boys all had a good grilling from the Police. Inevitably my reputation was quickly drawn as the Head's hatchet-man, or the "Prince of Darkness". It became apparent that whenever I appeared one or two pupils were going to be punished. The danger was that this image was the only way I could be seen by pupils and their parents. Fortunately the Head agreed that I needed to have an opportunity to present myself in a positive light as well.

We decided that a House System should be re-introduced to the school. Since the 1970s all intra-mural competitions had been rubbed out, being seen as too negative and too competitive. Andrew and I saw this differently, having both been at schools where the House Competition had been both healthy and positive in promoting fresh opportunities for the children. We selected four young aspiring members of staff to take on the role of Housemasters and then worked with them to design a range of activities and competitions to occupy and entertain the youngsters – sport, music and dramatic competitions and festivals were devised and staged with considerable success. We assigned the children into four different groups based initially on their homes' geographical location. Each House was identified with a famous historical character from St Albans School – Colin Renfrew (the archaeologist), Admiral Marsh (from the Navy), Tommy Hampson (Olympic Gold Medallist), and Stephen Hawking (the Physicist) - and the Houses soon found themselves engrossed in healthy rivalry. It was particularly important to ensure that the competitions were not just based on sporting grounds, so the House Music Competition with a House Shout was especially important. Not only was the competitive nature of these activities healthy but it allowed a larger number of pupils to take part in these activities – they might not have been selected to play for the school teams or act in the School Play, but they could all enjoy taking part in these House activities. Responsibility was handed to those who aspired to be leaders and they soon saw that they could make a difference themselves in the promotion and supervision of their House. An added bonus was that the frustrations of those who had wanted to escape into the city at lunchtimes were redirected into a fresh outlet for their attention and energy; gradually I was able to reduce the city patrols, and the complaints from the locals (who had suffered at the hands of some arrogant pupils) disappeared. Parents also approved the increase in extra-curricular activity for all.

The re-introduction of a House System also showed that the school's primary concern was to provide all pupils with an opportunity to take part and hopefully shine: they appreciated the chance to identify with a group within the school and it was seen as a force for good.

Something else that had an impact on my approach to being both a teacher and the member of staff responsible for discipline was having our son join the school. Jozef spent two years at a local Primary School in St Albans before passing the entrance examination to St Albans School. In that year group there were four sons whose fathers worked at the school – the Headmaster, the Second Master, the Head of Middle School and the Head of Science all had sons the same age who joined St Albans together. When you discover what your son feels and how he reacts to all the new experiences thrown at him in Secondary School, you inevitably feel differently about how those experiences should be handled. I even taught Jozef some Latin and again it made me think afresh about how all the children cope with what you ask of them. Needless to say Jo did not find Latin to his liking, but I was reminded of the maxim that my old Housemaster had said to me – "Our job is to find what the children **are** good at and encourage them through that success." Jo discovered History and orienteering, and drama, and made the most of his abilities in those areas.

It came as no surprise that someone would eventually have difficulties with my role as the school disciplinarian, but I was very disappointed when a parent decided to try to criticise me through an attack on my son. One day a relatively trivial incident occurred where Jo was accused of barging through a doorway and pushing another boy out of the way. Having asked the Head of that Year group to investigate it thoroughly, I was told that it was very much a matter of half a dozen of one and six of the other. Both boys had been in a hurry, no-one was hurt and no further action was needed except a talking-to by the Head of Year. The mother of the other boy was not satisfied and pursued the matter further accusing me of being biased towards my son and against the other boy. She was a solicitor in the City and had made it clear to the Head that she expected me to be dealt with. I was most reassured when Andrew batted the ball straight back at the mother, showing how the matter had been investigated: I had not been involved in the matter nor had I been party to how the boys were subsequently lectured. The matter went no further, but it had left an unpleasant taste, knowing that other parents might use my son unfairly to attack me. Jo was just as surprised at the whole issue but for other reasons — he was quite friendly with the other boy, and could hardly remember any "major clash" as the mother had tried to manufacture.

So, while the nickname Prince of Darkness remained, I believe that the pupils, and most of the parents, appreciated that my application of justice was always fair and proportionate. One particular incident highlighted this approach, and increased the respect the community had for me. I became aware that two Sixth Formers, a boy from our school and a girl from another school, had let their relationship go too far — the girl became pregnant, and they were planning to run away together. Their parents had to be brought into the school to be told what we had learnt. The boy and girl had been determined not to let their parents know before they eloped, but I persuaded them with the help of the School Nurse that the parents needed to be informed. As the kids had feared, both sets of parents were at first furious: neither family had approved of the relationship in the first place, nor did the girl's father want any solution except to "get his hands on the boy". What the father did not appreciate was that the boy was a talented young man with offers to attend a number of the top universities, and their proposed elopement had put all this at risk. However, the girl was an only child whose parents doted on her. I understood the anger of both sets of parents but I felt that these young people needed help: they knew they had gone too far, but running away was not the answer.

It took some time but eventually I was able to get the parents to see that what really mattered was the safety of the couple and health of their unborn child. I had had to organise several meetings with both sets of parents separately, and gradually they softened their mutual hostility. Inevitably the one family had blamed the other and vice versa, and neither side had seemed originally interested in the fate of the child. When eventually the penny dropped that everyone should show more care and compassion, especially for the mother and child, progress was made. It was agreed that the girl should take leave of absence from her school until the baby was born and the boy should ensure that he secured a place at one of the good universities close enough for him to be a good father as well. I cannot say that they lived happily ever after, but I can say that they were given the chance to give their child a good start in life, supported by both sets of grandparents.

A more trivial incident occurred a few months later, which had everyone agog. One of the teenage boys in the school suddenly started having fits of sneezing. At first these fits lasted for a minute of two, but gradually they went on longer and longer, sometimes lasting for up to 30 or 40 minutes. The boy, Peter, was clearly suffering and his parents tried all possible remedies and cures. Peter could not really explain what triggered the start of the sneezing: it did not seem to relate to any cold or disease, and he was not known for being allergic to anything. The various doctors that his parents consulted put Peter through all sorts of tests, suspecting that this might be a problem associated with certain food or perhaps contact with animals. Nothing emerged from these tests, and the boy kept having his sneezing fits.

I eventually became involved because his fits were affecting his lessons, and the other pupils, who at first thought it a joke, were getting more and more irritated by the regular distractions. I had witnessed one of the extended sneezing fits when the boy had attended an Assembly in the Cathedral. It started in a particularly quiet stage of the service, and at first everyone around the boy showed some sympathy, but gradually as the sneezing continued and the ceremony was interrupted by these nasal explosions, more and more people started muttering in complaint. Peter had to be removed from the Nave, and eventually his sneezes ceased when he reached the school car park and playground. I decided that we really had to find a solution to this matter: this sneezing could not go on and on and on....

I had the boy watched in secret for a few days: it was clear that the boy was certainly sneezing, but the only thing that suggested that there was a trigger was that he was more likely to sneeze when moving through certain corridors of the School. I interviewed Peter and suggested that I would like to try an experiment: I wanted Peter to spend some time at another school. I suggested that there might be something within the city air which was sparking Peter into sneezes. I had sensed during my interview of the boy that Peter was obviously very happy talking about his affliction: in many ways it felt as though Peter was enjoying the attention that this problem was causing. Digging a bit deeper into Peter's background I discovered that while he was an able scholar at school, he was not very popular: he adopted a rather superior attitude towards other boys and superficially showed no interest in girls. However, I had noticed that Peter sought out the women when he was having one of his fits: women were always more sympathetic towards his plight than men.

I organised a day's visit to a neighbouring school, Haberdashers' Aske's School, and Peter seemed to enjoy the time away from St Albans. Peter did not have a single fit of sneezes in the morning, but then much to everyone's surprise he burst into a sneezing fit in the afternoon. I suspected that Peter had worked out a stratagem: the sneezing fit lasted no more than five minutes but it was convincing, and no-one could work out what had been the trigger. However, I was not surprised when I learnt that it had started as he passed some girls who were also visiting the Habs' Boys School from the sister school for Girls.

I was determined to get to the bottom of this strange condition, and I remained sceptical about the origins of this problem – I was beginning to feel that Peter was more in control of his actions than he suggested. Peter's affliction became well known within the community and eventually St Albans School was contacted by the local TV company: they wanted to do a story on Peter and wondered whether they could come in to film him. Ideally they wanted to catch him in action, so to speak. His parents agreed to allow the camera crew to film him, since they were getting more and more desperate and they hoped that by publicising his condition someone might come up with a cure.

It all happened during an afternoon break between lessons. The TV crew had set themselves up at the end of a corridor where Peter was well-known to start sneezing. As Peter emerged from the corridor, he caught sight of an attractive woman, the TV Producer, sitting next to the cameraman, and he suddenly burst into sneezes. The woman looked up and immediately, in response to the boy's noise, collapsed in a fit of laughter. The TV Producer did not just giggle, but she let rip with loud guffaws of laughter, tossing her head back and hugging her sides with the pain of her amusement. Peter was completely stunned by this reaction – no-one had ever responded this way to his sneezes (everyone had been too polite!), and to be laughed at by an attractive woman was shattering for him. She kept laughing for a while, until she realised that Peter had completely stopped sneezing! I quickly took Peter away from the scene: the boy needed to confess how he had controlled the sneezing fits himself, and I did not need to suggest that Peter was desperate for attention from women – the shock of a woman laughing at him had shaken Peter from his dream-world and brought him back to reality. I knew that Peter would find it difficult to cope with the embarrassment of the truth being revealed at school, and so I urged Peter to spend a few days away from school while the dust settled. Meanwhile we spread the story at school that Peter was spending time with his grandparents, who believed they could cure Peter during a period of isolation. By the time he returned no-one wanted to talk to him about his sneezing, and he was happy just to get on with his life at school.

After my experiences in handling responsibilities at Norwich and St Albans, my philosophy was becoming clear: schools should aim to provide the pupils with encouragement and inspiration to explore the world within and beyond the classroom. Teachers should promote high standards and aspiration to succeed. All children need praise and respond well to clear and well-defined leadership. Everyone in school should be able to tolerate, even celebrate, each other's differences and if anyone did not accept this, then they should seek another school in which they could find a world that suited them. This might lead to some difficult decisions being made but if a solution could be found then every effort should be made to implement it.

As a parent I wanted the school to be caring, but firm, and having a clear approach to discipline was essential. My experiences from school trips, running academic and sporting departments, leading the Pastoral team and establishing the principles behind an intra-mural competitive structure, had all given me as well as the children under my charge a wealth of experience and enjoyment. With these principles becoming clearer in my own mind, I felt that it would soon be time to seek higher office!

Lessons Learnt
Always try to keep in touch with the children, no matter what high-ranking office you hold. Also try to maintain a sense of humour: you never know when you will need it!

7 – Sports Tours

Cricket in Holland

Sport had always featured greatly in my career and I had long hoped to take a sports team on an overseas tour. In Norwich the opportunity arose after we had played against the Dutch U17 cricket side when they toured East Anglia; I was able to make enough contacts to return the favour and travel to Holland in the following year. The biggest mistake I made on this trip was thinking that I could do the whole thing on my own. Driving a minibus with 13 senior boys via the ferry for a tour of four matches seemed relatively straightforward and it kept the overall cost down to £50 per head! But with hindsight I should not have gone alone.

    I hoped that our arrival in Holland was not going to set the tone for the rest of the trip. I drove the minibus from the ferry straight to Deventer, the small town for our first fixture, and we had arrived much earlier than expected. Therefore I decided to seize the opportunity to get our bearings before our hosts arrived to greet us. I had never been to this town before and I just hoped to find a quiet back street in which to park for about an hour. It seemed fairly easy to find a suitable spot – although I did not really know where I was. It was approximately 3 o'clock in the afternoon and we were to meet our hosts at the main town sportsground at 5.30pm. I could see signs to the main square which according to my guide book was reputed to be the site of an interesting church and indoor market. As the boys got off the minibus, they looked out for suitable landmarks. It looked as though we had parked in a street full of antique shops from the many examples of Chippendale-style chairs in the shop windows, and I instructed everyone to remember these shops to find their way back to the coach.

It was only a couple of streets away from there before we found ourselves in the Market Square, and the team were happy to stretch their legs even if it meant wandering into a church and then through the indoor market. I suggested that perhaps they might get some ideas for souvenirs to take back from the trip. The church was quite High-Church and the smell of incense drove most of them quickly back into the fresh air of the square. The smells from the stalls in the indoor market were similar yet different, and I quickly decided that the "spices" available here might pose one or two problems when passing through Customs! Typically the young men of my team found some sugary fizzy drinks and plenty of freshly grilled food to restore their spirits after the minibus journey from the ferry.

By 5.15pm I started rounding up the group and heading them back to the minibus. None of the locals had been very helpful when some of the boys had asked where the street of the antique shops was, but fortunately my good sense of direction soon found us re-entering the street with the minibus at the far end. I was certainly not expecting what happened next – as I brought up the rear of the group, I saw many of my young cricketers stopping and showing a great interest in the antique shops. I had not expected that so many of them would have had this interest before they set off on the trip. However, as soon as I came closer to the shops I realized my mistake on two counts – the boys were not budding fans of some Antiques Roadshow, and the fine chairs were not examples of old craftsmanship. In fact, the chairs were no longer empty, but now they were all occupied by scantily clad, young, and some not so young, women, offering their fine "bodywork" to all. The point of such foreign trips was certainly to have some educational experiences outside the pupils' normal lives, but this experience was not part of my plan. I quickly ushered the group on down towards the minibus, while at the same time smiling with as much charm as I could muster to the "ladies of the street"! Not surprisingly the ladies found the whole situation very amusing, but I sensed that I would have to keep a close eye on one or two of our young men, in case they tried to sample more of the local culture than had been planned later in the tour.

In fact, the Cricket Tour passed without further incident. We played entertaining cricket and were welcomed at the four clubs where we were warmly hosted (the game was not played at schools). The one thing we had to get used to was playing the matches on matting pitches laid on concrete: batsmen had to adjust to the unusual bounce, while the only bowlers to get any movement off the matting were spinners. The games were played from the middle of the afternoon until about 7.30pm, and then the team would all be taken back to their billets − homes of the players − where they were fed and looked after. There was little post-match socialising with the opposition teams, which was slightly disappointing in some ways, but everyone enjoyed the hospitality of our individual hosts. On the other hand, I was billeted with the Deventer team's scorer: my biggest problem with her was that she did not cook and we had to eat out at the club-house every night at about 10.30pm. She then insisted on staying out until 3am: there was a culture of drinking and smoking amongst the other young cricket players at the club, which I found very difficult to accept - especially when they appeared at the cricket club the next morning around 9am all looking excessively healthy and handsome! Our final match before catching the ferry back to England was at Rotterdam: the pitch was directly on the flight path to Schiphol Airport, and there were a number of appeals for caught behind which could not be heard because of the low-flying aircraft!

Lessons learnt: Never organize and go on a trip on your own!

Rugby in Canada

St Albans School had a highly efficient process whereby they raised funds to support various sports tours abroad. Led by the Master i/c Rugby, Chris, this group had organised tours all over the globe, and their Fund-Raising Dinners annually raised several thousands of pounds by inviting celebrity sportsmen to entertain with amusing tales from their time in sport, and then finishing the evening with an auction of sporting memorabilia. As Second Master I was asked to join the committee who raised these funds and then as a sports coach of both rugby and cricket I was asked to accompany the Senior Rugby Tour to Canada.

Travelling overseas with sportsmen usually created a different set of logistical problems – more often than not uniforms and equipment take up a great deal of space and always needs checking. Sportsmen often become pre-occupied with their own movements and do not always focus on what they consider to be the minutiae of baggage! Of course, Chris and Jamie, the two members of the PE Department leading the tour, were experienced in dealing with sports teams and appreciated that a close eye needed to be kept on their charges: at least that was what they told me. The Headmaster was particularly keen for me to go on this trip to see first-hand how well the Tour was handled.

One distinctive feature of a sports trip is that accommodation is often based upon the hosts providing billeting for the visitors. This not only makes the trip potentially cheaper than using hotels all the time, but also enables the young people to mix in a more relaxed and sociable way: the competitive matches are not the only contact that they have with the opposition but the chance to spend time in each other's company afterwards helps build friendships and a greater understanding. The proposal on this trip was that the teams should spend the first evening socializing after a training session and then to play a fixture on the second day.

Our first fixture was in Newfoundland, where a large colony of Irishmen had promoted rugby. We were met at the Sports Ground by Patrick, our host; the boys were keen to get onto the field and run away any of those cobwebs left over after the long flight over the Atlantic. I left Chris and Jamie to supervise this and tried to get an understanding from Patrick about the arrangements for the next two days. Patrick's Irish background soon became very apparent, not only through his accent, but also by the way he kept avoiding the subject of the billeting. I was concerned to get the details of where everyone was staying, since I was aware of my responsibilities to remain the Guardian of the group while they were not staying all in one place – the real downside of such arrangements for the organisers of such trips.

What I began to wonder was whether the billeting had been organised at all. Patrick kept reassuring me that he would pass on all the information by the end of the training session, but not before. Gradually a number of potential hosts, in other words players from the opposition, started arriving for their training session. As they arrived Patrick went over to each and was obviously checking off on his list who was able to host one or two of the visiting team and who was not. To leave such arrangements to the hour before the visitors would need to be accommodated seemed to me to be rather haphazard, and I decided to challenge Patrick on what had actually been arranged. "Oh, don't you worry now." drawled Patrick, the Irish Newffie. "It will all be alright by the time we end the session!"

Well, it was not quite alright: by the end of the training session, Patrick read out the names of our squad as they were allocated to a host player. When he got to the end what he had not accounted for were the three members of staff. That had not been part of his calculations and so I had to get a taxi with Chris and Jamie to the nearest and cheapest hotel where we could stay for the next two nights. Fighting back my annoyance, I convinced Patrick that it was his responsibility to get a message to all the hosts giving them the hotel's address so that all our visiting players would know how to contact us or find us in an emergency.

I had never been on an overnight trip with Chris and Jamie before, and once we were settled into our hotel, I was eager to find out more about the town in their company. It did not take me long to discover that I was going to have more difficulty with the coaches than with some of the players on the trip. Jamie was never ready when we had agreed to meet – he had always lost something or needed to find a toilet at the last minute. Meanwhile Chris wanted to spend most of his time either drinking the local brew or hunting for a shop with exotic underwear for women – apparently he always returned home after such a trip with a surprise for his wife! I hoped to find some intellectual distraction during the down time on this trip – even a local amateur dramatic society's production of "Hamlet – the Musical!" might be a better way to occupy my time than hunting for the latest bra!

The following day's match was a great success contested well by both sides: it clearly mattered to Chris and Jamie that our side won, which they did. During the after-match festivities it was evident that both sides felt that their honour had been satisfied. One thing we had not fully anticipated was the problem posed by the heat: rugby is played in Canada during their summer, because most of their land is covered by snow during the winter (which is when they play ice-hockey!). So we realised how important water breaks were going to be throughout this tour – almost as frequent as on a cricket tour to the West Indies!

Sports tours always have that element of the unknown – what standard are the opposition teams? It was just as possible to face a side which were full of international players capable of defeating any opposition, as it was to be confronted with a team of beginners who were very grateful to be taught a lesson on how to play the game properly. What rules will the hosts lay down for the billets in looking after our players? I had heard nightmare stories of other school teams being greeted by their hosts, who then loaded the visitors into pick-up trucks driven by youngsters not old enough to drive shopping-trolleys, never mind a pick-up truck loaded with testosterone filled young males. The staff were sometimes left helplessly watching the disappearance of their party into the outback with no control over their fate and no idea what they would be up to before hopefully seeing them again before the next match. I had raised these two issues with Chris and Jamie before setting off, but they had claimed that all would be well: I was not so sure.

Sure enough I was proved right. That evening when roaming in the downtown district Chris and Jamie had come across one of our party emerging from a Strip Club in the company of nearly half the opposition team. What Chris and Jamie were doing in the area, I never found out, but I was comforted that they had felt it right to report the incident to me.

The tour to Canada allowed us a number of opportunities for R'n'R. In Newfoundland, we went on Murphy's Whale Watching trip: we were lucky enough to spot one humpback, but just as interesting were the puffins flying alongside our boat. In Calgary we visited the site of the Winter Olympics and went to the top of the 40 metre Ski-jump where alongside photos of the greats like the Flying Finn, Matti Nykanen, we saw the grinning face of that great British hero, Eddie the

Eagle! Ironically, Maryta and I had met Eddie on a school ski trip at Colle di Tenda in Italy, before he became famous for his heroic exploits on the ski jump. He was not only an engaging young man and an excellent skier – the local Italian ski instructors had allowed him to take part in their New Year's Eve torch-lit procession (a privilege reserved only to an honoured few), but he was also completely bonkers – having already jumped over cars and buses on skis, he was next hoping to break the world land speed record by being pulled along on skis by a very fast car over one of the frozen Great Lakes between the USA and Canada, but he had not worked out how to stop (in a net, or on a specially built hill?). Almost as memorable, but not quite, was the Calgary Stampede, a great outdoor show of horse power and bravery from the cowboys. In Edmonton, we spent time in the huge shopping mall which also housed the largest indoor roller coaster. I had to draw a line at ushering the whole of our party into an eatery called "Hooters", once I realised what the title of the restaurant was referring to! Chris wanted to argue that it was educational to experience "culture" across the Pond, and he was equally keen to pronounce that "What happens on tour stays on tour!" However, I was determined to insist on a high standard of behaviour, and that all members of the party should be able to tell their parents about what happened on the tour. The few days break away from rugby in Banff and Jasper enabled everyone to have a walk on a glacier and, for some, a walk in the forest, only to be confronted by a grizzly bear!

The final match of the tour was against a strong Alberta District side that were eager to put their visitors in their place, and a tremendous match ensued with the game swinging this way and that. Chris and Jamie had managed the involvement of all members of the tour party very well, but it was customary to make sure that everyone actually played in the final match: the challenge was to achieve this without letting it affect the outcome of the game. As the game moved into the final quarter with the scores level, Chris decided to allow the most inexperienced of his substitutes, Charlie, on for a few minutes on the wing. This was clearly a risk but one worth taking, if it came off. The team all pulled together and tried to compensate for this potential weakness in the side: however, the opposition saw their opportunity and pressed hard for the winning score, by spinning the ball out to both wings. Just as the final whistle was about to be blown, Charlie had to make a try-saving tackle: much to our relief, Charlie managed to get his body in the right position bringing his opposite number down on top of him, and the ball rolled into touch. The final whistle went with the scores even, honour was again shared. However, as Charlie was congratulated by his team-mates, he groaned loudly: he had suffered a serious blow to his shoulder in that final tackle, and could not now move it. I was in no doubt – Charlie would have to visit the hospital, and sure enough there it was revealed that he had dislocated his shoulder in his attempt to save the touring parties fine record. After his shoulder was relocated into its socket – not a simple task, and not one achieved without a considerable amount of pain – Charlie had missed the final post-match barbecue and was only able to re-join the touring party for their journey home: a surprise hero, still suffering a certain amount of pain, especially when he tried to sleep. I was tremendously impressed by his resilience and admired his fortitude when called up to be counted. I was also delighted for Chris and Jamie who had shown more care for the welfare of their charges than I had expected, but even that had not stopped me having some sleepless nights over the course of this tour.

Lessons learnt: Never allow a Sports trip to go with just PE Staff in charge!

Hockey in Greece

When I became Headmaster at Eltham College, I did not take too long to decide that playing rugby for two terms was educationally imbalanced – I had not experienced this at any stage of my career: for most of my education I had played rugby in the Autumn term, followed by hockey in the Spring or Lent Term, and cricket in the Summer. So despite the popularity of rugby in Kent, and amongst the Old Elthamians, I was able to convince the Senior staff and the parents that having a break from rugby after Christmas might allow some boys to learn new skills and not be totally reliant on being physically strong in their sport. In addition I knew that hockey would help the cricketers at the school, not just from having more opportunity to hit a moving ball, but also build up their determination to face the physical challenge of cricket: for, no matter what anyone might say, hockey is a tough physical game!

Having appointed the right man to develop the sport, it became clear that to put it on the map, a tour abroad would allow the boys and parents to see the sport in a more positive light, rather than always seeing it as the 'bridesmaid' next to rugby. Alex, the Master i/c considered that the first tour should be to a country that was developing the sport – Germany and Holland were far too good – so he found a company who wanted to take schools to Athens, just before they hosted the 2004 Olympics. The opponents were unlikely to be that good, but being in the advance party before the Olympics was always going to be a positive experience.

Alex was keen to have Phil with him as his right hand man, but he needed a third teacher who knew the ropes about touring and perhaps something about Greece: I volunteered for the role. While I felt that the structure of such a tour would follow a similar pattern to my trips to ancient sites, the make-up of the group was likely to have a very different feel to those who had an intellectual interest in the lands they were visiting. Sportsmen are great company but they don't always want to stand and look at an old building. However, I had always felt that the point of visiting foreign lands was to learn about different cultures, and so I felt that this sports trip should include activities which enabled the pupils and leaders to discover more about a different culture and tradition. Such high minded ideals are certainly laudable but the manner of their execution can lead to surprises and inevitably some bouts of insomnia!

Athens was hosting the Olympic Games within the following three months and as tradition has it the Olympic Torch was beginning to make its passage around the country. We had learnt that the torch procession was going to one of the islands not far from where we were playing our first match and so we had arranged a boat trip out to the island. We set off early in the morning and after a three hour journey on what turned out to be a very slow "retired" fishing vessel, we arrived at the island - only to hear, as we entered the harbour, trumpets blaring and choirs singing. This was not a greeting organised specifically for us, but rather the final fanfare sending the Olympic Torch off on the next section of its journey to another island! We had arrived just too late to see the actual torch! As we disembarked it was clear that the only town on this island had made a great effort to welcome the torch, so much so that once it had departed the townspeople were ready for a rest or siesta! No shops or restaurants were open and the whole place had the feeling of being a ghost town. Nothing could be done except to sit quietly in the harbour area and wait for the next boat back – and the three hour journey back to the mainland was less full of anticipation and more full of frustration at what we nearly saw! So close and yet so far!

Our second fixture had been arranged against a school in the hills outside Athens: when we arrived we found a pitch that was only one third of the normal size, and our hosts were delighted to welcome us for a series of mini-matches with only half the team playing at any one time. Luckily our boys adjusted to these "local rules" and put on an excellent show.

After the match it was customary for us as visitors to provide our hosts with a small memento of our visit, and Alex was following the normal custom by donating a school tie to each of our opponents. I shuddered when I heard this ritual which might have been appropriate in a Commonwealth country where the schools were often founded along British lines, but in this hot European country where no school children wore ties, to pass such items on to our young hosts was ludicrous. Indeed once the handing over of the small packages took place the blank look on the faces of the recipients was no surprise. However, to my delight some of our lads tried to explain what to do with the ties and the younger hosts soon entered into the spirit of the rite, wearing the ties in whatever surprising way was possible. The good spirits quickly spread across the group and everyone was able to feel that the gifts were well received! However, I felt a degree of embarrassment at the end when a large and rather shiny trophy was somewhat unexpectedly presented to our victorious captain by our hosts. While the touring party felt that their mere presence had been the best souvenir for this inexperienced group of young players, it was obvious that the lack of a suitable response to the trophy was possibly considered to be an insult, and so our prompt departure was appropriate.

In truth, the tour was not that memorable: the level of hockey was acceptable without being demanding. Inevitably I enjoyed showing the hockey players some of the ancient sites of Athens, including the sculptural relief in the Agora Museum which showed the ancient Greeks playing a kind of hockey! I suspect the boys remembered more the night out at the entertainment complex near the Olympic site, watching a film and then enjoying fast-food. However, I do remember having a very intense game of ten-pin bowling at a sports café while waiting for our coach to take us to the airport. Both Alex and I were convinced that we were better than each other – as I have said before, sport is good at revealing character, rather than building character! The tour did achieve the result that Alex and I had hoped for: hockey now had some status at Eltham, and for once I was relatively happy with the principle that "what happens on tour stays on tour." If nothing worth reporting had happened, why did everyone else need to know about that!

Lesson learnt: Only allow Sports Trips to go to countries that actually play the sport in question!

8 - Close Encounters of the Third Man Kind

I suppose cricket was in my blood. My father was a keen cricketer himself, and I even had the pleasure of playing in the same side as him once – but his contribution was really only memorable for getting himself locked in the toilet before going in to bat! He took me from an early age to Test Matches at Headingly as well as the Scarborough Cricket Festival to watch the stars of the day: I vividly remember seeing Brian Close take on the West Indian fast bowlers, Wes Hall and Charlie Griffiths; I marvelled at the multi-talented Garry Sobers; I saw the South African greats, Barry Richards, the Pollock brothers, and Colin Bland, before the sporting boycott of their country; as for the home-grown talent Ted Dexter and Fred Trueman were great personalities as well great cricketers. As I learnt how to play the game, I found that I was able to spin the ball out of the back of my hand, so I took a particular interest in the Australian captain, Richie Benaud. Long before the advent of T20 and the Big Bash, I was enthralled by him as a leg-spinner, playing in a televised International Cavaliers game; as he bowled he predicted what he was about to bowl via a radio-mic. He was also a captain who challenged the potentially safe, and often English, approach to the game: he was well-known for making clear his belief that sometimes he had to risk losing a game in order to win it.

I learnt how to play at my Prep School in Sunderland: the standard was probably not that good: I think that I scored most runs in our first match aged 10 – 3 out of a total of 7! But it became obvious that cricket was the game I wanted to pursue. So when not at school I played local club cricket. This started with the club in Ryhope, the mining village in which we lived. The fact that my father was the local GP may have helped me get picked, and the standard was a good introduction to Club Cricket. The biggest problem was the different language the rest of the team spoke – most of them had worked down the coal mines and so used many expressions that only their 'marras' (mates) would understand. Apparently this was called "pitmatic" according to my mother, who only really knew about it from the man who used to work in our garden. After one season with Ryhope, I was moved to Sunderland Cricket Club, where I attended mid-week practice nets. Much to everyone's surprise, especially mine, I was quickly given a chance in the 1st XI in a Durham Senior League match against one of the top teams, Chester-le-Street. I am sure that my main talent of being a youngster who would run around enthusiastically in the field was why my name appeared on the team sheet. In fact, I had to bat out the last two overs, facing the Chester-le-Street and Durham County captain. His first ball wrapped my pads, but I had got them well down the track and his appeal was only half-hearted. I saw out the rest of that over – runs did not matter at that stage of the game - and left the final over to our other not out batsman. I did not play too many other games for the 1st XI that season, but life in the 2nd team helped me toughen up; as a batsman I learnt that you have to keep the runs flowing, no matter how difficult the bowling; at the same time I realised that bowling leg-breaks to get wickets expensively was not always what the team needed!

At school, now away in Cambridge, I was chosen to captain a number of sides from the age of 14. In some ways it was easier not to be captain especially when deciding who should bowl the next over. But it was great training ground for the art of leadership! Cricket is the one sport where the captain really does make decisions which can determine the course of the game: it is no longer the coach on the side lines who changes the bowler or the field placing – unless the square-leg umpires cannot resist interfering! As you grow older, you realise how the way you manage your team can influence how they all play. Again cricket is almost unique in the sporting world by combining individual skills within a team game. In addition, it is a sport which even before the arrival of the Twenty20 revolution at professional level can be played in a variety of formats: over one or more days, determined by declarations, or limited overs 60, 50, 40, 20 with limits on the number of overs a bowler can bowl, to say nothing about the laws governing the positioning of fielders! All of that makes it the most sophisticated game imaginable, and I confess that I really enjoyed being in charge on the field. I ended up captaining my school and University 1st XIs.

Before going to University, I spent nine months in South Australia as a Gap Student teaching English and sport at Prince Alfred College, Adelaide. This happened to be the school where the three Chappell brothers had learnt their cricket, so when I was asked to come down to the Senior Net Sessions by the Head Coach, I felt very honoured. By then I had lost the ability to spin the ball much and had turned myself into a rather steady medium paced in-swing/leg-cutter bowler, more suited to English green wickets, not Australian fast bouncy tracks! Nevertheless I enjoyed bowling at some of the future Australian stars. Eventually I was offered a chance to have a bat in the 2nd XI net, but it was no surprise that the 1st XI opening bowler decided to swap nets in time to have a bowl at me. It was also no surprise that his first ball was pitched half-way down the wicket and so flew towards my head (in the days when there were no helmets!). I suppose it was so predictable that, if I had not got in position to hook it, I would have looked rather silly. After I had passed that test, we got down to a serious test of my ability with the bowlers showing far more skill than that first bouncer. The coach, who was probably behind this introduction for a "Pom" to Aussie cricket, was a man of few words; the sun of Australia had clearly dried up any sense of generosity in him, but after this net session he asked me to play in the school 2nd XI at the weekend. I suppose what I really learnt in Australia was how hard you have to work at it to be successful: for a bowler the wickets rarely give much help, but for batsmen you cannot afford to make a mistake since once you are out you could end up not doing anything for the rest of the weekend – their matches are played for two innings over two weekends.

Life can be full of close encounters. For me, Australia provided one of the most extraordinary moments of serendipity. The Headmaster of Prince Alfred College often asked me to accompany him on the golf course, so that he could get away from the politics which is an inevitable part of the role, and I was a suitable golf companion because he could get many things off his chest without there being any hidden agenda from me. One day's golf took place at the Royal Adelaide Golf Club. As I signed the Visitor's Book, I thought the name above mine looked familiar; and as we played our round we gradually caught up with the two gentlemen playing in front of us. I was then able to confirm what I had suspected from the Visitor's Book: it was the great Sir Don Bradman. Unfortunately I cannot claim to have played golf with the Don, and he did not come into the Clubhouse for a drink, but at least I can claim to have my autograph next to his at the Royal Adelaide Golf Club! Bradman's great mastery on the cricket pitch was attributed to his powers of concentration combined with superb technique. Neville Cardus described him as "a terrible little man, but likeable, and with a wistful something about him, probably that melancholy which Aristotle says is the mark of all the great ones of the earth." I am sorry I did not get the chance to speak just one or two words with the great man.

Returning to Nottingham for three years at university was a complete contrast. The wickets off University Boulevard were often soft tops which suited my leg-cutters, and I was delighted to elected Captain for my second year. We even reached the UAU semi-final, losing to Durham who had three First Class County players. We then went on a tour to Hampshire via London. I had negotiated a sponsorship deal with Reg Simpson of Gunn & Moore in Nottingham and we enjoyed the summer sun of '76 playing 20 matches in 21 days after our exams! I haven't kept in touch with too many of the "gang" but my vice-captain (who was also our Best Man) is now Secretary of Suffolk County Cricket, the wicket keeper (and architect) has been Chair of the MCC Estates Committee for a number of years, and I meet a couple of others when I go up to Lord's for Test Matches. That was another thing I achieved after leaving school – the Master i/c Cricket at the Leys had nominated me to become a Playing member of the MCC. This involved playing 10 Probationary Matches over two years. One of these was in Harrogate against Ashville College. Since this was a match to celebrate the school's Centenary, the MCC produced a team with a number of ex-Yorkshire players: imagine everyone's surprise and delight when just as the game was about to start, a large Rolls Royce arrived driven by none other than Freddie Trueman. Although he was rather more portly than when I had first watched him playing for England, he still had that ability to perform and entertain. He was asked to bat just before we declared and he managed to hit a couple of quick sixes, but when he opened the bowling, he was extraordinary. He came in off about four paces, leapt into his bowling stride and let the ball go. It sped past the batsman and wicket-keeper (who had been a county player) and over the ropes for 4 byes! Fred just smiled and said the young lad who was opening the batting for the school "Duvvn't worry lad! Aah shan't pitch it short, just keep coming for'ard." True to his word, Fred bowled about six overs taking three wickets, all caught behind, and then went for a rest in the slips. After the match the MCC team retired to a local hostelry and enjoyed Fred's stories: he held court recounting many amusing tales, some of which he was about to include in a book he was co-authoring with Eric Morecambe. It had been an unforgettable day. I can't remember what I did in the game, but making sure that Fred's pint was always full seemed to go down well with the Match Manager who was writing a report on my 'contribution' to the day.

I learnt more about these reports when shortly after being accepted into the Club, I was asked to manage the MCC fixture against Ipswich School. It was not an auspicious start. The night before the game I had a couple of players cry off – Lord's can usually help by sending young Groundstaff players at short notice, but I only managed to get one. When we arrived at the school, it had rained overnight, making the pitch a real green-top. The tradition is that the MCC should always bat first whatever happens with the toss. Not surprisingly the school were delighted at this, and their opening bowlers made hay while many of the MCC team had to be called out of the Greyhound pub to get their pads on quickly. At lunch the score was 85 for 7! We eventually were all out for 135, which the school got with the loss of only 2 wickets, despite the young pro from Lord's and the Cambridgeshire opening bowler both trying to break down the school batting on what was now a flat track! I suspected I might not be asked to 'manage' that game again, but they were obviously short of good candidates and I was in charge of this match for ten years. Needless to say I made sure we had a strong side for the next two years at least. One of the tasks Match Managers have to fulfil is complete a form giving an account of any Probationary Player's performance. There are obvious areas to comment upon – batting, bowling, fielding, attitude to the opposition. But there is also a Section which asks whether you think that candidate would be a suitable person to represent the Club and the game. In ten years I only "black-balled" one person in that Section, and I doubt that I would have been the only Manager to do so!

At Cambridge during my Teacher Training year, I played regularly for the Crusaders, the University 2nd XI, and in one game managed a good fifty against Uppingham School whose opening bowler, Jonathan Agnew, found the wicket a bit slow! As 'twelfth man' for the Blues side against Leicestershire, over lunch I sat next to Ray Illingworth, but he was not very interested in a minion like me! I also found myself introduced to a side called the Sou'westers CC, who not surprisingly toured during the summer in the South West of England. They were run by a couple of bachelor schoolmasters, and while the standard could vary, fixtures against sides like the Somerset Stragglers, Gloucester Gypsies and Devon Dumplings rarely disappointed and took us to some wonderful grounds. I enjoyed the whole 'touring' experience but it definitely suited bachelors more than married men. Maryta joined me on one of these tours early in our marriage: I am not sure she was too impressed by the rather the 'Spartan' accommodation provided at a Prep School near Yeovil, and my commitment to the Sou'westers waned in the following years.

Once I moved into teaching I was determined to coach cricket alongside teaching Latin and Greek. My first job was at Colchester Royal Grammar School where they took their cricket very seriously. The Master i/c cricket Roger was a great example of a good player becoming an excellent coach. He could explain to players of all abilities what they needed to do to become better players. He just had a knack of encouraging the kids to try that bit harder while keeping a real sense of enjoyment in the game. I played for Colchester and East Essex in my two years at CRGS, but probably enjoyed more playing for Camul C.C., a team linked to the school with boys, staff and other guests playing in a number of local competitions. Camul gave a first chance at competitive cricket to Neil Foster before he was spotted by Essex and England as a fast bowler. That was typical of the culture at Camul – to give a chance to youngsters to develop their game alongside some more experienced players with a relaxed atmosphere, as opposed to the demands of senior league cricket.

When I was appointed as Head of Classics at Norwich School I was fairly sure that being a cricket coach helped, as they wanted someone to be Master i/c Cricket. Anyway I felt that it was time for me to improve my coaching experience and signed up for the ECB Senior Coaching Award. The batting coach on this course was Graham Saville from Essex, with whom I had played at Colchester. At the end of the first day he asked me to be his "guinea-pig" in the nets on the following morning. The point he wanted to make was that if the coach finds fault with every aspect in a batsman's technique, the batsman will only get worse; so the coach should concentrate only on one or perhaps two points at a time. After criticising my back-foot drives, then my cuts, then my cover drives and finally my forward defensive, he succeeded in making me play worse and worse. Finally, Graham concentrated on one particular stroke – the forward defensive. A number of First Class Players were on the course, and Graham turned to the West Indian Opening Batsman, Gordon Greenwich, and asked him:

"Gordon, do you play the forward defensive with your bat behind or in front of the pad?"

Gordon looked thoughtful for some time, and then displaying a typical Barbadian indifference towards any form of defence, he replied,

"Ah can't remember when Ah last play'd di forward defensive!"

Nice one, Gordon! I am sure that Gordon would have subscribed to the philosophy, outlined by an Englishman many years ago, that the greatest gifts of a batsman are "patience, serenity, and happiness." Wise words indeed, and probably applicable to life beyond the Noble Game!

We were also required to give a talk on an aspect of cricket which we felt strongly about. Gordon's was on the importance of impartial Umpires: pretty important, not just at International level. My talk was on the importance of the scorers! It is so important to record the score accurately at every level of cricket, and at Norwich School I introduced the awarding of 'colours' to the schoolboy scorers if they did an excellent job.

As a coach I quickly learnt that, while you need to start with a basic technique, many players thrive by doing it slightly differently. Just think about how different Thomson and Lillee were in their bowling actions, or how the batting styles of Boycott and Gower differed. As a coach you have to be careful of over-coaching, or even destroying natural flare by insisting on following the coaching manual! What is far more important is to develop the mental capacity in your band of players to play the game positively, with self-belief and confidence. So much of the game is a battle between two warriors trying to get the upper hand over each other: the bowler knows that the batsman only has to make one mistake, while the batsman wants to put the bowler off his length to gift him some free shots. Meanwhile the captain on the pitch is trying to outwit the batsman with subtle changes of field-placing, as well as keep his bowler following a pre-arranged plan. In many ways, cricket is a subtle form of multi-dimensional chess, with the opponents trying to out-think each other. As Master i/c Cricket I found that I had to deal with even more layers of engagement within the game. For example, quite apart from developing skills in the children, I had to delegate that same responsibility to other staff; I had to find and trust impartial umpires; some of the most important people in many parents' eyes were the tea ladies, while I knew how important the ground staff were. Your role requires you to seek constantly to maintain or improve the facilities at your school – I bought the first all-weather net from Tom Graveney at Norwich, as well as persuading the school's Design and Technology Department to create an electronic score-board, and in two schools I helped architects design new sports pavilions. At the same time it is essential to promote the success and manage the failure of your sides with the Headmaster, the other staff, the parents and governors, never mind the children! One thing that has become incredibly popular, and expensive, is taking senior sides on tours abroad. I started with simple UK Festivals in London and Durham, but eventually I succumbed to the inevitable tour overseas – although whether Holland would be that high on the list of many cricketers these days, I doubt. Nevertheless it was a tour which the boys all thoroughly enjoyed, and which promoted the sport most effectively within the school and beyond, without being hugely expensive (£50 per head!).

So I learnt a huge amount by being the Master i/c Cricket, and not just about cricket. In many ways it showed me all about leadership and management. I am not sure that I was the greatest coach, but I believe I tried to show the boys that you had to work hard to improve, and that with that extra effort they could enjoy their sport. I certainly learnt quite a bit about how to prepare a cricket square. In most parts of the country a specific time of loam or marl is used to help bind the surface together. In Norfolk it was Acle mud! While it worked as a binder, the major side-effect was that it killed off most of the grass, and without careful management gradually the areas around the batting creases become mounds above the rest of the track. When I persuaded the ground staff to relay the whole square in the Lower Close – what a delightful setting, even if the high water table meant that we would never have hard fast wickets – it was also an opportunity to remove the raised end sections of the square where Acle mud had been piled high! Following the retirement of the Head Groundsman I was presented with the challenge of replacing him. In the end I suggested to the Head and Bursar that we should opt for a local company of contract groundsmen. Having met their boss who was the owner of the company, I was convinced that they would do an excellent job, and while they might not be on call at every hour of the day and the weekend, I sensed that he wanted to prove that his men would care for our needs as much as a resident groundsman. And so it proved: their work at Norwich School became the 'jewel in their crown' when applying for other contracts, and I am pleased to say that as they grew they did not let their standards slip at Norwich. The other major decision I persuaded the Head to take after ten years was to appoint a Professional cricketer onto the staff, who could dedicate more time to develop the skills and techniques of our young cricketers.

That's not to say that we did not have a successful team or two. Most notably our U17 side reached the national semi-finals of the Barclays Bank Cup (50 overs), and two boys had trials for Northamptonshire. I came across very few young men who were naturals as captain as of a cricket side: as I have said before, the captain is left on his own out on the pitch to make the decisions where to put his fielders and when to change the bowlers: many coaches found it easier to manage the game from square leg, either by having the captain stand next to him and whisper the next instruction to him during the over. I tried to discourage this, and to spend more time before and after the game discussing the decisions to be made or which had been made. I also gave copies of The Art of Captaincy by Mike Brearley to those young men who showed a real talent in that direction. Brearley was an excellent example of a player who might not have been an automatic choice as a batsman, but who made a huge difference to the rest of the team through his captaincy. He managed to get the best out of Botham after he had been dropped as captain, and he had that knack of getting a team of disparate individuals to play as a team. His book on captaincy remains one of the best analyses of the task.

I continued to play some cricket whilst in Norfolk. Back in the 1980s Norfolk cricket was an intriguing mix: there was League cricket on Saturdays, and Cup and Friendly matches on Sundays. Some clubs, like the Cavaliers and the Barleycorns CCs, only existed on Sundays, which suited me since I was never available on Saturdays during the school term time. There were more traditional clubs putting out teams on both days of the weekend – Ingham CC, who were full of quality Gentlemen cricketers, played on a tiny village ground; Swardeston CC were by contrast built around a cricketing family who could be described more as Players rather than Gentlemen. There was no specific Norwich Club: two clubs that only played on Saturdays, CEYMS (Church of England Young Men's Society) and Carrow CCs, were the major teams, the latter was founded originally for the staff at Colman's Mustard and played at Lakenham, the Norfolk County Ground. I joined Cavaliers CC, captained by another member of staff at Norwich School, and, when I was available after the end of the summer term, I joined many of the Cavaliers on Saturdays at Carrow. On Sundays, you could play at a distant Norfolk village in what was nominally a friendly! In reality, there was often at least one batsman wearing a big leather belt to hold up his not very white trousers who relished the opportunity to dispatch our bowling all over the park by means of his ample forearms – yes, he was the blacksmith! Similarly it was more than likely the opposition would have a young opening bowler who was very fast without being that accurate – you just never knew where the ball was coming from next! It was normal for Norfolk to discover that many of these village players had never been out of the county, and a trip to Norwich was a big adventure.

The big knock-out competitions in Norfolk were the Carter Cup, over 60-overs and the Biss Cup, over 50 overs, played on Sundays. I soon discovered that a number of Club Chairmen vied with each other to attract semi or retired professional players to join them for these competitions to secure glory for their sides. One Chair even bought a whole club with the money he had gained from his caravan park in attempt to be the top club. Cavaliers reached the finals of these two competitions, on more than one occasion whilst I was in Norfolk. We were never winners but pretty good at coming second! It is interesting to see that on returning to Norfolk after 25 years some of the sides remain dominant – Swardeston in particular, Norwich (who were the amalgamation of Cavaliers and Carrow in my time, and subsequently joined with Ingham), and Vauxhall Mallards – while new clubs like Great Witchingham have emerged with presumably a financial backer behind them. Meanwhile the Clubs at Cromer and Kings Lynn (known as North Runcton) are now in the second tier of competitions. A particular disappointment is that the County Ground is no longer at Lakenham: it was a large open ground with a superb square, and the most impressive thatched pavilion. Apparently the ground was eventually sold to developers, and houses now sit on top of that sacred turf!

When I left Norwich to become Second Master at St Albans School, one of the challenges was to give up any responsibility for cricket. In fact, in my interview one of the Governors announced that he was bowling me a 'googly' when he asked me how I would cope with not coaching any sport. I was delighted to discover that this Governor was not only a member of the MCC but also a Friend of the Lord's Taverners, a charity who raised funds for children in need. I even played in one of the games he organised under this banner. To my delight I was on the same side as John Snow, the England opening bowler, whom I had admired for many years. After I discovered that he had the fiercest handshake I had ever come across, I was pleased to see that he still had that ability to deliver the ball with real pace and movement off the wicket. I was relieved not to be batting against him.

I believe that we should all have heroes, and I have been very fortunate to have had a number of 'close encounters' with some of my heroes. What should come as no surprise is that these heroes are usually ordinary people, just like the rest of us, and that should encourage us to aspire to greater things ourselves. One of my heroes had to be Mike Brearley: as I have already mentioned he was not an outstanding player, but he was an exceptional leader. After retiring from professional cricket, Brearley set up a practice in psychoanalysis. I was fortunate to hear him talk about leadership at the Headmasters' and Headmistresses' Conference: he focussed on getting know your 'team' well and realising that each individual has to be treated in accordance with their differing personalities. I decided to invite Brearley to be the Guest of Honour at Eltham College's Speech Day. Unfortunately he declined, most courteously but indicating that he did not approve of the awarding of prizes that excluded others. Ever the team man, I suppose, my hero did not quite match my hopes, but then that's part of life, isn't it

It is true that I did miss close involvement in coaching cricket once I started to climb up the ladder of responsibility. But what I had learnt as a captain, coach and Master i/c Cricket helped me during my time leading and encouraging pupils and staff in the rest of my career. Captains have to make decisions every minute of the game – how to set the field, when to change the bowling, when to declare, what the batting order should be, and what advice to give the incoming batsman. Just like every cricket side, so every staff common room has the equivalent of temperamental bowlers of different styles and skill levels, egotistical batsmen who want to bat early in the innings or go in just for the slog before a declaration. Heads always need a safe pair of hands amongst their Senior Management Team who will catch the problem parent first, and there are so many aspects of school life beyond the classroom that the Head will need a complete set of quality fielders. Knowing how to communicate to and manage the moods of parents and Governors is all part of the psychological game; similarly a Head needs to present a plan for their 'team' to face the next challenge - whatever the 'wicket', whatever the 'weather' might present. And one must never forget to look after the folk who make the teas!

Lessons Learnt

Criticism heaped on an individual only makes matters worse; show your pupils how to solve one problem at a time.

Remember that you may not be the most talented 'batsman' or 'bowler' in your 'team', but as 'captain' you can have a greater influence than everyone else, by getting the rest of the 'team' to 'play' better.

Always have heroes and aspire to emulate them.

Chronology I

1967 - 72   The Leys School, Cambridge: went as a pupil on Villiers Park Trip to Greece

1973   **Prince Alfred College**, Adelaide: work experience during Gap year

1973 - 76   Nottingham University: BA (Hons) Classics
1976 - 77   Cambridge University: PGCE - **Ipswich School** teaching practice

1977 - 79   **Colchester Royal Grammar School**:
Classics teacher
Classics trip to Greece (1978) with Ipswich School

1979 - 94   **Norwich School**: Head of Classics,
Master i/c Cricket,
(eventually) Director of Studies

Classics trip to Italy - 1980
Classics trip to Greece - 1981
(Villiers Park Educational Trust: Classics trip to Greece 1981)
Classics trip to Egypt - 1982
Cricket tour to Durham
Skiing trip to Italy - 1983/4
(Villiers Park Educational Trust: Classics trip to Greece 1983)
Cultural trip to Moscow and Leningrad, USSR - 1984
Classics trip to Italy - 1985
Cricket tour to Holland
Skiing trip to Austria - 1985/6
Classics trip to Greece - 1986
Classics and Art trip to Provence - 1987

Classics trip to Turkey - 1988
Classics trip to Italy - 1989
Classics trip to Greece - 1990
Classics trip to Provence with Norwich High School for Girls - 1991
Skiing trip to France - 1992
Classics trip to Italy
Classics trip to Turkey - 1993
Classics trip to Greece with Norwich High School for Girls – 1994

1994 - 2000   **St Albans School**: Second Master

Classics trip to Italy – 1996
Yr 7 Trip to France
Yr 7 Induction week at Pen Arthur, Wales – 1997
Rugby tour to Canada
Yr 7 Induction week at Pen Arthur, Wales – 1998
Classics trip to Italy - 1999

Part II –The Eltham Years

9 - Headship

I suppose once one takes on the role of Second Master, there is an assumption that there is only one way to go – up! Certainly there were staff at both Norwich and St Albans who made it quite clear to me that they expected me to become a Head somewhere: were they just hoping to get rid of me, or were they genuine in their assessment of my ambition? As Second Master, I had become used to a silence falling over the room as soon as I had entered the room – this was not just with a classroom of pupils but also in the Staff Common Room, a clear sign that I was "management" and no longer one of the "people". I was even shocked to learn that one of the Middle Managers had gone out to buy a new pair of trousers before coming to have dinner with Maryta and me.

One of the best things that Andrew, the Head, had insisted on when I was appointed as Second Master was that I should attend all Governors Meetings. For most of the "ground troops", this was a no-go area, but it is an essential learning ground for anyone hoping to become a Head. Governors are a key element within any school, but one needs to appreciate how they work and who are the key players. At these Governors Meetings I got to know Tony, who eventually became Head at Eton, his third Headship, an invaluable contact for someone hoping to move on upwards. Intriguingly most of these meetings were held on Saturday mornings – there was no Saturday school at St Albans – but a guillotine was applied to all discussions when an International Rugby match was being played at Twickenham, and half the Board had to leave to get to the match in time!

I began to apply for Headships in my fourth year, and concentrated on schools that were similar to those I had experienced ie day schools which had a good sporting or musical tradition. I was still very conscious of the fact that my academic background would not fit certain schools: a 2:2 from Nottingham University would probably not suit many schools, even if the degree was in Classics! I was interviewed at Yarm School, where at least I could claim some association with the North-East! The school was only c.25 years old, having been created after the demise of Grammar Schools, and the Chairman of Governors had been in post since the beginning; the rest of the Board were either from ICI or other key businesses in the area. In many ways this was a major factor in my approach to the post. The process involved two days of interview with an overnight stay for Maryta and me along with the other candidates: wives were given a view of the surrounding area while we were interviewed. Once we headed home, I said to Maryta that I hoped that we had come second – which was exactly what had happened. I had found the Chairman quite difficult: he wanted the school to remain as he saw it and he had invested so much of his time and effort in establishing it that way that I sensed we would fall out, and I suspect he sensed that as well.

I then applied to Eltham College and Wells Cathedral School. I confess that I had never heard of Eltham, and had had to ask Andrew what he knew about it. His reply was not too helpful, except that it seemed to fit the profile I was looking for – day school with a good range of extra-curricular activities; being in South-East London also meant that Maryta would be able to continue working at the London Evening Standard. I was somewhat disappointed when I received a letter from the Chairman of Governors indicating that I had just missed out on the Long List for interviews – probably the curse of a non-Oxbridge degree, I concluded. So I turned my attention to Wells Cathedral School, set in a delightful South-West country town and with a wonderful musical tradition. It was however a complicated school with two types of children: the normal child who entered after passing a traditional entrance examination, interview, and with parents who could mostly afford to pay the fees; the other children were Music Scholars whose fees were paid by the State, and who were clearly regarded as the "cream" on whose success the school's reputation was based. Maryta and I visited it the school for a tour before any interview, just to get a feel for the place. It felt confusing.

At that point, someone intervened in my fate. I have always wondered who that person was, if only to thank them. One of the ten long-listed interviewees at Eltham College had dropped out, and I received a phone call informing me that I was the first reserve and they wanted me to attend the first round of interviews. I suddenly found myself rushing to find out more about the school. Founded by non-conformist Missionaries for the education of their sons in Walthamstow, moving via Mornington Crescent (!) and Blackheath to its present site in Mottingham, this school had been adopted into the State system as a Direct Grant School until opting for Independence in 1976. It had a good, but not outstanding academic reputation – there were plenty of competitors in South-East London – and it claimed to have a strong musical reputation, based mainly on a relationship with Classic FM. I then saw on the Governing Body the name of a Headmaster who had rejected me as a Deputy at his school a few years earlier – he was an Old Elthamian and a Governor at Eltham College!

The first day of interviews involved a series of sessions with different panels of Governors, covering various aspects of school life, pastoral, academic, financial and governance. I enjoyed the day and felt that it had gone pretty well. Following this, the Long List was reduced from 10 to a Short List of 5 candidates, and I was one of those invited to attend some Tests at the Oxford Brookes University – I don't think they could be called Psychometric Tests, but rather they attempted to provide role-play opportunities relating to various tasks one might allegedly face as a Head: a review of the school finances with the Chair, a group session with all the candidates putting forward a bid for grants from a local authority/charity against each other, and a presentation of one's vision to prospective parents. I have to say that I was not convinced by this process, which seemed rather contrived especially when all five candidates were pitted against each other in open debate. I shared this in the car park with the other short-listed candidates, all of whom seemed to agree. There was a certain irony here, since it transpired that the assessors apparently considered me to be the best candidate based on these tests!

The final round of interviews clashed with the first round at Wells Cathedral School, and so it was with some reluctance that I asked them to accept my apologies in the South-West while Maryta and I headed to our hotel in Bromley. By this stage I was getting to know the other candidates pretty well, and I was pleased to see three of the other four as we were given the usual tour of the school and Head's house. The fourth candidate was the person who had beaten me to the Deputy's post at that Governor's School, and he had then gone on to become a Head in a school in Wales. I feared that with an ally amongst the Governors he was already ahead of the rest of us, and that we would all find it difficult to move up past his experience. Actually all the rest of us eventually made it to be Heads, and remained good friends, while we never saw him again – it transpired that his Boys' School had amalgamated with a Girls' School in Wales, and he was the Head who did not get the over-arching role, which is why he was looking for another Headship. I often wondered what happened to him.

Before commencing the final stages of the selection process, Maryta and I decided to visit the local pub, partly to calm the nerves and partly to get a feel of the place. I don't suppose that many Headmasters of Eltham College were regulars in The Porcupine – it probably had been the haunt of the Sixth Form Boarders, and some of the staff, when desperate. As we walked in there was a sudden change in the atmosphere – conversations at the Bar stopped and every eye in the Lounge Bar turned towards the couple who had entered, Maryta in a smart cocktail dress and me in my smartest suit and MCC tie. We quickly decided to have just a coffee, which was served in 1950s china. Finding a seat was more of a challenge: the benches around the room were upholstered but when you touched the material it felt like it had been coated in a grimy grease – in fact, I was not sure I would be able to get up again having sat down. Anyway we did sit down, trying to look nonchalant, but not feeling it at all. I don't think this brief visit to The Porcupine either calmed our nerves or gave us a positive image of Mottingham.

By contrast, our final set of interviews began with a 'Trial by King Prawns' – a meal was served to all of us with the Governors arranged on five tables, and we were to move on at the end of every course. The first course was a plate of king prawns, and Maryta and I afterwards joked that this had been part of the test – how do you deal with these in civilised society? Maryta was happy during that evening to bat back questions about her interest in music (which was not great compared to mine), and we left the meal fairly relaxed. I had even received an encouraging invitation to meet one of the Governors, no matter what happened in the final selection, at the Real Tennis Bar behind the Lord's Pavilion at the next Test Match!

One of the areas of the school we had not been shown at any stage during the tour was the Boarding House – the school had originally been founded as a Boarding School for the Sons of Missionaries, but it seemed as if it was an area of the school which everyone wanted to keep in the background. I therefore asked to be shown around the building before my final interview with all the Governors. Apparently none of the other candidates had asked for this, and it enabled me to ask some questions about the Governors' view of the future of Boarding at that final interview. This certainly helped some years later when I proposed that we should close the Boarding House permanently and turn the building into a Music School.

I am not really sure what I expected from this whole process: I did not believe that I was necessarily cut out for being a Head. Alongside many other Heads I have often felt that their presence and charisma were far more significant than anything I could offer. I suppose I wanted to become a Head because I hoped that I could make a real difference to a whole school rather than just individual pupils as one can as a classroom teacher. I was happy as a Second Master working for someone who knew very clearly what he wanted – or at least he gave that impression. I cannot deny that I wanted to rise to the top and enjoy that feeling that I was in charge, but good leaders serve the common good for everyone, not for their own gratification. In my career at Norwich and particularly as Second Master I had seen how heavily the burden of responsibility could weigh on the Head. I was fortunate to have served under two excellent Heads with very different styles, and even what I had observed in my time in Australia with the Head of Prince Alfred College had helped me work out how I wanted to be as a Head myself.

So, it was a genuine delight and surprise when I received the phone call offering me the post of Headmaster of Eltham College. Apparently the vote was unanimous amongst the Governors with only one abstaining – Stephen, the Old Elthamian Head whose Deputy had been a candidate: fortunately we became good friends when we worked together. Maryta was also delighted for me, while our children were somewhat bemused, I think. We naively believed that it had fallen well for Holly who finished her A levels when we moved, and so we thought she would move to South London without too much difficulty – in fact, she never identified with our home in Mottingham, having spent a Year in Industry in Dorset before moving on to Edinburgh University. In contrast, we were concerned that our son, Jozef would find it difficult: he was just beginning his GCSE years in September 1999, so we offered him the chance to be a boarder at Eltham in advance of our arrival there the following year (the appointment was made in May 1999 for a start in September 2000). He opted to stay at St Albans which meant that for his first year living in Mottingham, he had to get up early to take the train to London Bridge and then get a connecting train to St Albans. His commuting exploits became fairly legendary in St Albans – falling asleep in French lessons, for example – but we admired the way that he never once refused to get up and make the train.

And so it came to pass that I became the Head of Eltham College and we, with or without our two children, took up residence in the Chantry, Mottingham. As I had experienced myself not many people had heard of Eltham, and this allowed a number of quips from staff and Governors at St Albans to comment that it was going to be quite a challenge to take charge of the Borstal at **Feltham!** The only reason most people had actually heard of Eltham was because it was where Stephen Lawrence was murdered, and it didn't help that my new Chairman of Governors had shared the same name with one of the alleged perpetrators of this racially motivated crime! Just to add to the confusion, the school site was actually not in Eltham but in Mottingham, which most people assumed was just a mispronunciation of **Nottingham!**

Anyway before we moved in, we had insisted on several alterations in order to make the residence feel more homely, and we were determined to make all visitors welcome there, something that had possibly not been the case for many years previously. I wanted to create a culture that valued everyone, from the highest to the lowest in the school. I knew that this school was neither the largest nor the wealthiest in South-East London, but I hoped that it could aspire to being one of the happiest and I believed that if this could be achieved it would then be successful.

Becoming a Head of a school founded by Christian Missionaries certainly made me reflect on the role God had played in my appointment. I had been brought up by my Anglican mother and Methodist father to have a sense of faith. At The Leys School (Methodist) I was confirmed in that faith at an ecumenical service led by the Chairman of the Methodist Conference and the Bishop of Ely. My Gap Year in Adelaide was thanks to the Head of Prince Alfred College who was a lay preacher in the Methodist Church, and then I married Maryta, a Catholic. Therefore I had no problems filling in application forms which required my religion by saying Christian – when challenged on which denomination, as I was when I became a "Beaver Leader" in the Scouts, I stuck with Christian! I had always considered myself decidedly fortunate to have taught in two schools whose venue for Assemblies happened to be Cathedrals – Norwich and St Albans. I was reasonably comfortable delivering homilies during acts of worship, sometimes recalling the faith of my wife's Polish family during the War, sometimes using some of Rabbi Lionel Blue's 'Thoughts for the Day' as prompts for further reflection: indeed, I was challenged by one boy (and his parents) for reading a small section by Rabbi Blue about "it" (sex) in Norwich Cathedral!

Eltham College was founded by Non-Conformist Missionaries, mainly Baptists and Congregationalists, so Maryta, my Catholic wife, feared that the College Chapel roof might fall in when she entered. I took three decisions about the

Chapel quite early on at Eltham: first of all, there should be a cross somewhere within the building, and one of the teaching staff (Elaine, who claimed to be an Atheist) created an embroidered hanging for the Lectern with the school symbol on it – a cross with two Missionary staffs. Secondly, the Chapel itself needed a face-lift: I was delighted when the PTA agreed to finance the cleaning of all the varnish from dark-stained wood (pews and panels) and we improved the lighting and replaced the flooring with diamond-patterned black and white tiles. The point I wanted to make was that the Chapel was at the centre of what this school was about, with all pupils attending it at least two or three times a week; it needed to be a welcoming building, not a cold dark place. Even the non-Christians should feel comfortable to attend the Services – they nearly all believed in God and I wanted them to realised that He wanted them there as well: when I was asked for a room in which Muslims could pray over Ramadan, I pointed them in the direction of the Chapel as a place of prayer – they accepted this without too much debate. I am not sure how the founding fathers of the school would have reacted. I was taken to task by a former member of staff, then Archivist, when I introduced a Carols by Candlelight Service – the candles were clearly a sign of papist leanings and the non-conformist Old Elthamians would not stand for it! Well, the pupils, parents and staff all loved it – it was often said that that Service had just the right atmosphere to begin everyone's Christmas!

Being able to talk to young people about Christ in a way which means something to them is quite a skill, and not many of us have it. I confess that leading Acts of Worship was something I did, but I doubt that I ever converted anyone – I just hope I did not put anyone off! What was important was being able to bring large groups of children together in Collective Worship, to remind them of our Christian heritage (singing hymns, listening to reading from the Bible - especially the poetry of the King James' Version - and pausing for thought or prayer). The most powerful occasions were when our communities had to cope with tragedy: it is a hugely powerful experience feeling the emotions of a whole community come together on such occasions, and this can sometimes be the only positive thing that comes out of death and family tragedy. I have been blessed by the support of a number of school Chaplains, in particular Robin and Philip at Norwich, and Peter at Eltham. All understood how to talk to children of all ages, and I was particularly pleased to be able to appoint Peter at Eltham – if anyone could convert young people he was the man to do so.

My Day One as a Head

Following the principle that Tim Smit established at the Eden Project, I was determined to ensure that anyone I met at the start of the day received a warm greeting, groundstaff, cleaners, teachers and pupils. What one learns very quickly as a Head is that you are the focus of most people's attention, especially on Day One: in many ways people look at you to decide what kind of day they are going to have. I hope that doesn't sound too arrogant. Next, I broke from the tradition of having two separate Assemblies on Day One - the Chapel could not hold the whole school – so we all gathered in the Sports Hall. The one element I had not rehearsed in my own mind was the Chaplain leading the school in prayer. Bob, the Baptist Chaplain, suddenly grasped my hand to ensure I was joined with him delivering the prayer, symbolically if not literally!

The next thing that happens is that you return to your office, and wait for something to happen: in reality, something will happen but you just never know what or when, and in that empty space I decided to take a stroll around the school site. If the first day gives out any messages, then I wanted everyone to know that I was not going to be a Head who sat permanently behind his desk. Secondly, I had always intended to follow the lead of Geoff in Australia during my Gap Year and make sure I got to know the pupils. In order to achieve this, I was determined to teach all the pupils in Year 7 over the course of the academic year. It did not really matter what the subject matter was, although I was delighted that I could be accommodated within Latin on the Timetable. The added bonuses of my teaching (even if it was only 3 or 4 lessons a week) were twofold: it reminded the rest of the teaching staff that I was one of them, and that my views on teaching in the classroom might carry some weight. It also made it clear to the parents that I was a practitioner in the education of their sons. On more than one occasion I was able to make significant contributions to discussions about the abilities and behaviour of the children in the classroom to both teachers and parents.

The only other thing that cropped up on the first day that I remember was my Secretary asking me how I wanted to be addressed: I had not thought about this until she raised it – I had always been Paul, Mr Angry or the Prince of Darkness, none of which seemed appropriate now. I asked her how my predecessor had been addressed - "Headmaster" she replied. Well, I had known some Heads who had liked being called by their Christian name, but to me it suggested an informality which could be misconstrued, and I felt it necessary to remain behind a more formal barrier at this stage. So, "Headmaster" it was.

I don't know whether it was meant as a joke or a dig at me, but Maryta was called "Mrs Headmaster" by a number of staff, and however it was meant she took it in good part. She had often been called "Mrs H" on various trips in the past, so imitating Alan Bennett's King George III addressing his wife as "Mrs King" didn't seem that bad an idea – delusions of grandeur or what, from both of us! Perhaps we should have Coldplay's Viva La Vida played at our funerals?

The first time I appreciated the pertinence of the lyrics of this song was when Peter, by then the Chaplain, as part of his final Assembly before Easter, played this song in Chapel to accompany a montage of images of Christ – it certainly made the school sit up and listen to his message. Somehow it seemed appropriate for a school founded by Christian Missionaries.

Lesson to be Learnt

Like all conquering Roman generals celebrating a Triumphal Procession in Rome, have someone close who will constantly remind you that you are human and not a God!

10 – *One thousand and one sleepless nights*

I had always found getting off to sleep difficult, but once I became a Head I found it even more of a challenge to switch off: there were so many things buzzing through my head, it was almost impossible to enjoy a restful night. After discussing this with various colleagues, one suggested that I should make sure that I read something distracting last thing at night, and if this failed try to write down the ideas still running around my brain.

Shortly afterwards while rummaging through a second-hand bookshop in Blackheath, I came across a title which struck a chord – "One thousand and one sleepless nights". I could not resist it and hoped that this might help me with my own insomnia – how naïve can one be! Here is a selection from some of the tales about a Sultan called Vasilis.....

Dramatis Personae

Prince Vasilis   The Sultan
Princess Shirin   his wife
Argos   her devoted hound

Chates   Vasilis' loyal Captain
Eryx   An athlete, one of Vasilis' friends
Mezentius   The son of a rival Sultan

Jafar   The Vizier
Fatimah   his wife
Duban   Chief of the Palace Guard
Al-Haddar   Chief of Security

The Sirens   High Climbers
Scylla   The wife
Charybdis   her son

Harun   The Great Architect
Kassim   his successor

Elithorn   Minster of Culture
Merry   An Alchemist, turned Artist
Belladonna   his wife

Bacbouck   An Alchemist

Zumurrud   Someone with an interest in figures
Adelpha   his distraction

Alibaba   A generous silk-trader

11 - *The Dream: with reverence to Virgil*

Men shouted, ropes screamed, clouds suddenly blotted out the light of the sky. The winds came from every direction falling upon the sea all at once, whipping it up from its bottom-most depths, creating huge waves all around them. Oars broke, the prow was wrenched round, and as the ship lay beam onto the seas, there came towering over them a sheer mountain of water. Vasilis stood firmly on the poop-deck, looking strong and determined whilst silently praying to the Gods for protection. Despite his reverence to the Gods, he feared that for some reason the Gods were this time abandoning him. All that his sailors could see were the mountainous waves crashing down onto them and the huge valleys that opened down to the ocean bottom as their ship was tossed yet again this way and that. They had escaped from the one-eyed monster who eats people for sport in his cave; they had avoided being trapped on the island of the Lotus-Eaters; but now they sensed that the challenge of the whirlpool and the clashing rocks was going to bring about the end of their great adventure. Vasilis may be a charismatic leader, but even he could not save them now.

And yet…just when they thought they could hold out no more, the seas lost their anger and grew calm, the clouds were blown away and the sun came back to cheer them. They had avoided the rocks – goodness knew how – and they were able to raise the sails once more and accept a welcome rest from their vain attempts to row in the stormy sea. Vasilis hid his exhaustion for the time being, and walked the length of their ship patting his crew on their backs and giving them all something to cheer about. The Gods had obviously relented and decided to let him and his men get home safely. They were heading for port after twelve months' voyage and this last trial had been the worst. It would not be long now before they reached their homes safe and sound. Eventually he left faithful Chates in control of the tiller and made his way to his cabin, where, after a small glass of wine, he lay down on his bunk worn out from the day's exertions, and quickly dropped into a deep sleep.

Suddenly Vasilis sees himself standing all alone in a strange but wondrous land, with verdant meadows stretching away until they meet the foothills of a mighty mountain range capped with unblemished snow. He traces the path before him as it rolls over hills, with sparkling brooks babbling their way gently down into valleys. His senses are all filled with a feeling of purity: the sun appears to be shining brighter, the birds on the wing are singing a captivating melody, and the sweet smell of jasmine blossom wafts across his way. Before he can make out where he is, he becomes aware of an Old Man emerging from a wood. Vasilis does not recognise him and finds it difficult to make out this stranger's face as the Old Man is wearing a hood and cloak which conceal most of his features. The Old Man greets Vasilis by name and instructs him to go into the wood:

"You must find an animal, any animal, which is resting at the foot of the large Plane tree. When you have found one, catch it and bring it back here: it will bring you luck and we can take it as a gift to the gods."

Vasilis does not question what he has been told and rushes into the wood searching for the Plane Tree. As he wanders he realises that a small bird is guiding him, hopping from rock to branch just ahead of him. The bird chirrups as if giving Vasilis a signal that he should follow. Sure enough led by the small bird, Vasilis comes upon the tree. At first he can see no animal in sight; but as his eyes focus more in the gloom of the forest, he spies a chases a small furry creature with pointed ears. He is not sure what animal it is but its golden fur makes it easy to follow when it moves. After creeping up quietly behind it he makes a leap to grab hold of it. But the rabbit, for this is what it is, bounds beyond his grasp. Three times he jumps to catch it and three times it evades his clutches. Frustrated by his lack of success, he decides to collect some leaves from the plants the rabbit obviously favours and lays them in its path, while he prepares to trap the creature with a net he has mysteriously found within his cloak. With one pounce the rabbit is caught and accepts that Vasilis is now its master. Vasilis then eagerly returns to show the Old Man his prize.

"Good! I thought you would never work that piece of deception out. The Gods will be pleased you have passed this test. We must hurry on now and take the rabbit as an offering at the Temple."

Vasilis can see no town, never mind a temple, but he follows behind the Old Man who strides off over the nearest hill. While they walk the Old Man talks a lot about the importance of Fate and Destiny: Vasilis feels that this is important but he struggles to see what importance it might have for him. Nevertheless he keeps agreeing with the Old Man, hoping that all will be revealed when they arrive wherever they are going to.

Without any warning they suddenly arrive in an open meadow with a huge table in the middle. It is piled up with food of all kinds as well as wine and other fine drinks. The table is surrounded by men who are scoffing the food almost without pausing for breath, and drinking wine without restraint: upon noticing Vasilis and the Old Man, they invite Vasilis to join them in this orgy of feasting. But Vasilis is not impressed by their behaviour, and he politely but firmly declines their invitation. The Old Man has remained silent watching Vasilis decide how to respond to the greed of these gluttons. He now praises Vasilis' refusal to join the feast, and advises Vasilis to look at what happens next. Suddenly there is a screeching in the sky, and harpies, monsters in the shape of half-vultures and half-women descend on those at the feast attacking anyone still left eating at the table. The slaughter by the harpies is horrific.

Vasilis is glad he disapproved of the gluttons' behaviour, but he is struck dumb by the harpies' attack. The Old Man urges him to make haste, and moving away from this meadow they next climb up a hill going past a man who is trying to roll golden shield up the hill; but just as he nearly gets to the top the weight of the shield overwhelms him and it falls back to the bottom of the hill. Vasilis offers to help him, but the man stubbornly refuses any help. It is clear to Vasilis that the stubborn man is only interested in the gold for himself. Looking back Vasilis can only watch as the man tries for the umpteenth time to get the shield to the top of the hill.....and fails once again!

"Keep your eyes open and your wits about you" The Old Man tells Vasilis. "If you learn from everything that you see, you will grow to become a worthy leader."

After reaching the brow of the hill, they can see before them a town. As they descend the slope towards the town, Vasilis watches girls picking sweet-smelling jasmine and lotus blossom. As soon as he enters the town, Vasilis is immediately struck by the great numbers of happy people, and they are of all ages. The old men and women are enjoying each other's company sitting in the main square chatting and drinking wine together, being served and waited upon by younger men and women. In some of the open squares there are children playing games and sport with great enthusiasm and passion. But what seems most striking to Vasilis is how they are all praising and supporting each other: the message is clear that the team is always stronger than the individual. Next Vasilis hears the sound of sweet music being played and accompanied by choirs singing; Vasilis is also overwhelmed by the brilliant colours of the paintings that decorate the outside walls of every building, and the life-like statues standing in every square.

Suddenly two of these statues appear to come to life – one is a lion and the other an eagle. They take on the role of guides and lead Vasilis past a scene where two women are taking great care of a large group of African children, dividing them into small groups and showing them how to read, write and play games. In another area there is an athletic-looking man who is in charge of some oriental-looking children inside a dining hall. The children are struggling to eat the food they have been given because they have been told to use huge (six-foot long) chop-sticks. The athlete is telling the children that instead of trying to feed themselves with the chop-sticks, they are to use the long implements to feed each other. By this simple change of approach everyone is able to enjoy the food.

Next Vasilis hears the sound of sweet music drifting over the roof tops with choirs singing praises to the gods. The Old Man urges him to keep following the statues which are leading them to the source of the music. They turn a corner and come to a site where a new temple is nearing completion. Vasilis is overwhelmed as he looks up at the spires of the temple which appear to reach up to the clouds; they glitter with jewels that shine like a rainbow. A gentle breeze brings the heavy fragrance of incense as the choir of young boys and girls sings a hymn and dancers scatter roses in their path as they approach.

Upon instruction from the Old Man, Vasilis deposits his gift, the rabbit, outside the temple's great wooden door; and it immediately disappears down a hole just beneath the threshold. Almost at once a peal of thunder rings out in the cloudless sky.

"Do not fear! The Gods are acknowledging that your gift is welcome." The Old Man reassures Vasilis, who was afraid that he had failed to present his offering appropriately

And so they go inside the temple, followed by the bronze lion and eagle: these creatures climb on top of two huge bronze men and suddenly lose their vital spirit becoming an integral part of two huge statues, representing 'power' and 'speed'.

While Vasilis is amazed and confused at everything he has seen, the Old Man tells him to open and read the first few pages of the book which he finds on a lectern at the end of the building. Vasilis does as he is told – on the first page of the book, a number of prophecies are foretold. Among them, he reads:

"It will not be easy to keep hold of your throne and you must be prepared for a fight with the one closest to you to maintain power;"

"You must beware the dwarf and the hunchback; you must avoid the pride of lions, and don't listen to those sirens."

Confused even more by what he sees and reads, Vasilis turns to the Old Man to ask for some explanation. Before he says anything, the Old Man removes his cloak and hood, and Vasilis at last recognises him: for it is none other than the Sultan – or at least it is his spirit, for it – the spirit - reveals that the Sultan has just died. The spirit tells Vasilis that what he has seen is to inspire him for the future – the sights he has witnessed are some of the achievements that will happen during his time as Sultan, and what he has read in the book are warnings of the challenges he is likely to face. While Vasilis remains confused, the Sultan's spirit reveals that he has recently died of a heart-attack, and urges Vasilis to return to the Sultanate in time for the Funeral Games which traditionally take place one month after the ruler's death. "If you remember and understand what you have just seen and read, then you will stand a good chance of becoming a true and just Sultan." the spirit of the Old Man reminds Vasilis.

The spirit concludes that he can help Vasilis no more and guides him to two ornately-carved Gates, one made of horn and the other of ivory. It advises Vasilis that he must choose which Gate he must pass through to return to his ship: the Gate made of horn will make him forget everything that he has seen, while the Gate of ivory, being the path of false dreams, will enable Vasilis to remember some of what he had seen, but he will always have doubts as to whether they are true. After much thought, Vasilis chooses the Gate of Ivory.

When Vasilis woke up he had a mixture of feint memories, and he was not sure what was real and what was not: he thought he remembered many positive images, but there were just as many odd or unaccountable ones – how did the rabbit fit in? One thing was clear: he needed to return to the Sultanate as quickly as possible. His crew, with the quiet encouragement of Chates, and with their own desire to get home as soon as possible, eagerly pressed on. As soon as they arrived in port Princess Shirin, Vasilis' wife greeted him with the sad news of the Sultan's death.

"When and how did it happen?"

"Almost a month ago: he just collapsed while taking a stroll in the Palace grounds. The only conclusion the Wise men have reached is that his tired heart just stopped." she explained. "We could not wait for you to return, so he has been buried with due pomp and ceremony in the Royal Mausoleum. The Vizier has been very active in your absence!"

"Has he, indeed? I suppose he has made all the arrangements for the Funeral games – to suit him!" said Vasilis under his breath.

"They are to take place tomorrow." Shirin explained. "You are just in time to take part. But let us go to the Palace, and we can discuss everything there…away from prying eyes and listening ears!"

"Of course. But first I must go to the High Temple and dutifully give thanks to the gods for watching over me and my ship during our last voyage. I must ensure that they continue to support me as I approach the next stage of our lives. I have a feeling that I am going to need their continued support for some time!"

For a number of decades, a new Sultan's reign had traditionally begun with a series of Funeral Games being played out in honour of the previous Sultan. It was expected that the next Sultan would take part in as many contests as possible; so, after making an offering at the High Temple to the Gods, Vasilis prepared for the challenges of the next day. He wanted to show the people that he would be a worthy successor to the Old Sultan. Since the opening contest was a boat race, he sent word to Chates to warn his crew that they would be needed again so soon after returning home. Chates was tremendously loyal and Vasilis was confident that he would rally his crew to support the new Sultan.

After the opening ceremony where again Vasilis was able to show his duty to both the Old Sultan and to the gods, huge crowds moved down to the harbour where the boat race would take place. Following this, there would be a foot race, an archery competition and a game of "Soldiers" which is played out on a huge board marked out in the main square between two players: one player would be Vasilis, but the Vizier had broken from tradition by not choosing a suitable opponent from within the Court, but had unexpectedly invited a prince from a neighbouring country. Vasilis suspected that the Vizier was hoping to embarrass him, especially when he learnt his opponent, Mezentius, was well-known for his skill at "Soldiers". Vasilis knew he would have to use a high level of strategy to win this match.

Fortunately the boat race did not demand too much from Vasilis; Chates was able to gauge how best to win against the three other boats. He held their boat back initially while two other captains jostled for the leading position; and, as Chates expected, one of these ships ran aground after getting too close to the turning post, and the other was pushed so far wide to avoid the sinking boat that the steersman was thrown overboard by his angry captain, Prince Mezentius. That left Vasilis' boat with only one serious contender, but Chates' ability to get his rowers to pull together as a team won out just as they reached the finishing line.

Vasilis could not just sit back and let others do all the work for him in the foot race. Many young men wanted to show how quick they were, if only to impress him. When they reached the final bend Vasilis was in third position behind Mezentius and Vasilis' close friend Eryx. Just before the finish line, as Eryx was moving up to go into the lead, it looked like Eryx was tripped by Mezentius. The crowd all shouted angrily, claiming foul-play, but after talking to Vasilis, Mezentius was allowed to keep the winner's prize, a golden torque, while Vasilis consoled his friend Eryx who had failed even to finish the race.

The archery contest required archers to shoot a pigeon that had been tied by a rope fixed to a tall mast outside the High Temple. Vasilis had never liked this particular contest but he was known to be a fine archer, and so was expected to take part. Again many others try to shoot the pigeon, but it appeared as though the gods were protecting the bird. Every time an arrow flew near the pigeon, the bird darted in the opposite direction avoiding the fatal dart. Even Mezentius failed when his arrow only hit the mast. Vasilis went last and, as if to make the point that the bird did not deserve to die, his arrow flew true and straight, cutting the rope and setting the pigeon free. The crowd raised a loud cheer, as the pigeon disappeared over the roof of the High Temple.

The final contest was organised for the afternoon of the Games. "Soldiers" was a real game of strategy, in which the protagonists were to marshal their troops effectively over difficult terrain and take out as many of their opponent's forces until they were compelled to surrender. Vasilis had learnt that his opponent, Mezentius, was particularly talented in this game, and that he was notorious for adopting a merciless approach towards his opponents. After a cautious beginning by both players, Vasilis gradually became aware that he had let his troops move into a number of traps, cunningly laid by Mezentius: it looked as though Vasilis was going to be beaten. A short break in the proceedings, when the Vizier had tried to insist on both players having a drink of wine, enabled Vasilis to gather a fresh strategy together. He had declined the Vizier's wine, taking a glass of water from Princess Shirin instead. With his own head somewhat clearer, Vasilis realised that his opponent was becoming over-confident because of the relative position of both sets of soldiers on the huge board. By offering up a few less important pieces to his opponent, he was able to distract Mezentius from his counter-attack. His opponent was no longer concentrating properly, but instead was playing to the crowd and showing off the golden torque he had been awarded for winning the foot race. Enflamed with anger for the defeat of his friend Eryx, Vasilis makes his counter-attack with dramatic effect. Furious that his friend had had to lose so unfairly, Vasilis demolished his rival's soldiers on the board and snatched a great victory from the jaws of defeat. Even the Vizier was surprised at Vasilis' passion. Mezentius left the square without a word, trying not to show how angry he was in defeat. Vasilis suspected that their paths would cross again.

    The crowd were amazed at Vasilis' stunning victory and acclaimed him as a great strategist. It came as a fitting end to the Funeral Games, when he and Princess Shirin were hailed as the new ruling couple, and he was welcomed onto the throne as Sultan. Vasilis was excited by the events of the day, but in the back of his mind he seemed to remember that there were a number of other challenges to watch out for, and he only hoped that he could face them all as well as he had done on this first day.

12 – Inspiration: Divine or otherwise

Given Eltham College's heritage as a School for the Sons of Missionaries, I expected the Chapel and the Chaplain to be close to the heart-beat of the school. My own background was fairly ecumenical, having been educated at a Methodist school but confirmed in my faith under the auspices of both the Chairman of the Methodist Conference and the Bishop of Ely. To confuse matters completely I had married a Catholic; and I was not sure how the Baptists of Eltham would view this.

After my first real encounter with the Chaplain at the beginning of term Assembly, I had no great confidence that our views on Christianity would complement each other. However, Bob the Chaplain was an intriguing mixture of non-conformism and pragmatism. His assemblies in Chapel often seemed rather apologetic about Christianity: almost to a fault, he never forced his faith on anyone, and I worried that the pupils did not consider what he had to say seriously enough. When the first Christmas approached I suggested that we have a Carols by Candlelight Service – Bob seemed happy with this idea: it was the then College Archivist, David, who questioned how the Baptists amongst the former pupils would view such a "papist" move. Bob came up with the laudable suggestion that our Carol Services should rotate through the different versions of the Christmas story as presented by the Evangelists, thus avoiding a muddle of too many different images all at once. He and the Director of Music set to work deciding what music and reading would work together. In contrast, Bob hardly ever mentioned Easter when we reached the end of the Spring Term.

I was very proud of the fact that during my time at Eltham only one pupil ever requested permission not to attend Chapel Assemblies, and he was a Seventh Day Adventist! I suppose it was an indication of the gentle nature of the Services led by Bob, myself and other staff: many of the pupils, if pressed, would have described our Christianity as Anglican, and those who were agnostics would have seen much of what happened in Chapel as humanist and inoffensive. Bob tried to organise Services of Holy Communion at least once a term, and this enabled him to give a role to a couple of pupils he had identified as Chapel Wardens: they were to help distribute the Bread and Wine. However, the numbers for such Services rarely reached double figures – until Bob had the bright idea to invite the whole of Year 10 to attend one Service as part of their GCSE Course: it may have increased their understanding of the Service but it did not encourage greater attendance on other occasions.

Religious Studies was part of the curriculum for all leading to a Short-course GCSE: Bob was pretty effective at teaching this, and the boys responded well to his traditional methods in the classroom. I was always surprised by the popularity of the Religious Studies Trips to centres like Iona: the older students, especially those who had opted for Philosophy and Ethics (as Religious Studies A Level was rebranded), all returned from these long weekends inspired and positive about their time away. I always wondered by whom they had been inspired.

Bob's final Assembly in Chapel rather summed up my lack of appreciation of him. Bob had been accepted as a volunteer at the 2012 Olympic Games – he had been a Missionary in Brazil and so spoke good Portuguese. We invited him back after retirement to talk about his experiences with the Brazilian Team with whom he had been an interpreter. His talk focussed solely on Bob with pictures of him in the Victory Parade, and revealing very little of interest about how the Brazilians responded to being in London. His talk seemed interminable, and the pupils were clearly bored; the new Chaplain had to interrupt him so that the pupils could leave to attend their lessons. It was a disappointing, but perhaps typical, final memory to have of a good servant of the school.

I had had to wait some time until Bob had decided to retire: but when this vacancy arose I had no doubts about who I wanted to appoint. I had met Peter on a number of Old Elthamian functions: as a former pupil he understood the school very well, and after University he returned to teach English at the school. However, he then felt the calling to become a member of the Baptist Church, and eventually became Assistant Chaplain at Berkhamsted Collegiate School. I had invited him to preach at a couple of Services in the College Chapel and I was impressed by his ability to talk about God and his faith. He had been selected to go to the Seoul Olympics – as a Chaplain! – and he was a sportsman and a musician, as well as being a thoroughly pleasant chap.

Peter had let me know that if the opportunity arose, the post of Eltham College Chaplain was something he had always wanted. I had very little doubt about wanting to appoint Peter when Bob announced his decision to retire, but we had to go through the correct process of interviews as well as putting him through his paces. Unfortunately Peter was late for his interview day, which should have started with him leading Assembly in Chapel: he rather bizarrely missed the turning off the M25 to his old school! However, we re-organised the Assembly and his talk about the disappointment of Derek Redmond who broke down in the 400 metres at the Barcelona Olympics, only to be supported to the finish line by his father was incredibly moving: he made the story of an athlete's utter despair and then being overcome by a father's love and determination so pertinent for the pupils. I knew that through stories like this Peter would be able to make a genuine religious connection with the pupils. I was very happy to appoint him. Many of his assemblies stand out but I particularly remember Peter's first Assembly to the Junior School, which was a version of the story of David and Goliath, performed in rhyming couplets and with actions to match! I knew he was going to be a breath of fresh air at Eltham.

If I had been frustrated by Bob's aversion to address the Christian Easter story, I shall never forget two of Peter's Assemblies to coincide with Easter – one ended with a series of visual slides to the musical accompaniment of Coldplay's *Viva La Vida Or Death and All his Friends**, and the other focussed on the last fifteen minutes of Spielberg's *Saving Private Ryan* when the Tom Hanks character charges Private Ryan with his dying words to make his death worth it - fancy that, a Chaplain addressing the topic of Christ's Death and Resurrection in language that kids can relate to!

Peter decided that he was going to retire just before me, and he announced that he was going to go and work in Tanzania. While I was disappointed that he wanted to leave – I even accused him of seeking out a 'Foreign Legion' retirement – I was equally delighted when the Tanzanian government made it difficult for him to stay: all non-Tanzanians over the age of 50 were no longer provided with work permits, and typical of Peter he chose not to fight this but return to the UK. I was delighted because I had failed to replace him as a Chaplain, and I immediately offered him his post back on a part-time basis. He accepted and I was even more pleased when my successor agreed to keep Peter on for at least the following year. Even at a school founded by Missionaries, it is not always easy to hold the attention and get everyone in the school to reflect on our relationship with God: Peter is one of the few who in my experience can do it successfully.

*The Lyrics for *Viva la Vida* appear at the end of the Chapter

One of the claims made by Eltham College in 1999 was that it was a strong musical school, enjoying a special relationship with both the Orchestra of St John's Smith Square and Classic FM. In truth, neither of these two links actually had a significant effect on the musical lives of the pupils at the school. It was true that the school provided office space to the OSJ, and I did attend a concert at the school just prior to taking up the post of Head at which some pupils played strings alongside members of the Orchestra. But that concert was the exception rather than the rule, and it was more memorable to me because of a particular parent introducing herself to me as a former student from Nottingham University that I had dated some twenty-five years previously: fortunately she was now married to a local vicar and her son was an able Eltham pupil.

Similarly the link with Classic FM was a somewhat over-promoted story: somehow the Bursar had become involved with the financial supervision of a Charity being run by the radio company, and so a plaque on the outside of the school proclaimed that the Office of the Classic FM Charity was resident at Eltham College. My attempts to develop a closer relationship with the radio Company proved fairly ineffectual. Whenever Classic FM hosted one of their concerts live at the Royal Albert Hall, the Bursar somehow retained control of one or two boxes (not being used by the debenture holders) so that we could entertain Governors or potentially influential associates of the school. I tried to enlist one of the Directors of Classic FM to become a Governor at Eltham, but the one who accepted "the honour" hardly ever attended and eventually he moved on to greater things in the Arts Council.

My own enthusiasm for music was essentially that of a budding amateur. I had sung in school choirs throughout my own education (most notably at The Leys under Ken Naylor whose tune Coe Fen for the hymn "How shall I sing that majesty" remains one of my all-time favourites); I had even sung back in Sunderland with the Bishopwearmouth Choral Society who entered a national competition and ended up at the Royal Albert Hall, being conducted by Sir Colin Willcocks. I was then inspired to take singing lessons, but I confess that at the age of 18 I was more enamoured of the attractive female teacher than the actual lessons! But singing in choirs had played a huge part in my adult life. During my teaching practice at Ipswich School the Director of Music, Geoff, showed what could be achieved with school choirs and Choral Societies, and I shall always remember singing under him in Elgar's Dream of Gerontius. I am less happy remembering a performance of Haydn's Nelson Mass, when a year later Geoff asked me to sing the Bass solo: I don't think I pitched all the notes accurately, even if they were probably in the right order! At Norwich I thoroughly enjoyed the music made by the children under Colin's baton, and was happy to join in singing when available. Colin's philosophy was to engage as many pupils in music as possible: a good example of this was his improved version of the House Music Competition (which I copied shamelessly at St Albans and to a certain degree at Eltham): the event was not just about the "star" musicians, it was about musicians of a variety of standards making music together in ensembles, brass, strings, woodwind and choral. As the staff coach of one House I thoroughly enjoyed training the 60+ non-professional singers in the House Shout! Inspired by Colin's approach of choosing music which performers and audiences could enjoy, I used the theme tune from the TV comedy Cheers!, the Lord's Prayer from Fanshawe's African Sanctus and *Non Nobis, Domine* from Kenneth Branagh's film of Henry V: none of these were particularly familiar to many, but once the boys had heard them the simplicity of their melodies proved to be absolute winners. Colin was a model Director of Music: his choice of music for the children and his belief that everyone should enjoy the music-making remained influential in my decision-making in the future. Colin even persuaded the 1st XV to form a choir called "Eight in a Bar"! He and I shared a similar sense of humour, which we put to good use when coaching junior rugby sides together – he could never remember the names of the players and received a lot of stick for being the last man out of the staff changing room. Two other personal memories stand out: one of the candlelit Carol Service in Norwich Cathedral which ended with the great West doors opening to snow falling – just the start to the Christmas we all hope for! Two distinct memories stand out: one of the candlelit Carol Service in Norwich Cathedral which ended with the great West doors opening to snow falling – just the start to the Christmas we all hope for! On another occasion I was asked to sing some plainsong chant with three other staff: we stood on the galleries above the side aisles in order to sing the chants over all the pupils in assembly. I am afraid that I got totally carried away and sang my little bit as if it was from a Verdi opera. After we climbed down from the balconies, I was greeted by one of the other singers with the comment – "It is called PLAIN song for a reason, Paul!" I had been disappointed by the quality of music making at St Albans School, although joining the St Albans Bach Choir allowed me to enjoy something completely away from school life, while singing some of the most demanding works in the Choral repertoire under two outstanding conductors.

Therefore I was determined to promote the value of music-making at Eltham: I knew of its value as a corporate activity and building confidence amongst individuals, never mind the uplifting joy and inspiration it can produce! Therefore I had asked my predecessor to allow me to be involved in the appointment of a new Director of Music – there was an interregnum for a year, following the late departure of the last one in post. I stuck my neck out after meeting and watching one of the candidates in action with the school musicians: here was a young man with limited experience, but I had watched all the candidates conduct a choir and small string ensemble, and he had an ability to inspire others as well as a passion for the kind of music that I appreciated. He was well ahead of every other candidate, including the Deputy Master of Music who had been the interregnum. I had a sleepless night waiting for him to accept the post, for not surprisingly he had been offered the chance at another of the schools to which he had applied; I think the attraction of being in London convinced him that there would be greater opportunities here. I was never to regret this appointment, and Eltham was to enjoy a rich vein of musical experiences, and its reputation for fine musicality grew under Tim's "maestro-ship" deservedly.

As well as setting out to increase the quantity of music performed by the pupils he set standards which were to increase the quality almost overnight. In some areas it was going to take more time – the Junior School was key to improving both quantity and quality, but until we were able to replace the teacher who had been given responsibility for music there, the progress was bound to take time. The introduction of the Eltham College Community Orchestra Instrumental sponsorship was one step that could take place sooner rather than later: all children in Year 3 and then 4 were given the chance to have lessons first on a stringed and then on another instrument for free for one term, and then with a reduced fee for the rest of the year. This increased the take–up of music being played and it convinced the Visiting Music Teachers that we were serious about quality as well. Recruiting Junior School boys to sing in the Chapel Choir also helped develop their voices along the lines of a Cathedral Choir, enabling them to sing a wide canon of music for at least four years.

Tim was keen to promote music so that it became popular to be part of the music scene at Eltham. One idea, the introduction of Choir Tours, made the idea of singing in the choir much more interesting. In Tim's second year a trip was organised to Rome, and just to add a little depth to the lower voices, Tim invited two 'friends', or some might call them 'ringers', from Cambridge (King's College!) along for the journey as well. They both had wonderful voices, one a bass and the other a counter-tenor, and upon meeting them at Gatwick Airport I realised that they were going to be a welcome addition to our company.

As Rome was one of my favourite cities, Maryta and I went along to support. We stayed in a little Hotel at the top of the Spanish Steps while the choir stayed in a hostel near the Stadio Olimpico near the Tiber: this hostel had a reasonably sized group room that enabled the choir to rehearse every morning before moving off to one of the concert venues. I used my position as Head to convince Tim that I might sing along with the choir in return for me taking the group on a couple of cultural visits to the ancient Roman sites. Tim quickly realised that ensuring that we had an audience was never guaranteed so it was agreed that some of our boy trebles should spend time before each concert handing out leaflets about the choir in the vicinity of the venue: having smartly dressed angelic English schoolboys promote the concerts certainly helped attract tourists if not the Italians! We enjoyed being able to sing in a few amazing churches, including the Basilica of Mary Magdalene. We did have a slight problem with this as we had asked to perform on Good Friday, but the Vatican had blocked all services being performed then. Fortunately Prue, a French Teacher and someone who seemed to know everyone important (including the Duke of Edinburgh!) managed to convince the authorities that we could sing a mass in one of the side chapels on the Holy Festival of St Mary – somehow she seemed to have enough influence even to change the Pope's mind!

I managed to give a short guided tour around the Roman Forum – "This was the centre of the Roman World" – but the most memorable trip was to the Catacombs which happened to be relatively close to one of our concert venues. The Catacombs are not one of the most attractive sites in Rome but they are near to the old Appian Way, an ancient Roman Road, as well as impressive tombs outside the ancient city walls. What sticks in my memory is actually our return journey back to the centre of the city by local bus: with approximately 40 of us standing at a bus-stop, I urged everyone to cram into the next bus – Roman buses are always crammed full and the boys responded to the idea of a rugby scrum. What I had not expected was how the younger boys found places even on the window ledges at the back of the bus and luggage racks, and it took some time for us all to disembark at our destination as all 40 disgorged from the bus much to the bemusement of the local Romans!

Later that evening, we sat down at a restaurant on one of the side streets, with all 40 of us enjoying the balmy autumn air of Rome. During that meal I spent some time talking to the second Tim, the counter-tenor: he impressed me greatly. He turned out to have a real ability to communicate to the children, as well as an affinity with the whole concept of improving the quality of singing. That evening I decided that if he ever considered becoming a teacher, I would happily find a way of employing him. Six months later he started as the Eltham College's first Musician-in-Residence, and subsequently became a full-time teacher with us before going on to run his own departments at other schools.

Choir Tours became a regular feature of the Music Department with trips to Estonia, the USA and Italy, separated by a week singing Services at Anglican Cathedrals in alternate years. I again joined the party to the East Coast of the US starting in New York and ending in Boston via Yale. The biggest problem on this trip was trying to sing during Lent – not many churches wanted a choir and audiences were hard to come by. The first service was in a Chapel just off Times Square: there was plenty of incense which would have raised a few eye-brows amongst the non-conformist founding fathers of the school, but the congregation were very appreciative. I managed to take some of the older members of the choir to the Metropolitan Opera to see Beethoven's Fidelio at greatly reduced prices since they were students. We then travelled north to Yale where we sang a Service of Compline at Yale University to about twelve Dons – being Lent they didn't even want us to use the organ, but they appreciated the choir's a capella singing. Finally we spent three days in Boston: the Cathedral allowed us to give a lunchtime concert, but since they were 'between' Musical directors no publicity had been given out to the congregation, and the audience was sparse, but included Maryta's Jewish journalist friend from twenty years ago! In contrast, we then performed an evening concert inside a basement Chapel in downtown Boston with a large and delighted audience, who lapped up the boys' singing and gave them a standing ovation. The final event was on Palm Sunday in the Irish Quarter of Boston: I confess that we were very well received and the choir sang very well in a most memorable service, but I was not the only one to notice that there were very few women attending this service, and our boys attracted a lot of attention from members of the congregation. We did not delay our departure too long after completion of the service!

With the growing popularity and quality of music within the school, I decided it was time to provide better facilities for the Department: rehearsal rooms and classrooms were at a premium and all the different ensembles were struggling to find any free space in which to prepare. This coincided with the decision to close the Boarding House: having a dedicated space for only five boarders and three boarding staff neither carried out the principle of a good home environment nor was it a good use of the space. Once the decision was made to convert the Boarding House into a Music School, I planned for an Official Opening. At last I was able to use the apparent relationships with both the Orchestra of St John's and Classic FM. The Musical Director if the OSJ, John Lubbock, agreed to put on a concert combining with some of our musicians which would be performed in the College Chapel. I persuaded a Governor to sponsor the composition of a piece of music specifically for the event, and through the Bursar's links with Classic FM we approached Karl Jenkins. I know that the Music Department wanted someone more high-brow than this, but my instinct told me that his music would appeal more to an audience of parents and musical enthusiasts and he won Tim over with his willingness to help. He finally agreed to create a choral work accompanied by strings, brass and percussion (strong musical areas at Eltham), and after working with Tim on its form "Sing we merrily" was composed. The final piece of the jigsaw was securing the services of a dignitary to open the rebranded building: Karl Jenkins himself was not available, but again through the good offices of Classic FM the Duchess of Kent agreed to honour us for this occasion. She was absolutely delightful and showed a particular interest in the music-making of the children. What she eventually confessed was her passion for Big Band music and she urged us to invite her back to our annual Jazz Night: I am afraid we never did manage to get her back.

Music continued to thrive, particularly now it had excellent facilities; musicals became a popular activity for senior pupils, even members of the senior rugby squads thought it was 'cool' to be part of the Chorus in shows like Chess, and West Side Story. Another Choir Tour returned to Italy, this time in the northern region around Verona during a very hot July, with the highlight being invited to sing a mass in St Mark's Basilica in Venice. Staying in a Sports Hotel just outside of Verona did not allow them to rehearse as they might have wanted, but it did enable the staff to take all the choristers to see one of the Grand Operas in the Roman Amphitheatre in the city – we saw Zeffirelli's memorable production of Carmen. Alastair, the next Director of Music, continued with the idea of Choir tours, and he invited Maryta and me to accompany them to Malta; this tour was notable mostly for one boy fainting in the heat during one concert and another having to wear his Headmaster's black trousers because he had failed to bring his own on that day's trip across the island – his parents who had arrived for the concert were none the wiser until after the performance when he revealed how large the trousers were compared to his own!

I am not sure whether the presence of the Headmaster on any of these tours was particularly welcome, but I was pleased to be able to observe at close quarters how the various Directors of Music inspired the children, as well as giving them the opportunity to visit some special places within the Christian world. I also enjoyed singing in the choirs!

Lessons learnt

When you find excellent staff, try to keep them as long as you can. However, no-one is indispensable, and, when the time comes to find another inspirational Head of Department, you never know who will be amongst the applicants.

Music can be as much a team activity as any sport, and should be enjoyed by as many as possible.

- The Lyrics of Viva La Vida:

I used to rule the world
Seas would rise when I gave the word
Now in the morning I sleep alone
Sweep the streets I used to own

I used to roll the dice
Feel the fear in my enemy's eyes
Listened as the crowd would sing
Now the old king is dead long live the king
One minute I held the key
Next the walls were closed on me
And I discovered that my castles stand
Upon pillars of salt and pillars of sand

I hear Jerusalem bells a-ringing
Roman cavalry choirs are singing
Be my mirror, my sword and shield
My missionaries in a foreign field
For some reason I can't explain
Once you'd gone there was never
Never an honest word
And that was when I ruled the world

It was a wicked and wild wind
Blew down the doors to let me in
Shattered windows and the sound of drums
People couldn't believe what I'd become
Revolutionaries wait
For my head on a silver plate
Just a puppet on a lonely string
Oh who would ever want to be king?
(Berryman, Buckland, Champion and Martin – 2007)

13 - The Pilgrimage

No-one can appreciate the ethos of Eltham College without understanding the role of the Missionary fathers and, in particular, the story of Eric Liddell played in the collective memories of the school's alumni. After acknowledging the anniversary of his birth, I decided to discover more about Eric Liddell and how his life had helped shape this ethos within the College. Furthermore with the introduction of Mandarin as the only foreign language taught in the Junior School, I felt that a trip to China would enable me not only to learn more about Eric, but also to establish links with Chinese schools from Eric's life: this might lead to exchanges with the UK in the future.

The legend of "Uncle Eric" was familiar to most of the Eltham Community, and there was much to admire in the man. I had frequently used his life as a model for the pupils encouraging them to aspire to develop similar admirable qualities. He had earned the description "Uncle Eric" because of his caring nature and his determination to look out for others, often at his own expense. But perhaps Eric Liddell was best known for his exploits at the Paris Olympics in 1924. Eric had been an extremely talented athlete at school and then after playing rugby and athletics at University, as well as rugby for Scotland, he had gone on to be selected for the Olympic Games. He had a speed which none could match and his enthusiasm for running was only matched by his belief in divine support and guidance. Before each competition, Eric could be found at the local church, praying to God and dedicating his life for the greater good. He believed that he had been blest with the gift of running fast, and that it was his duty to celebrate this gift. So wherever he travelled, Eric would try to pass his experience on to others so that they could also share a dedicated and wholesome life. He visited schools and universities, talking of his faith: his message was that everyone had some talent and it was thanks to God that this was so: what every individual needed to do was recognise that talent, whether it was in athletics or music or mathematics or engineering, and to work with God in developing that talent for the greater good. It was during these visits that he became widely known as "Uncle Eric" for his warmth and caring attitude to all.

Eric Liddell had made it clear to the British Olympic Committee that while he was prepared to compete in the Olympic Games, he planned like his parents and brother to pursue his calling to spread the word of God to distant lands; he especially wanted to be a missionary in China, where he had been born. While celebrating his talent for running, he also wanted to help establish the belief of "loving your neighbour" with peoples who had not heard the 'Good News' yet.

Liddell's particular strength was in the sprinting disciplines, and his fame had spread so widely that he was respected by all the other athletes. Before the Olympic Games began, Liddell discovered that the heats for the 100 metres, which was his best discipline, were to be held on a Sunday. Immediately he had reported to the British Olympic Committee that he would not be able to take part in these heats, because Sunday was the Lord's day. Although many efforts were made to try to persuade him to change his mind, Eric stood by his belief. This meant that he would have to miss the 100 metres, but he was still able to take part in the 200 and 400 metres competitions.

So great was Liddell's reputation for sprinting that his rivals were disappointed in his absence from the heats of the 100 metres. However, the story of his success in the 400 metres race – not considered to be his strongest distance - became the legend which has been well told in the film *Chariots of Fire*. The two quotes from the film which still stick in my mind come from the reading Eric delivers in the Church of Scotland in Paris "He shall mount up with wings as eagles: he shall run and not be weary." (Isaiah 40:31), and from the note which he allegedly received from one of his American competitors: "Those who honour Me I will honour." (1Samuel 2:30). His victory in the 400 metres has rightly been celebrated, but what is not often mentioned is that he also came third in the final of the 200 metres.

Everyone at Eltham knew this legend well: what is not so well known is what then happened to Eric Liddell after the Olympic Games. I decided that a journey to China would help me understand more of his story and give me a greater appreciation of Eric the Missionary. Maryta agreed to accompany me, and I asked Eltham's first Mandarin teacher, Angela, to join us on the trip to act as an interpreter and guide. On arriving in Beijing, our first evening had some unexpected delights: first of all we went with Angela to a restaurant famous for its 'Peking Duck' dishes. What I had not realised was that you eat the whole duck over a series of courses: so the first course starts with the webbed feet, served with a horse-radish sauce, and so on. At the end of the meal you are presented with a small lead tablet which identifies the duck you have eaten! Following that eye-opener, we went to the new Beijing Opera House – an extraordinary building shaped like a dome sitting in the middle of a lake: it is apparently nicknamed either 'the cow-pat' or 'the egg'! To enter the building you walk down a tunnel under a glass roof which supports the lake. We learnt that Kiri Te Kanawa was giving a recital in one of the smaller concert halls, and we had no problems getting tickets to hear this wonderful singer. The rest of the audience seemed to be made up from the New Zealand Embassy and a group of enthusiastic Chinese students. We thoroughly enjoyed the recital, applauding only a little less enthusiastically than the New Zealanders!

With Angela's help we had established contact with a Beijing school that looked suitable for an exchange with our Junior School. This school rejoiced in the wonderful title of "The Experimental Primary School at the Beijing Normal University". Upon our arrival we were asked to go through a specially erected electronic gate in the playground – this was able to read our temperatures – we had arrived during an outbreak of "Bird Flu" and the school were only allowing visitors to enter the school whose temperatures were normal. It was obvious from the crowd outside the school grounds that parents needed to be convinced that we were acceptable visitors – our temperature read-outs on top of the gate were visible to them standing in the main street!

I confess I could not see what was so "experimental" about this school – lessons were very formal and the children were reasonably well behaved - except in the music lessons we watched, where not everyone's attention was on the teacher. I think the fact that art and music were on the curriculum was probably the "experimental" side of the school. During the lunch break the children came out into the playground and the most popular game was to keep a large shuttlecock off the ground by kicking it up to the next player. Angela was keen to show us how this was done! I am afraid that she was no expert, but claimed that our English children would find the game difficult – my feeling was that her own son might have found it difficult, but I knew many of our Eltham sportsmen who could perform this trick with ease!

Because we hoped that any exchange with the school should include a Homestay, I had asked to visit some of the children's homes so that I could go back to London and reassure our parents that an exchange was feasible, that the homes of the children in China were smart, and most importantly that the parents were kind and understanding. It was not a surprise to be taken to homes both in tower blocks, and both families only had one child (in accordance with the Chinese Government's policy). In one flat the son was required by his parents to perform on his saxophone to show us what a cultured boy he was, and in the second flat (which was really quite spacious) we were offered bowls of sweets and fruits – the son of this couple had a clear preference for the sweets!

In the evening we were taken to a restaurant for what we were to discover was the obligatory formal dinner, or "banquet", with the school's management. Sitting around the table were not only the Headteacher and several senior staff but also the 'Party Secretary', who seemed to have more power than anyone at this gathering. Various dishes were produced and placed on the largest "Lazy Susan" you can imagine; this was then rotated so that everyone had a chance to take some of each dish. The most difficult thing to eat with chopsticks was greasy fish! The drink we were first offered was a purple liquid with a milky consistency: we were told it was a type of potato drink, but it tasted revolting. Maryta really struggled to drink any of it, so I had to show an enthusiasm for it to compensate! We learned that it is important to show the correct deference to our hosts by lowering your glass below theirs when you chink together before drinking. Another interesting aspect of the evening was that I was easily the tallest person present: this apparently gave me a significant status - the Chinese admire you more the taller you are! At the end of the meal, I was presented with a document in Mandarin, which set out terms for establishing an exchange between Eltham College and the Experimental Primary School at the Beijing Normal University. I had to ask Angela to read this quickly before I could sign the two copies, and once she assured me that I was not committing Eltham to anything too impossible, I was happy to sign. The Party Secretary seemed very pleased with the night's work – he had really enjoyed the potato drink! – at that point Maryta was presented with a large bunch of white lilies. What we were supposed to do with these as we were heading off to Tianjin by train the next day, I was not sure, but we accepted them gratefully – coincidentally it was actually our wedding anniversary, so it seemed more than appropriate.

The train journey to Tianjin was very fast and smooth – we went by Bullet Train, which reached nearly 400 km per hour according to the read-out in the carriage – this is easier to achieve when you don't have to stop at any station on the way, and when some of the villages had even been moved to accommodate the recently laid track! In our carriage there was a large group of trainee drivers who were being shown the ropes: they were suitably excited by the speed and performance of the train. I dutifully took a photo of Maryta standing on the Tianjin platform next to the train, but what stands out is the cleaner in the background polishing the gleaming white livery of the train as soon as all the passengers had disembarked.

When we arrived in Tianjin, our hosts met us just at the exit to the Railway Station: they were two old gentlemen who had been alive during Eric Liddell's time in China. As we drove through the vastness of the modern city, one of them, Mr Hua, told us in a pleasantly lilting English accent his story about "being ball-boy for Mr Eric Liddell when he played tennis at the hospital where his parents lived". At that moment our car pulled up outside a building which had formerly been the hospital accommodation. Then, as if it had all been planned this way (and it probably had been), our attention was directed towards a building site on the opposite side of the wide road. This had been the site of the school at which "Mr Eric Liddell had taught science" and it turned out that he had coached Mr Hua in his studies so that he might pass the entrance examinations for that school, at the age of 11. Unfortunately the school had been badly damaged by an earthquake in the 1950s and so no longer existed. The pupils and staff had been distributed to other schools in the city, and this was why these two gentlemen had planned visits for us on the following day to two different schools, both of which wanted to claim Mr Eric Liddell as a former member of staff, and as a hero of China!

However, the main focus of our car journey before arriving at our hotel was a district to the west of the main city, and a road formerly called Cambridge Street. This is where we found a house with a sign outside saying "The Home of Eric Liddell". I was amazed that such an honour had been bestowed on an Old Elthamian. When we entered the house it became clear that Eric was still held in high regard in China. There was a board giving an account of his athletic success, and then more stories of the good deeds that Eric had performed in this city. The house was now used by a small banking firm, but they were delighted to show us around the small property and make sure we knew how highly regarded Eric Liddell was. Further research has suggested that this house actually was where Eric's fiancé, Florence Mackenzie, lived and while it may have been that Eric boarded there for some time, it was perhaps stretching the point to call it "The Home of Eric Liddell". Notwithstanding this, we were left with no doubt of Eric's status within Tianjin.

The following day, we were taken on a tour of the other sites linked to Eric within Tianjin. First of all we visited the two schools which proudly claimed a link to him because of the distribution of the pupils and staff as a result of the earthquake at the school where he did actually work. Both schools had large Honours Boards giving accounts of Eric's success at the Olympics and his work in Tianjin. At both schools we attended Receptions with Senior Staff and the Party

Secretaries, where our two elderly gentlemen guides were held in high regard – it is still part of Chinese culture to follow the Confucian principle of showing great respect to the elderly. We were not absolutely sure what they both said at our meetings – Angela did try to keep us quietly informed of what was being said – and it appeared that the links to Eric were being repeated for all concerned ie the elderly gentlemen, the school and us. At Morning Break we were invited to watch the whole school exercising in the school playground – it was like a formal PE session led by a prefect from a dais, including exercises for the eyes and ear muscles. There were so many pupils that there would have been very little space for the type of activity one expects in English schools at break time, and the exercise drills were made to fit the space in a regimental fashion!

In the afternoon we were taken to a small side street close to the second school, where we were shown a brick wall – the only surviving element of the church where Eric and Jenny were married. Then we went to a Sports track which Eric had helped design for the local children, but was now used for stock-car racing; it still had classical columns outside it and was revered as part of his legacy to the city. Eric had even raced there against the sprint World Record holder from Germany, as we learnt when we visited a local-history museum, and the people of Tianjin had cast a gold medal, which had pride of place in the museum, in honour of Eric's triumph in this friendly contest. Again we were impressed at the esteem in which Eric's achievements were remembered.

In the evening as we sat enjoying a meal of local food, I was able to ask our gentlemen what else they remembered of "Mr Eric Liddell", as they liked to call him. One story stood out: when China was invaded by Japan, many people were killed or injured. Eric was known for finding ways to protect and hide many of them. His philosophy of putting others before himself was always apparent, and on one occasion Eric had found a young man who had been attacked by some Japanese soldiers: he was very ill, but Eric picked him up and carried him in a wheel-barrow over ten miles to the nearest town where Eric's brother, Robert, provided medical help and they both spent the next few days looking after the injured man and getting messages to his family. They concealed the young man in a hiding place when more Japanese soldiers arrived and risked torture by keeping him safe.

Eventually Eric Liddell was arrested by the Japanese and taken to a prisoner of war camp, some distance away from Tianjin. There he tried to keep spirits high by reminding the other internees of their faith in God, while helping to distract the younger children in the camp by organising athletics competitions for them to enjoy – even on a Sunday! We also learnt that Eric Liddell's death should be considered as part of his legend: in 2012 it became public knowledge that Winston Churchill had negotiated a permit with the Japanese to have Eric Liddell released from his Prisoner of War Camp, but Eric had refused to accept this and instead insisted that this permit should be passed on to a pregnant woman. One month later Eric died from a brain tumour in the Camp. His body was buried near the Camp. The Christian philosophy of putting others first remained central to Eric right up to the end of his life. Unfortunately it was not possible on our trip to make it all the way to Wuhan, where a memorial to Eric had been set up.

On our last day in Tianjin, we said our farewells to our hosts: the two elderly gentlemen had always remembered "Mr Eric Liddell" as someone who had shown others how to live their lives honourably. His Christian message of 'helping others as if they are your own brother' was still strong in their minds. As we were about to climb aboard the train for the next part of our journey, Mr Hua grasped my hands and asked us to pray with both of them. He then recited in excellent English the Lord's Prayer which he had learnt from Eric Liddell all of seventy years previously. It was a most moving experience for us and one that reflected the influence that Eric had had on those who had known him.

As we travelled on, the mere mention of Eric Liddell was enough for the locals to welcome us with open arms and to treat us as special guests. It was clear that Eric was honoured and respected more in this country than in the UK. I hoped that this was something that we could put right when we returned home to Eltham College.

The final stage of our journey took us to Beidahuh, the small town on the coast where Eric and his parents' family had spent many of their holidays away from the heat of the city in the summer. It felt surprisingly European to us, with many buildings resembling French, Swiss and German houses – it had been frequented by many Europeans, missionaries and merchants in Eric's time. Angela booked us into what seemed from the outside a rather grand-looking hotel on the sea front: it was, however, inside it was rather down-at-heel, mixing grand Art-Deco decadence with torn curtains and broken doors. We spent the early evening going for a walk on the beach as the sun set – at which point huge floodlights were switched on to allow the few tourists and rather more locals to enjoy some more light before retiring to bed. It was a very strange and yet atmospheric place, made even more intriguing when one thought of Eric Liddell and his family enjoying the coastal air here before the war.

I always kept the story of Eric Liddell firmly in my mind: here was a man who was respected by all who knew him, who kept his faith in God and was granted honour accordingly. He led his life following a philosophy to help others, right through to his death. I think we all hope that we can achieve a little of what "Uncle Eric" did. As we headed back to the UK, I resolved to ensure that the pupils at Eltham appreciated much more about Eric than just his victory at the 1924 Olympics. In addition it seemed right to establish closer links with China – we had learnt much during our visit, and I was sure that even more could be achieved in the future with those pupils at Eltham who had an understanding of Mandarin.

Remembering how Eric Liddell was honoured in China, I set about creating an Honours Board recognising Eric's Olympic achievements, similar to those in the Chinese schools we had visited on this pilgrimage. During our Centenary Year, 2012, this was hung in the refurbished Sports Pavilion on College Meadow. We were honoured to have his eldest daughter, Patricia, who was visiting the UK from Canada, unveil the Commemorative Board after our own Sports Day. One month later this facility was used by the London Organising Committee as a training venue for eight international football teams during the 2012 Olympic Games.

Lesson Learnt

It is very difficult to appreciate fully the effect of individuals on others just from reading about them. Only when you meet someone who knew them and spent time with them, can you get beneath the surface and begin to appreciate properly their worth.

The Bullet Train to Tianjin being cleaned before we travel!

The two elderly gentlemen who had known Mr Eric Liddell.

14 – *Always pay due reverence to the Gods...*

Vasilis knew his country's success lay firmly in the hands of the Gods: he had been brought up to believe that the support of the Gods was essential for the continued prosperity of the whole nation. This should be achieved by acknowledging their role regularly with prayers, sacrifices and festivals in their honour. If problems arose, he would turn to the Gods for their additional help, support and advice. Vasilis was dutiful in showing his reverence to the Gods.

The vast majority of the people seemed to accept this view of the Sultanate's prosperity: Vasilis believed that his people were loyal and supportive. They appeared content with their lot and followed Vasilis' assertion acknowledging the Gods' role in this. Vasilis had urged his people to strive for success, and he was happy to celebrate their achievements. Most people seemed content to acknowledge the Gods' role watching over them by regular attendance at the Holy Festivals. In addition they were prepared to make generous offerings to whichever God they considered to be their personal Guardian.

Vasilis saw himself as a benevolent ruler: he was always prepared to meet regularly with representatives of the people to discuss any concerns that they might have. He was reassured that their main concerns related to the matters that seemed trivial to him, for example, the quality of food in the market, or the slowness of construction of good roads outside the city. The cost of taxes was rarely discussed, nor were the appointments of Courtiers to high-ranking Office ever brought up at these meetings. By meeting regularly with their representatives, Vasilis felt confident that the people were happy: they seemed to appreciate that he cared about them, and he believed that his leadership met with their approval.

So when there was a riot in the suburbs of the City, Vasilis was completely taken aback; what had caused such disquiet and why were so many people angry? He demanded a full report from Duban, the chief of the Palace Guard:

"It seems to relate to the closing of a laundry in the suburbs, my Lord. The woman in charge was forced to abandon the site and is being driven out of the Sultanate."

"Why? What had she done?"

"It is more what had she not done! Her laundry was the worst: most of the clothes appeared dirtier after they had supposedly been cleaned, and many items of clothing just disappeared. Hardly anyone used the laundry because it was so unreliable."

"So why has there been a riot? It sounds to me," said Vasilis, "that the people should have been glad about her removal."

"It seems that a recent arrival in that part of the town, a Magus, has stirred up the people to defend the woman's rights. He has persuaded them that the manner in which she was removed was draconian, and that they might be treated in a similar fashion in the future."

"What nonsense!" cried Vasilis, "Who is this Magus? Why is he stirring up trouble?"

All that Duban could find out was that the Magus had a reputation throughout the land for adopting 'lost causes' and volunteering to act as a spokesman for those who had little education or confidence. He was a persuasive speaker and clearly experienced in winding up crowds to follow his adopted causes. Many towns in the Sultanate had discovered that, soon after the Magus arrived in their locality, there were a number of complaints lodged against the authorities. He rarely stayed long in any one place and moved on as soon as he had satisfied his own desire to 'rock the boat'.

Vasilis was both surprised and upset that many of his people were now voicing concerns against his rule. Soon there were gatherings organised by the Magus, at a time when only the disaffected could attend; the Magus easily found ways to fan the flames of their discontent. Where before he had thought the people were happy under his rule, now he found complaints being hurled at him as he passed through the streets of the city.

"There's too much tax! Our houses are crumbling, while you spend money on the High Temple! The price of bread has gone up again this year! This year's harvest has failed – it's clear that the Gods don't care about us….and neither do you!"

Vasilis was particularly hurt by the last complaint: he passionately believed that the Gods did care about his people, as he did. He spent many a night pacing up and down the corridors of the Palace, wondering how to stop this situation getting out of hand. Inevitably he made many visits to the High Temple to pray to the Gods for guidance. He remained particularly bemused by the support for the laundress whose case seem to have started all this unrest. Again he turned to Duban for more information.

Meanwhile in his meetings with the Council and the Vizier, Vasilis tried to discover if he was deceiving himself, and that his rule was genuinely unpopular. Most of the Councillors reassured him that this uprising did not reflect the mood of the nation:

"The people remain loyal to you and acknowledge the Gods as our protectors and guardians. This small uprising stems from one man stirring the pot and encouraging any grumblers to join his campaign. It will pass. Be patient, my lord." Jafar tried to calm him.

But the complaints did not go away, nor did the Magus. He seemed to have a personal grudge against Vasilis and his crowd of supporters appeared to be growing. Finally Vasilis decided against his Councillors' advice that he needed to confront the Magus. He was not sure what to expect, but he was determined to find out face to face what was driving the Magus.

Their meeting was brief, but not unproductive: the Magus made it clear that he was only interested in righting wrongs in the world, and that a wrong had been done to the laundress. Vasilis asked for more details, and the Magus explained that although the laundress was not good at her job she had been beaten and removed from her house by the Guards with no warning. She needed somewhere to live and she deserved to be treated with greater dignity.

Vasilis sensed that there was a sense of injustice driving the Magus' actions, and he realised that if he was prepared to acknowledge this injustice then the Magus would be satisfied. The Vizier was not so convinced:

"If you give in on this matter, the Magus or his followers will just find another scapegoat to roll out. There will be no end to this without more drastic action!"

However, Vasilis wanted to trust his own instincts in this matter: if the cause of the unrest stemmed from the treatment of the laundress, then he should see that this was put right. He instructed Duban to punish the Guards who had beaten her, and told the Vizier to find another house for the laundress. Vasilis also instructed his Councillors to let it be known that if mistakes were made like this in the future, he wanted to know about it first hand and that he would try to correct them. He finally went to the High Temple to pray to the Gods and ask for their approval of his actions.

Instead of an increase of complaints of injustices, and requests for redress, which is what many of the Councillors had predicted, the civil unrest gradually died down. The Magus left the city, probably to find a different venue to right injustices. Those who had complained about the harshness of their lives soon found that without a spokesman for their complaints their lives could be more productive through their own efforts. Vasilis thanked the Gods for the wisdom to trust the honesty of the Magus, and to guide the people back into a more harmonious way of life.

Vasilis regularly visited the High Temple, to seek the approval of the Gods in his dealings over State matters. It was not only the people who could cause him sleepless nights: several members of the Council also caused him headaches, but Vasilis had always felt that it was important to listen to their complaints – he did not necessarily act upon them, but a fair hearing was always important. One infamous event, however, led him to take action against one of these difficult Councillors sooner than he had expected. During one of the many Holy Festivals the Professor, as he was known, initiated an event where the whole Court was taken to an oasis for a feast accompanied by display of horse-racing. His idea was that everyone should been able to relax together in the pleasant setting of the oasis, while the entertainment would provide some excitement. With the benefit of hindsight, the Professor should have included an act of worship to the Gods during this event – after all it was meant to be part of a Holy Festival. Secondly he did not appreciate how important it was to treat everyone equally: tented pavilions had been erected around the oasis, but he allocated the best pavilions to members of the Council and the Court who had helped him in the past: the food and wine was of a higher standard here than in the other pavilions. Organising the pavilions in such a way to provide a good view of the horse-riding had not even occurred to him: as a result many courtiers saw hardly anything. Just to add insult to injury, when they attempted to enter those pavilions with the best views they were ejected by Palace Guards. This bungled event just upset everyone: its purpose had been to promote a feeling of harmony as well as bringing the Court closer to the

Sultan. The end result could not have been more of a failure. Vasilis was left with little option but to consider an alternative role for the Professor, who quickly decided to travel to distant lands to help everyone forget his failings. Vasilis knew that the Professor had not shown due reverence to the Gods, and they in turn had given him a message from which he had to learn.

Inevitably when citizens were caught committing crimes they had to be punished – something Vasilis never enjoyed, but found necessary. He would always seek guidance from the Gods on the fate of these criminals. Their broad message in punishing criminals was that actions must have consequences. During his own travels, Vasilis had seen the pain and distress by bright and able young people who failed to show any respect to their parents or elders: Vasilis wanted to demonstrate how their fresh new ideas could be introduced without the complete abandonment of the old traditional ways. However, the younger generation within the Court were less enthusiastic; and more than this, they did not see why they should support Vasilis' reverence to the Gods – that is until the Sirens arrived in Court.

There was a tradition in the Sultanate to celebrate the Sultan's birthday every year with another large Festival, and the Sultan was expected to choose a theme for each year. Vasilis enjoyed this more than the Festival itself which he always felt occasionally veered towards anarchy rather than good humoured merriment! One year the theme was related to a topic close to Vasilis's heart, that of the Ancient Romans; this meant that those attending the Festival could wear alternative costumes, and the Palace craftsmen decorated the Palace grounds with model buildings and decorations suitable for this theme.

During the evening's festivities, Vasilis and Princess Shirin, dressed as though they were a Roman Consul and his wife, were approached by a couple who wanted eagerly to tell

Vasilis how impressed they were with the Festival. It transpired they had recently moved into the Sultanate from a neighbouring country where they revealed they had found life not to their liking. After making considerable efforts to flatter Vasilis, they became quite outspoken about their time elsewhere - so much so that, after the couple had moved on, Princess Shirin commented "I suspect they will find it difficult to settle in any land. They seemed too ready to find fault with anything and everything! I hope that we don't have too much to do with them in the future."

Princess Shirin's words were to haunt Vasilis a few years later. Sure enough, the Sirens, as they were known, settled in the city and quickly ensured that they were part of the social group linked to the Court. Their style of flattery and obsequious praise became well-known in the Court, and Scylla, the wife, was notorious in her over-zealous praise of Vasilis. However, it was not long before a seemingly trivial encounter occurred which reached Vasilis' ears. It seems that Scylla had attended another event at Court, and during some light-hearted conversation when she had yet again been praising the Sultan, she had been mocked for her accent: her foreign background had never really been successfully ignored. She was obviously mortified and demanded an apology. The offending courtier had quickly apologised, but later he laughed off the incident. It soon became clear that the Sirens were not prepared to drop the matter. They insisted on having an audience with Vasilis, who had tried to avoid any direct dealings when such courtly matters occurred. The Sirens continued to press for a meeting, and Vasilis eventually agreed to meet them, if only in an attempt to take the wind out of their sails, by showing his concern. The meeting was not pleasant, and Scylla became quite emotional: she wanted the courtier to be publicly punished and she was not prepared to accept a simple verbal apology. Vasilis eventually agreed to take steps to put the matter right.

"You should not feel unwelcome in our land and I shall put in place measures to ensure nothing like this will happen again."

"But I want to know how you will punish that rude man."

"That will be for me to decide and I don't want you to be concerned any more about the matter."

That did not satisfy Scylla, and she left the meeting threatening more action if she was not satisfied. Vasilis had decided to suspend the courtier's rights to attend Court Functions for a year, and while accepting this gracefully the courtier apologised for putting the Sultan into a most uncomfortable position. Vasilis hoped but doubted that this would be the end of the matter.

To no-one's surprise, this was not the end of the Sirens. Like most parents, they were particularly keen to support their son, Charybdis, in his pursuit of a career at Court. Although he certainly had talent, unfortunately he was unable to speak the Court language correctly: he had been brought up abroad and he struggled to master the nuances of pronunciation effectively. This was bound to put him at a disadvantage when seeking for any high office in the diplomatic service. The Sirens were determined that their son would rise to high rank within the Court: but the Council could not decide in which area he might be best placed given his difficulty with language. His native wit was apparent to all, but when he was instructed to address a particular issue with the Vizier's friends, the Pride of Lions, he failed to communicate the Council's decisions clearly, which only led to more difficulties with the Pride. After a number of incidents like this, there were few councillors who were prepared to support his promotion.

That did not suit the Sirens, and Scylla soon made it known that she expected more support from both the Council and the

Sultan. She seemed to believe that his promotion should be a matter of course. When she was told that this was unlikely, she again sought an audience with Vasilis. After much deliberation, he declined to meet with her. Her reaction was to spread false allegations against Vasilis, reminding everyone that he had not dealt with the courtier who had insulted her promptly or appropriately (she had expected him to be exiled), and that the Sultan was now displaying huge prejudice against her son Charybdis. As is often the case, Scylla's comments successfully attracted malcontents within the Court and the city: given the chance to complain, the grumblers readily found a band-wagon upon which to hitch a ride. The Sirens then found other complaints to add to their initial dissatisfaction: "Vasilis had always been prejudiced against foreigners seeking promotion in the Sultanate; the Court was dominated by men, and women were not given any chance to prove themselves; her husband had been over-looked because he had absented himself from a Palace Reception without seeking the permission of the Sultan to attend a distant relative's coming of age ceremony!" How was anyone to achieve recognition in the Court of Sultan Vasilis?" became her slogan.

Vasilis realised how potentially dangerous these charges might become, even if they were wholly unfounded. He spent much time discussing with the Council how to deal with the Sirens, and there were concerns that an increasingly ugly mood in the city had the potential to lead to an uprising against Vasilis. Vasilis had initially believed that Scylla had only wanted to have her moment in front of the Sultan, but it was clear now that she wanted more. As was his custom, Vasilis decided that he needed to turn to the Gods for their support. He spent considerable time at the High Temple praying to the Gods in the hope that they might give him guidance. In the end he decided upon a challenge with the Sirens before the Gods: if the Gods felt that the Sirens were in the right, they would display their support; if not, the Gods would make their decision clear. Much to Vasilis' surprise, Scylla leapt at the opportunity of having even more attention and agreed to the Divine Contest – her husband seemed less comfortable with the idea.

The challenge was for the Sirens to pray loudly to the Gods appealing for their support in front of the Temple where a sacrificial goat was tethered. A crowd gathered to see the event – something which they had never seen before – and waiting to see how successful the Sirens might be. Scylla, with her son Charybdis in tow, launched into a series of prayers, appealing to the Gods. When nothing happened, Vasilis told her to call the Gods louder. She tried again, but to no effect. "Call them even louder!" but even after three attempts nothing had happened. Vasilis then stepped forward, and rather pointedly removed the wax he had put in his ears to stop him hearing the appeals of Scylla. He then bent down on his knees and silently prayed to the Gods for a judgement. Almost without a moment's hesitation the clouds started massing over the city, a wind blew up and there was a powerful display of thunder and lightning. One of the flashes of lightning struck the post to which the goat had been tethered and a flame shot along the chain and killed the goat. The crowd were amazed, even more so when the storm passed almost as quickly as it had arrived and a stillness settled over the Temple forecourt. Scylla was dumbfounded by this dramatic turn of events, and her husband led her quickly away. Meanwhile Vasilis proceeded to sacrifice an additional bull along with the goat and offer thanks to the Gods for their judgement.

Nothing was heard of the Sirens ever after this. It was rumoured that they were stunned by the Gods' rejection and had left the city that night travelling to one of the neighbouring countries. Vasilis suspected that their story would be repeated wherever they went, with many criticisms of this Sultanate being mixed up with huge amounts of flattery of the next Sultan they met. However he wondered whether Scylla's husband might be able to moderate his wife's excesses; he did not hold out much hope – but perhaps the Gods' judgement will have been a revelation to her and the Sirens would not have to sing loudly again in the future!

Vasilis' faith in the Gods in this public demonstration also served to enhance his reputation with the Court, and particularly amongst the younger courtiers. The reward for his reverence to the Gods was a relief to many members of the Court who had become uncomfortable at the dissent within the city as a whole. It had been made clear how to maintain the prosperity of the Sultanate – remain faithful to the Gods and show reverence to their representative, the Sultan.

15 - The Fairy Godmothers

Knowing who you can trust is often the most difficult aspect of coming into office. Many staff and managers have shown a loyalty to your predecessor, and they don't know which way you are likely to take them. Some of them see the change of power as an opportunity to curry favour and seek promotion, and others resent the fact that you are even in power believing that they were more qualified than you in the first place. Someone once advised me that even when you spend the first two years trying to work out who you can trust, in the end, you realise that you should probably trust no-one except yourself.

The first six months is often called the 'honeymoon' period when everyone will more or less supports whatever changes or decisions you make, and only after that their true colours start to emerge. Elaine stood out from the start: she was not someone who agreed with everything I did and she did not feel the need to keep quiet during the first six months. If she felt that I had got it wrong, she would be ready to volunteer her opinion, right from the word go.

Elaine, a Physics teacher, also took on many of the jobs which no-one else was prepared to do. She had strong views about discipline and bullying, and she was always ready to urge me to adopt a more sympathetic view of the children. She would spend many hours after school returning lost property, or as she would prefer to call it "found property", to their rightful owners, when other members of the Common Room would have happily just disposed of all this "rubbish". She spent an equal amount of time ensuring that both young and old members of staff received a fair deal from the Head. Often I discovered her fighting someone or other's cause, when she felt that some wrong or unfairness had been perpetrated. I considered Elaine to be the Staff Common Room's conscience: although she claimed not to have a Christian faith, or even to believe in God, she recognised the ethical principles behind the school's religion and regularly she could be found leading Chapel Assemblies on the subject of what was right and proper behaviour, and it often sounded to me more like a religious homily than a simple philosophical statement. She was the member of staff who volunteered to create a embroidered drape with the school crest on it for the lectern, so that the Cross was given a visible presence in the chapel. Whenever there was a charitable activity at the school, Elaine would be on hand to help with its organisation; for example, when a disco was organised for the younger pupils of Eltham College and some of the local girls' schools in Bromley, she could be found still active into the early hours of the morning ensuring that everything was safe, sound and ready for the return to normality. She was also dedicated to support the many cultural activities at the school, and so that the producers of the plays or conductors of the concerts did not have to worry about the "front of house" arrangements, Elaine would be there sorting out the tickets and programmes. As if this was not enough, Elaine was also ready to volunteer to accompany many of the less glamorous school trips and exchanges, when help was needed.

    I soon began to realise that, although Elaine asked many difficult questions and posed as many problems as she solved, in the greater scheme of things she was always working towards the 'Greater Good'. It was also clear that the Senior Management held her in great respect and if I wanted a straight answer to any question I could rely on Elaine to give it. After a number of years listening to Elaine's advice, I worried that Elaine would eventually decide to step back from her work, and I doubted that I would be able to find anyone to take her place, covering all the valuable roles she fulfilled. Indeed, it seemed likely that the whole school might suffer if she was not involved in some way working for everyone's good.

Sure enough, I was eventually approached by Elaine who announced that she intended to retire: she wanted to look for a role that gave her greater satisfaction. In some ways I had been expecting this, and I was not surprised to hear that she was looking to find a job within the VSO scheme – she felt confident that there would be many opportunities for her teaching skills abroad. I could just see the potential consequences of her departure.

Elaine had always been an enthusiastic traveller either in the company of other teachers or on her own. She was legendary for arriving at the borders of a foreign country and being able to talk herself into that country, even apparently without the proper paperwork. Many men were quite envious of her determination and confidence at going where they might fear to go. She had over the years always offered her services as a host to foreign teachers from any visiting schools on exchange trips and had thus built up a strong range of contacts as well as a level of confidence in how to deal with foreigners in their own land. Her initial 'retirement' plan, she explained to me, was that she would apply through VSO to work in a Third World country teaching Science, an area in which she had considerable experience. However, much to her and my own surprise, she found that she was not welcomed with open arms by VSO – apparently they wanted Primary School teachers, not Secondary ones.

Shortly before this disappointment to Elaine's plans, I had been approached by a national charity to help support a Festival of Rugby with children from a Third World countries – I agreed to host the party from Rwanda. The principle behind the Festival was that by introducing these children to a new sport a spirit of harmony and happiness might be created that they could take back to their own countries. I was sceptical from the outset that this would be truly effective in transforming these young people's lives, but the charity had secured a good level of corporate sponsorship for the Festival – air flights and kit were all paid for by large companies - I decided that it could do no harm. The main requirement from us was that the "Rwandan Gorillas", as they were called, would be billeted within the families of boys from Eltham College who would also play in the Festival. I hoped that this would be a good way of getting the children to mix together and, at the very least, enjoy their time at the festival; I was delighted that the parents of our boys were happy to support the idea by offering to host the "Gorillas".

When the Rwandans arrived we carefully allocated them to their host families. Two adults had accompanied the group, and they were invited to stay at The Chantry with Maryta and myself: I had wanted to show my personal support of the project and by looking after the guardians of the children I felt I would be better able to understand what they had faced in their country's recent troubled past. However, when I met the two supervising adults, I felt confused: we thought that they were going to be teachers, or at the very least sports coaches - but the eldest, Mbleme, was reluctant to talk about any sport and eventually admitted to being a building contractor for most of his life. As for the second adult – he was hardly that: Mborake was still in his teens and hardly spoke at all. He didn't speak much English, but he rarely spoke to his fellow coach, Mbleme, in his own language. I soon became very suspicious of other aspects of the whole visit.

Disturbing reports started coming back to me from our hosting families. The visiting children were clearly overawed by the living standards in which they now found themselves; they were not very sociable and very few of them seemed interested in sport. The host families all had children themselves who had agreed to take part in the rugby festival –

they were not our best players but it was a great opportunity for them to play and represent their school - and it had been hoped that this would open doors and build bonds between the children of different backgrounds. However, matters took a turn for the worse when two families reported that several items had gone missing from their homes, and when the Mbleme and Mborake were asked to investigate, the stolen items were found in some of the Rwandan children's bags. I did not want to over-react to such behaviour, but it became increasingly clear that the whole idea of transplanting these children from their world into our much more affluent world was a mistake – it was like showing them paradise, but telling them that they could not even touch it! I was not surprised that they wanted to have the possessions they had taken, but they did not seem to understand that stealing was wrong; they just wanted to have a life which was not available to them in their own country.

But I was not expecting the next turn of events: one of the 'Rwandan Gorillas' disappeared – his host family said that he had just asked to go out for a walk, but he then never returned. The Rwandan leaders did not seem terribly upset or surprised, and when they were questioned in depth by the Police, they revealed that this child had been the nephew of one of the Rwandan politicians. Apparently he had been a late addition to the rugby group, and it was now obvious that he had been sent to the Rugby Festival as a means of escape from the war-torn country. This was later confirmed by an anonymous telephone call left on the school's answerphone over-night, indicating that there was no need to hunt for the lost boy – he was "…in safe hands and would be looked after by relatives in Manchester". I was very angry at this, and it just confirmed my concerns that the whole trip had been flawed in conception from the start. Just to add salt to this wound, on the last day of the visit, after the Rugby Festival had finished, Mborake, the younger of the two 'leaders', also disappeared. It transpired that he had agreed to meet some "friend of his family" at a local café, and after excusing himself to go to the toilet he had slipped away, never to been seen again. Mbleme revealed that he had not known this young man before the trip, and he had eventually realised that he had been sent away with a view to him starting a new life in the UK as well.

After this whole episode, I was determined that if Eltham College was going to support any more "charitable" projects assisting Third World countries and their people, it would not be by enticing them away from their own land into a country where they would get a false picture of the "good life", without understanding how it was achieved. If any progress was to be secured for such people, it had to take place in their own country; support in education and by showing how hard work can achieve positive results: I felt that these were key to genuine progress, and I hoped that I would find such opportunities in the future.

I suppose the experience with the Rwandan Gorillas influenced how I approached the project which Eltham eventually established in Tanzania, and it helped me find a way to help Elaine after her disappointment with VSO. Eltham College's missionary heritage had remained very strong until the middle of the 20th Century, and, as we approached the centenary anniversary of moving to Mottingham, I had hoped that there might be an opportunity to initiate some project which could be based on similarly philanthropic principles.

At about that time, and somewhat serendipitously, another member of the teaching staff put forward an interesting proposal which might provide a solution for both Elaine as well as become the Centenary Heritage Project. Christine was a Mathematics teacher with hidden talents: not everyone knew about her early married years in the Middle East, nor how she had spent many years fostering children from South-East

London - I recall an extraordinarily moving Assembly she had delivered to the Sixth Form in which she related her experiences with those children who had been rejected by their own parents.

Christine, along with her husband, Bill, and their friends, had spent much of their holiday time working with a local charity on a project to help a Primary School in Tanzania. Kisasa Primary School in Dodoma hardly had any completed buildings, so the children were forced to sit in the dirt while being taught how to read and write by the few available teachers. She and Bill, a retired engineer, had raised funds with their friends to help build suitable classrooms and even to find a few tables and chairs for the children to sit on: no longer would they need to bring a brush to school to sweep away the dirt before sitting down on the floor. Christine approached me for help in the next stage of her 'mission': she was worried about the quality of the next school that the children from her Primary School would attend once they were older. Christine asked me to accompany her and Bill on a trip which she was organising from Eltham College to Tanzania; this way I could see the situation for myself and consider whether I might agree to extend her project to help the Secondary School. I was certainly interested in the proposal, but after the experiences with the Rwandan Gorillas I was more cautious about this sort of project without a more complete analysis. Therefore I agreed to accompany Christine and Bill on the visit to Tanzania to establish for myself whether anything could be achieved that would make a real difference in the lives of these children.

So, after the seven hour bus journey, in the company of chickens and goats, from Dar Es Salaam to Tanzania's new capital city, Dodoma, our party settled into the Nam Hotel, where the incomplete floor of rooms above ours promised a greater standard of comfort than the level of the existing rooms! When we made our first visit to Kisasa Secondary

School, in a suburb of the main town, we discovered that this Secondary School was very basic with limited resources: class groups of 90 children, in breeze-block huts without any books, led by teachers some of whom had just left the school and some whose knowledge was either inaccurate or insecure. As we tried to assess what could be done, we agreed that there was little point in sending engineers to build brick walls and cut down trees for roofs – there were plenty of local craftsmen capable of doing this in Tanzania. After spending time with the school's Headteacher, Joseph, I appreciated some of the problems that improving the fabric of the school might cause: if the school suddenly had modern facilities with running water, electricity and computers, the Headteacher would have to employ many extra Security Guards to protect the buildings both night and day – modernisation without security would only lead to greater problems. I even proposed that we could raise money to provide every pupil with a solar-powered lamp, so that the children could read books at night when they went home – the Headteacher's response again was disheartening: he predicted that the children's parents would just decide to sell such a wonderful lamp to get money for themselves. When I talked to the Tanzanian Education Department about providing facilities for science, they responded by assuring me that every school would have a fully-fitted laboratory within two years – what they meant by a fully-fitted laboratory was a room with four walls, a number of desks and chairs, but no water, no electricity and no gas!

After spending nearly a week in the Secondary School, I suggested that something could be done to help the teachers, by giving them a more secure knowledge which needed to be expressed in confident English, and with a more engaging style of pedagogy. Christine and I felt confident that this would be beneficial to all concerned. In an attempt to show the Headteacher and his staff what might be possible with a little help, we suggested dividing one class (of 90 pupils) into three different groups of about 30: Christine would take one group for Mathematics, her specialism; Maryta and some of our Eltham Sixth Form students on the trip would lead the second group in a debate on the "Importance of educating girls as well as boys" - just up Maryta's street! And I would take the final group in a lesson on English under the title "Who is your neighbour?" I used the Christian story of the Good Samaritan first by getting Bill and a couple of other members of our party to perform the story as a drama acted out in front of the pupils, and then I tested the pupils' understanding of the story and their English in writing. The purpose of all this was to show how much more effective the engagement and therefore the education of all the pupils might be with smaller numbers in each group, and by a variety of presentation. The Headteacher was enthusiastic about this approach, but of course without more teachers he could not adopt this style. Unfortunately, not many of his current staff seemed that interested in our ideas: very few bothered to observe what we were trying to do in the different classrooms. So, although the Head prioritised financial help for books, a new classroom, creation of a sports field, as well as completing a house on the school site for him, we agreed that we would try to help with some of these, but there would be an emphasis on providing more teachers.

Once back in London I reflected on the best way to proceed, and I quickly realised that many of Elaine's talents would fit into our proposals for Kisasa. Both the Primary and Secondary schools, as identified by Christine, were trying to improve their status and hoped that, with improved facilities and a better quality of teaching, the next generation of pupils would be better prepared to find their place in a modern world. The Primary School had enough teachers but it was still struggling to provide desks and chairs for the children: the first load of desks that Christine and her charity had provided had fallen apart or mysteriously disappeared, so our Junior School at Eltham undertook to find money to help pay local Tanzanian craftsmen to build much more sturdy desks so that the children did not have to sit on the dusty concrete floors. The Secondary School needed more teachers and I hoped to provide a solution for that too.

I discussed my proposals for both schools with Christine. With her approval, I then approached Elaine: I suggested she should go to work as a science teacher in Kisasa for two years; she was to work alongside the teachers of the Secondary School, ensuring that accurate Science was being taught delivered in good English. Regular expeditions would come from Eltham College led by Christine, to help support Elaine's work, and she would be expected to coordinate these visits. In return, Eltham College would pay for her board and lodging during her time in Tanzania. It came as no surprise to me that Elaine agreed to all of this, except for the regular payments: she wanted to consider herself retired and responsible alone for the task in hand. We eventually reached a compromise. Finally we agreed that if a real difference could be achieved in Kisasa, we would have to find more teachers to go out to help Elaine during this time. I therefore undertook to find other teachers to spend some time there with her.

It was typical of the woman that Elaine prepared thoroughly for her visit to Tanzania: she attended a course at a local college to learn how to teach English as a foreign language. She identified a number of her Eltham colleagues who might visit her and spend time helping the Tanzanian teachers discover different methods to get through to their pupils. Elaine decided to take with her a number of items which she felt would be helpful in winning over the children at both Kisasa schools: sports clothing, books and pencils were all in short supply, and she hoped to be seen as a helper rather than a foreigner who just wanted to interfere.

I had tried to strike a deal with the educational authorities in Dodoma and they had made a number of promises, which I was sceptical about them completing before Elaine arrived: they had promised to ensure all the schools had more teachers of English and Science, as well as having classrooms fully fitted with desks, chairs and other basic facilities. Having also discussed our plan with the British Council in Dar Es Salaam, I remained doubtful that such promises in Dodoma would be honoured; I feared that Elaine would be daunted by the challenge she faced on her arrival.

Elaine was prepared for the Kisasa teachers' resistance and resentment at the arrival of a foreigner coming to "solve" their schooling problems. What she had not anticipated was the teachers' treatment of the children. Her first email to me after she arrived began "If you had told me about the caning of the children, I would never have come!" I confess that I had not known about their use of corporal punishment. Elaine's email explained how the children were summoned into the Teachers' Common Room when they were to be disciplined; they were forced to kneel on the ground and then were beaten with a cane on their hands in front of all the staff – a degrading and disturbing experience. The challenge that Elaine faced was convincing the teachers that children could be disciplined without the use of such violence. I agreed to help by sending further resources (books and pencils to be rewards for good behaviour) to Elaine. Meanwhile she worked hard at convincing the teachers that by commending good behaviour those who were inclined to behave badly would see the disadvantage of their ways. It was a long and uphill struggle; Elaine had many meetings with teachers and, although corporal punishment was technically against the law in Tanzania, few members of the authorities were prepared to enforce this law. She welcomed the arrival of one of her Eltham colleagues who joined the campaign, and slowly but surely the Kisasa teachers began to adopt a more positive approach to the children.

The other main issue to the success of education within these schools was the size of the classes: as we had all seen on our investigational visit, often the numbers were as high as 90 in the classroom. Even when Elaine went into the school and suggested that the groups would learn more effectively if they were divided by half, she found that the other teachers would resent having a small increase in the number of teaching periods in order to facilitate this, and they would often just leave the smaller groups to their own devices. Only when other colleagues from Eltham and young Old Elthamians fresh out of university, supported by the Old Elthamian Association funds, came to stay and to help Elaine, was it possible for her to demonstrate the real benefits of teaching to smaller numbers in a class. She was not convinced that the local teachers would necessarily continue to adopt this approach, for she considered that many were inherently lazy. However, she had shown them what was possible and hoped that given a 'following wind' enough teachers in the future would recognise the positive impact this change could have. As with so many other areas of education, when a critical mass moves in the right direction, others will eventually follow.

As to the basic task of improving the children's language skills, Elaine realised that the earlier they started, the better the children would be. And so she found herself visiting the Primary School to help with their English and sow the seeds of effective learning there. I was not surprised to discover that she also became a regular visitor at an orphanage to help the staff with art sessions for abandoned children - in return, staff helped her learn some Swahili. She found suppliers of books and promised them hard currency in return for sourcing books from the UK and sending them directly to the schools – she feared not only that any orders which had to go via the local authorities would be delayed, but also that unnecessary costs would be added. Soon it became a possibility to start talking to the Secondary School about establishing a Library. One key point was to open this after school as well as on days when the school was shut: that would require paying staff to be able to do this. Elaine contacted me with a proposal, and I agreed to find the funding to support this idea for at least the first year.

It came as no surprise to Elaine that the girls in African schools were not encouraged as much as their male counterparts. Despite the fact that many of the teachers were women, power rested with men, and so there was a culture to ensure that the boys' success was the priority in most schools. Girls were often the most able in each class and typical of most cultures they were committed to their studies, while boys often saw little point in trying hard. Then there was the 'curse' of monthly periods which all women have to deal with; when this happened it often meant that the girls of a certain age were regularly absent. There were no facilities at the schools to give them privacy or hygienic space. Finally, hardly any of the mothers of children worked and, if they did, they expected their daughters to stay at home to look after the younger children.

Equally it came as no surprise to me that Elaine wanted to correct this situation. At first, she promoted discussion and debate amongst the teachers confident that they would see the value of encouraging both sexes equally: "You will get better results for the schools overall if the girls are encouraged to stay at school, and you will find that the boys will respond better to the challenge of girls doing better than them in examinations, and thus try harder." She then introduced similar debates with the pupils, and found that this sort of thing was well received. Open debate and respect for other's opinions became part of their culture more than it had ever been.

However, Elaine still feared that the girls would never be as confident about attending schools during their period times, and this would always put them at a disadvantage. She contacted me again hoping that I would appreciate the problem. It only took a brief discussion with Maryta for the matter to be addressed; we quickly found a former pupil of Eltham College who was prepared to donate the necessary funds; Elaine was then able to employ local construction workers and to oversee the construction of suitable washroom facilities at the school, just for the girls: privacy and hygiene were both addressed in one solution, and hopefully the girls would not be so reluctant to attend school during the "curse".

By this stage, I considered that Elaine was being something of a 'Fairy Godmother' to all her children: she had come to Dodoma and had tackled a number of key areas in education in just a couple of schools, but her concern for the children and her wisdom was apparent to all. The success of using the 'carrot' rather than the 'stick' was on reflection simple, and her insistence that all children deserved to be equal was paving the way for the Kisasa Secondary to become a forward-thinking school.

Christine and Bill always visited Elaine whenever they were in Tanzania continuing their work with the Primary School. One particular area that Christine wanted to tackle was to encourage all the children in Kisasa to start school at about the same age. This would avoid the problems of classes eventually having children mixed in with young adults who had started school sometimes as much as seven years later than the others. Christine had heard of the success another charity had had at a Primary School with attracting the children to come to school: this involved the construction of a kitchen run by the locals to provide a cereal breakfast for all children before school. This had had the effect that parents were happy to send their children into school to be fed for free. Christine felt that she could not turn to Eltham College for further funds to support this idea, so her Sidcup-based charity found support from the local Rotary group to provide the funds to pay for the cereal crop to be grown locally, and then Christine encouraged some of the mothers to volunteer to serve the breakfasts on a rotational basis. This needed managing, but once the system was seen to be effective, Christine was confident that they would be kept going.

I wanted somehow to recognise the amazing work of these two "fairy Godmothers", Christine and Elaine, in Tanzania, but typical of both women they made every effort to avoid being seen in the spotlight. They were satisfied with the knowledge that they might have had a positive effect on the lives of children who might otherwise have been left in a world that did not recognise their potential. It was enough that they would always be remembered with affection by those children, and I am sure they will be.

Lessons Learnt

It is not easy to guarantee any long-term effect within someone else's country or culture: a change of Headteacher, or a change of Government policy can sweep it away in a trice.

Elaine teaching Physics to a class of over sixty pupils.

With Christine and the Kisasa teachers in front of the Head's house.

16 - *The Grand Vizier:*
with a puff of smoke!

Vasilis knew that it would take time to learn whom he could trust and whom he could not. The Grand Vizier certainly did not give him any confidence when he appointed his own wife as the Keeper of the Palace Keys on the first day that Vasilis had assumed to the Sultan's throne: but perhaps that was Jafar's message. Although Jafar, the Grand Vizier, had been the Old Sultan's closest adviser for a number of years, the old Sultan had blocked this proposal some years previously. But Jafar obviously saw his opportunity to make this move just as the new Sultan was pre-occupied with other matters early in his reign. By the time that Vasilis became aware of the appointment, it was too late to take any preventative measures, and he suspected that any rash response was more likely to produce greater problems than this one appointment. Nevertheless Vasilis quickly feared that this appointment was one which would lead to a number of sleepless nights.

There were six members of the Grand Council, and their role was to advise the Sultan; but the Grand Vizier had always refused to sit with the Council – he had preferred meeting with the Sultan on his own: that way he had more power. He had an "unhealthy disregard for the other Councillors" which led to a feeling of mutual distrust and enmity. Vasilis initially proposed that Jafar should become one of their number, the Councillors all rejected the idea as preposterous. Of course, Jafar was the most hostile to the idea, claiming that he saw no point in such "democratic discussion" and that he could see nothing positive in the idea. In reality Jafar suspected that it would undermine his personal influence on the throne. Vasilis remained determined to break down this resistance, and spent a number of weeks working on individual members of the Council weakening their resolve to block this idea. However, it was during this time that Vasilis discovered much about Jafar, which explained much of the Councillors' distrust of the Vizier.

The Vizier's appointment of his wife was not the first time he had members of his family appointed to positions within the Court that should have gone to others more worthy. His sons had both been given roles within the Palace Guard, but they had found it difficult to maintain the respect of their colleagues. So they had moved on by the time Vasilis returned to take up his role as Sultan. The position of Keeper of the Palace Keys was a position that the Vizier had created for his wife, Fatimah: there already existed a Chief of Security and a Preserver of the Beautiful Palace, but the Fatimah's role was an additional office putting her in charge of these two supervisors. She was not a well-educated person as far as Vasilis could make out, but the Vizier assured him that greater efficiency would be achieved in the Palace under her supervision. It gradually became evident that part of her role was to undermine both the Chief of Security and the Preserver of the Beautiful Palace to such a degree that they would have to be removed, leaving her in a position of even greater responsibility.

It was not long before those that stood in her way were brought before the Vizier accused of mismanagement: the Preserver of the Beautiful Palace had allegedly established a friendship with the gardeners from a nearby village to provide flowers at a reduced cost for the decoration of the Palace, but Fatimah claimed that the Preserver was presenting accounts which had higher costs. Despite the Preserver's protestations, Jafar dismissed her with immediate effect. No-one spoke up in her defence, and Fatimah was now in charge of beautifying the Palace.

Meanwhile the Chief of Security, Al-Haddar, had become too comfortable in his post – he had apartments within the Palace, and because of this he was expected to patrol the grounds late at night and then unlock the Servants' Gates early in the morning before all the dignitaries in the Palace got up. In fact, Al-Haddar enjoyed his lie-ins as much as the next man and was often found on his first patrol after Jafar and Fatimah had enjoyed their breakfasts. To ensure the unlocking of the Gates took place on time, Al-Haddar had appointed Hussain, his young nephew, to carry out the task. He was grateful for the responsibility and quickly established a good rapport with the rest of the servants. Matters came to a head when Hussain began appearing late at night, patrolling the grounds with a large bunch of keys. Al-Haddar was clearly taking delegation of Security a little too far! Fatimah had left some of her spies to keep a watch on Al-Haddar's movements. She again passed this evidence on to her husband, Jafar. When summoned before the Vizier, Al-Haddar was confronted with the evidence:

"Al-Haddar: you have the position of Chief of Security within the Palace, and so that you can carry out these duties most effectively you are granted accommodation within the Palace Walls. Is this not so?"

Al-Haddar nodded agreement.

"I now discover that you are abusing this position of Chief of Security: you live within the Palace, but you do not lock and unlock the Gates to the Palace yourself. You are not fulfilling your role as I expect; using your nephew in your place is not acceptable!"

Al-Haddar had no response to this.

In an attempt to reach a compromise the Vizier ruled that Al-Haddar could keep the title of Chief of Security, but as he was unwilling to operate during the expected hours, he should surrender his apartments within the Palace to someone who would. So the Chief of Security found himself evicted from the Palace in favour ironically of his nephew, Hussain, who eagerly accepted the duties that he was already performing, along with the rather smart and convenient apartment. The fact that the nephew was also completely in awe of Fatimah was never a factor in the Vizier's decision, but it certainly influenced the way the Chief of Security viewed the matter – Al-Haddar disappeared within the month, and it was discovered that he had moved to a small-holding in the country. He knew when he was beaten.

The other member of the Palace Staff who decided to step down shortly after Vasilis' ascendancy as Sultan was the Great Architect, Harun: he had served for many years within the Palace and was respected for his wisdom and ideas. However, he had reached an age where hard work was no longer his priority. He had helped with the inevitable modifications and improvements to the Sultan's quarters, but he informed Vasilis that he was unlikely to continue in his present post for much longer. Once the Vizier's wife was appointed, Harun immediately decided to retire from public service. Naturally Vasilis was concerned at all these officials leaving the Palace early in his reign, but he could not be sure that any of them were a great loss. What he could be sure of was that the Vizier was ensuring that he and his wife had more control over what happened in the Palace.

Vasilis asked the Vizier to search for a replacement as soon as possible: he felt that the Great Architect had earned his retirement and wanted to allow him to enjoy his retirement. At first Jafar argued that there was no need to replace the Architect, since he could oversee any projects himself that Vasilis intended to develop within the Sultanate. Vasilis refused to accept this and pressed Jafar for more positive action, and so the Vizier found and appointed a courtier who had no experience in design or construction, but who was popular in the bars and cafes frequented by the Honourable Guild of Builders. Vasilis quickly realised that this man could not carry out the role that he expected, nor could he achieve what the Vizier wanted - which Jafar claimed to be reduced costs combined with efficiency. What really influenced the Vizier was the fact that Jafar was used to receiving small favours from the builders and other merchants in return for their contracts; he quickly suspected that the newly appointed Architect was benefitting from some favours which had normally come his way. It was therefore no surprise when Jafar announced that the Architect had resigned and the search for a more suitable replacement had been recommenced.

Eventually an appointment was made: Kassim was a young man who had originally been a Eunuch within the Palace, but he had also shown his talents by advising on a number of building projects. He was unlikely to cause the Vizier any problems – Kassim was not a trained architect, but he had a relaxed and informal relationship with the workers, and he knew how to get the best out of them; he had never struck any deals with the Guild of Builders, and so would not get in the way of the Vizier and his benefits. In addition, he had a particular interest in training the young courtiers in the art of falconry – so Jafar always knew that he could control his new Architect by withholding his time from this past-time. And, finally as long as the new Architect kept the right side of the Vizier's wife, it was obvious to one and all that he would fit the bill as far as those with the real power were concerned.....

The specific role that the Grand Vizier performed was the oversight and administration of the Sultan's Treasury, and, despite some rumours put about by the hostile councillors suggesting some dubious activity in previous years, Vasilis could not find fault with Jafar's work in this area: in fact, Jafar had that uncanny knack of coming up with the funds just when they were needed. It was almost as if he has found a magic lamp with a Genie inside granting wishes whenever he wanted. When the Sultan had wanted to build a Turkish Baths complex in the city for the people, the Vizier had found over half the funds as if by magic, and so the task of raising the rest of the money was relatively easy. Vasilis had pressed Jafar to reveal where the money had come from, but Jafar only said "I have my sources." Another experience of Jafar's ability to use his "magic lamp" was when, shortly after Vasilis assumed the throne, the Vizier arrived at the Palace on a new "Flying Carpet"! The images of wild cats, lions, leopards and jaguars sown into the intricate pattern of the carpet all added to the impression that the Vizier wanted to create: here was a man with power! The Sultan was lost for words.

Vasilis often found it difficult to understand what were motives behind many of the Vizier's actions: the fact that he was reluctant reveal too much to the Sultan only increased Vasilis' distrust of him. The following episode was a good example of the Vizier apparently acting on behalf of the state, but with a heavy level of self-interest as well.

After meeting some of his neighbouring Sultans on State visits, Vasilis realised that many were quite envious of his fine country: his Sultanate was neither too large nor too small either; it was surrounded on two sides by small enclaves which belonged to small religious sects, not allied to any ruler, but who had always enjoyed good relations with Vasilis' ancestors. The rest of the Sultanate's borders were coastal allowing for good trade and opportunities for exploration. The land produced enough food for everyone and the people seemed content with their lives. His capital city was particularly prosperous and other towns were able to thrive in one or other area of manufacturing: the cloth trade, pottery and metalwork all brought sufficient wealth into different parts of the country. However, as Vizier Jafar was quick to warn Vasilis, there was little surplus anywhere in the Sultanate, and if he was planning to build new Palaces or temples, the Treasury would not be able to help:

"We just don't have that sort of money; the taxes that we collect from wealthy merchants help pay for the State Festivals and other cultural events. I know that these are the envy of other nations, but they use up what little money we have in our coffers."

Several years into his reign, Vasilis was approached by the Vizier with some interesting information. It concerned one of the two small enclaves immediately adjacent to the borders of the Sultanate – the one which was under the control of the Guardians of the Sun Temple. The Guardians had become increasingly worried that their land was being threatened by one of their close neighbours: they even suspected that this land's Sultan hoped to exert pressure on Vasilis by occupying the Sun Temple's land – this would potentially block a number of beneficial trade routes from Vasilis' Sultanate. Jafar reminded Vasilis that his predecessors had always had a good relationship with the Guardians of the Sun Temple, and in the recent past his father had sent some craftsmen to help the Guardians of the Sun with repairs to their Temple complex.

"I think that we might be able to reap a real benefit, thanks to your father's goodwill. An embassy from the Guardians is approaching the city, even as we speak. I understand from my informants that the Guardians are very interested in handing over control of their Temple Estate to us. Sorry, of course I meant to you, my Lord!"

Vasilis was very surprised at this news – not that Jafar had informants, but that the Guardians were proposing a deal. "What will they expect in return?"

"I believe that they will seek protection for themselves and the Temple Precinct; they know of and respect your reverence towards the Gods." Jafar replied.

"Make the necessary arrangements to make their embassy welcome, and let us hope that your informants are correct. We should try to secure such an agreement with the appropriate consideration, but without over-zealous haste. I shall join you once you indicate to me that you have reached a proposal suitable for me to support."

As Jafar left, Vasilis couldn't help wondering what advantage the Vizier hoped to secure for himself from this arrangement. However, even Vasilis could see that his country's merchants would benefit from the control of the Temple's Estate falling under his authority. It would be essential to step in before anyone else seized control of this plot of valuable land; and he was sure that the approach from the Guardians of the Sun Temple was genuine – they were a peace-loving holy sect that was well-known for its attempts to mediate between rivals, seeking amicable solutions rather than confrontation.

Within a surprisingly short period of time, an agreement was reached and signed whereby the whole enclave belonging to the Sun Temple would fall under the aegis of Vasilis' Sultanate. The protection of the Temple Precinct from any outside threat or danger was identified as a specific commitment from Vasilis. Notwithstanding this, it soon became apparent that the Vizier saw many ways to manage the estate land beyond the Temple Precinct, so that a regular income could flow into the Sultan's coffers. Vasilis was concerned about the reaction this might cause amongst the Guardians of the Temple and urged the Vizier to be cautious in the first instance: he did not want the Guardians to believe that he was only interested in their land for profit; nor did he want to create such a profit from this meadow land that his neighbouring Sultans might become even more eager to acquire this land by force.

"The first thing I wish you to do, Jafar, is send our best craftsmen to the Temple Precinct to see whether they can again carry out any necessary repairs. We must be seen to show our respect to the Guardians and their religious observance." Vasilis insisted.

The Vizier was nevertheless keen to pursue those ventures which he claimed would bring benefit to the whole of the Sultanate. After carrying out the Sultan's wishes, he contacted the Pride of Lions, a group of tribesmen who were notorious for their revels in hunting and feasting. They had established close relations with the Vizier's family in the past, and he knew they were keen to use the meadow land to train their youngsters in the rituals of their sport, and significantly they agreed to pay a not-inconsiderable amount of gold for this.

While Vasilis was not sure that he wanted a close association with the Pride of Lions – and he was most sceptical that the Guardians would approve of the Pride's hunting and feasting - he knew that getting money into his Treasury would be extremely helpful. Therefore he agreed to the Vizier taking this matter forward, but he insisted the presence of the Pride of Lions on the meadow land should have little or no impact on anyone, but particularly not on the Temple Guardians.

"As far as the Sun Temple is concerned, I am confident that the Pride of Lions will respect the Guardians' wishes and keep well clear of the Temple Precinct." Jafar assured the Sultan.

The Vizier was most thorough and persistent: his proposals appeared to focus on benefitting the Sultanate as a whole. To appease the Sultan's concerns, he placed a condition on the Pride of Lions that they were allowed this opportunity, under close supervision, for a period of five years only. The Pride of Lions accepted the terms and moved into the meadows to practise their sport with their younger tribesmen. Vasilis was impressed at how strict they were in controlling their youngsters and it was clear that they had accepted the Vizier's warning that this option to use the meadow land was very much under scrutiny by the Sultanate's authorities.

But Vasilis remained unsure that Jafar was acting only on behalf of the state. Why did he want to arrange for the meadows to be used by a group whom most people considered to be uncivilised? – they were a riotous bunch who seemed to enjoy their celebrations after the hunt more than the hunt itself, and their reputation amongst the other tribes was not good – "Nobody likes us, but we don't care!" seemed to sum up their attitude. Vasilis challenged Jafar on the wisdom of allowing such an unpleasant group into the grounds:

"I don't think we should support the hunting of lions: all our young courtiers are encouraged to learn the courtly art of hunting but smaller prey and mainly through falconry. I am not sure we get anything out of this arrangement other than a bad reputation by association?"

"We receive much gold in return for this small gesture." was the Vizier's swift reply; and so Vasilis accepted this, hoping that the Treasury coffers would swell without a significant loss to the Sultanate's reputation. The Sultan maintained his distance from the Pride of Lions, but he was also aware that Jafar spent many a long drinking session with them after their lion hunts, enjoying their wine and roasted meat. Vasilis always suspected that there was more to the arrangement between the Vizier and the Pride of Lions than Jafar ever admitted.

Jafar rejoiced in his ability to solve problems and made it clear to Vasilis that he would put himself out to find a solution for the Sultan. However, once that had been achieved, his interest in the project rarely continued. A typical example was the Grand Bazaar that had been completed just before Vasilis ascended to the throne. The Vizier had somehow found much of the money needed to build this – another example of his magic lamp trick - but once the Bazaar was up and running he showed very little interest in overseeing its management. Vasilis soon discovered that Jafar had hardly ever visited the Bazaar itself and after an initial level of popularity it was beginning to fall into disrepair though a lack of interest. Vasilis soon learnt from members of the Court who were regular visitors to the Bazaar that it was in need of immediate attention. Vasilis confronted Jafar with this, and after a visit by both of them, the Vizier sprang into action to solve the problem. But Vasilis noted that Jafar did not admit that his lack of interest had caused the problem, nor that the Sultan had been correct: in this way the Vizier could be seen to be coming to the Sultan's rescue again.

Once it became clear to Vasilis that it was impossible to trust anyone, and most of all the Vizier, he made it clear that he was not an easy Sultan to manipulate within the Court. Vasilis recognised that Jafar wanted to have a sense of power, but his ambitions did not appear to stretch beyond that. Vasilis just hoped that he could ensure that the Vizier could continue to work for him without undermining him. Gradually Vasilis and Jafar established a relationship which showed respect on both sides: the Sultan trusted his Vizier to manage the Treasury and work with him for the good of the country, while the Vizier acknowledged his Sultan's place as Head of State as long as Vasilis did not interfere too much with his methods.

After many years of working for his Sultan supportively, the Vizier turned his more of his attention to interests outside the Sultanate. He was often absent from the Court claiming that he needed to visit the Sultanate's allies or colonies to ensure that they maintained their close relationship. Vasilis was convinced that Jafar had another agenda, and he was really maintaining close relationships with these allies for himself. All that Vasilis could discover was that Jafar enjoyed many hunting trips or feasts at our allies' expense. Too many times Vasilis discovered that Jafar was absent without telling anyone where he was going, and Jafar rarely reported the details of what had been achieved on such trips: "It was rather tedious and you really don't need to be bothered by the details, my Lord." he would explain. All that this achieved was the Sultan's suspicion, but again perhaps that was the Vizier's plan: Jafar knew that control of information was one of the routes to real power, and by keeping all the necessary information close to his chest meant that he would remain invaluable to the Sultan.

In contrast to his reputation as a party animal elsewhere, Jafar rarely attended any of the parties Vasilis and his wife, Princess Shirin, organised in the Palace. If Jafar did attend them, it was only after Vasilis had insisted; Fatimah and he, almost out of indignation at being required to attend, made little effort to enjoy the festivities – they rarely talked to anyone except themselves, but they made the most of the wine he had specially ordered for his table.

The Vizier's regular absences and his increasing unwillingness to engage in affairs of the state eventually forced Vasilis to consider replacing him. It all came to a head over another important facet of the Vizier's role at the annual prophecy ceremony at the High Temple. At this ceremony, the Gods passed down to the people their prophecies for the forthcoming year: a priestess uttered the Gods' thoughts whilst in a trance. The Vizier was to transcribe the divine utterings as they were interpreted by the Priests and the Sultan, so that they could be published to the people. What Vasilis discovered was that Jafar spent a lot of time re-working these prophecies before publishing them. So much so, that by the time they were published, no-one could remember how accurate they were. It was another example of the Vizier using his position to control what was happening in the Sultanate. However, Vasilis had kept his own records of the prophecies. He confronted Jafar with his inconsistencies:

"Why have you changed the Priestess' utterances? What are you hoping to achieve? For many years I have suspected you of plotting for your own gain? Now I have the evidence."

Jafar just shrugged his shoulders and left the throne room. And that was the last anyone saw of either the Vizier or his wife. They just disappeared almost as if in a puff of smoke: the only trace left of them in their rooms was the hooker pipe used by the Vizier. No-one had any idea what had happened to them, and no-one could find any evidence of them leaving the city. Magic carpets don't leave much of a trace, but Vasilis believed that they had finally gone to seek their fortune elsewhere. Even without a Vizier and a Keeper of the Palace Keys, Vasilis felt that he would at last be able to sleep better in his bed now that they had gone – once all the locks in the Palace had been changed!

17 - Adventures in the Small Screen Trade

I was contacted by a television company inviting Eltham College to take part in a programme about the competitive world of securing a place for children in Secondary Education. I had been concerned for some time by the extraordinary lengths to which some parents went in order to get their children into a "good school". The TV programme was to be titled "Admission Impossible". It sounded to me as though it might be a suitable venture in which to be involved: South-East London is a very competitive area with both Grammar Schools and Independent Schools vying for the best children. Eltham College was normally seen as being a First Division academic school along with Trinity and Whitgift in Croydon, and Alleyn's and Dulwich College a bit further west, and City of London just over the river; these five all had both good reputations and a lot of money, so our attraction had to be different - location and size – we were not as large as the others and we were considered better than the other closer Independents. However, the real challenge came from the local Grammars – St Olave's in Orpington was probably one of the most selective schools in the country, but Dartford Grammar and the four Bexley Grammar Schools were not far behind – and from a parent's point of view if you could get a good free education for your child, why wouldn't you?

"Admission Impossible" focussed on two boys taking our Entrance Examination: one was a good all-rounder with academic ability and some musical talent. The other was hoping to secure a Sports Scholarship. The boys were filmed as they went through the process which included an interview with me. In the final cut, the programme included none of the footage shot about the first boy, who was successful with us and accepted the offer of a place, only for him to withdraw once his parents had been successful in their appeal for him to go to Dartford Grammar – his story worked well on TV when it only concentrated on his drive to secure a place at a Grammar School and his application to Eltham became irrelevant.

The Sports Scholarship boy was just what the TV company wanted: he came from a second or third generation immigrant family; his elder brother had dropped out of education as soon as possible and his father was determined that the second son should make the most of what a good school could offer. They seemed to have little money and so were desperate to secure a Scholarship. And most crucially, the boy stood almost no chance: he looked over-weight; his only sport was football, but he was hoping to get a Sports Scholarship at a school which played rugby and cricket. I had to go along with all of this: in interview, we asked all candidates to bring along something which they would like to talk about – he had brought a football. So I asked him which team he supported – Arsenal – and who was his hero – he could not remember! I asked him if he had ever played rugby – he was the right shape for a forward, but, no, he had never played it! Why did he want to come to Eltham? – his dad wanted him to come here because it was a good school!

After the interview, the film crew followed him as he was put through his paces in our physical tests: sprinting, and longer distance running, as well as catching and kicking (a rugby ball!), and batting in a cricket net. Suffice it to say that when the cameraman had to slow down for the boy to catch him up during the running tests, it was pretty obvious that the poor boy was not Sports Scholarship material for us. The programme showed the family at home as my letter declining the offer of a place, never mind a Scholarship, dropped on the doormat. Emotions ran high, but our decision was no surprise to any discerning viewer.

I am not sure how the general public interpreted "Admission Impossible" when it was shown on Channel 4, but the following year we had an increased number of applicants, not necessarily for Sports Scholars, but just in general terms. We still had the problem of many children sitting sometimes seven School Entrance Exams, which could not have been good for the children; and it just created more problems when the results were published with frequently seven offers on the table from which to choose. Most of the Independent Schools tried to tempt good candidates with offers of Scholarships or Bursaries, and parents often tried to play one school's offer against another – quite invidious in my view!

Our second foray into the world of television came under the dubious title "Young, Dumb, and Living off Mum", eventually broadcast on BBC3. The producers of the show were putting a group of unemployed youngsters through a series of tasks, and their mothers then decided who should not be allowed to continue to the next round. The visit to Eltham College was about the third challenge: the five surviving contestants had to prepare a form for a presentation to the rest of the year on a Personal Social & Health Education topic. Upon arrival at Eltham, the "kidults" as they were described, were presented to me, and I had to react to their appearance: one had a Mohican haircut, and another did not have a tie, so I had to suggest that they should improve their appearance if they were going to spend time in my school. The producers then decided to throw some of the candidates completely off-balance by requiring them to take a PE lesson in our Sports Hall. Now if you have never dribbled a hockey ball before, it is not an easy task to pick up, especially if sport is not your thing. Quickly one of the kidults revealed how anxious he was about sport, and when he clearly struggled to step up to the challenge, one of the producer's assistants was sent in to goad him. The resultant tears were what the director wanted to film! Just before the final scene was shot with the PSHE presentations, our Year 7 boys were interviewed about the candidates: they came out with some brilliant lines, questioning why these young adults did not take work more seriously, and what a shame they had wasted their years of education!

The final programme was shown after 9pm on BBC3, but I was sent a censored version (cutting out the bad language) to show our children. The right decision on the day was reached by the parents but it became obvious to me who would eventually win the overall competition – the young man with the Mohican haircut: he had some charm and wit, but he also seemed manipulative and lazy. Somewhat ironically the prize for the winner was a trip around the world: so the person, who showed enough commitment at the working tasks over the five programmes, was then given the opportunity to 'swan around' for another year! The best result from being part of this show was our own children's response not only to the personalities involved, but also to how the TV producers were manipulating the programme the way they wanted it to go. If nothing else, it will have made them particularly sceptical about all Reality TV shows in future.

Lessons learnt:
No publicity is bad publicity. Reality television is rarely real.

18 - The Hunchback: in case we forget!

Bacbouck, the hunchback, had been brought up in the Sultanate, but had then spent a number of years learning his trade as an alchemist in other countries. His family were very keen for him to return to his home land and frequently petitioned members of the Court to find a suitable post for him within the Court. Eventually a possible opening arose and Vasilis asked members of the Council to advise him how to proceed. They had been completely divided between support and opposition: some indicated that they felt Bacbouck would bring a huge commitment and diversity of experience to the Court, while the others were doubtful of his ability to conform and toe the party-line, so to speak. Perhaps he should have investigated their response more deeply, but at the time it seemed worth taking a risk.

Eventually Vasilis offered Bacbouck the post of Assistant Alchemist to the Court: in this role he was expected to oversee the education and development of the future alchemists within the Sultanate. His reputation suggested that he was a good communicator and so this role was designed to give him plenty of opportunity to inspire and sow seeds for the future. The Chief Alchemist knew Bacbouck from before and was eager to bring the hunchback under his wing. The Sultan hoped that his country might enter a time of huge progress and fresh ideas.

What became apparent soon after Bacbouck's return to the Sultanate was that he had not lost his passion for travel. He persuaded the Chief Alchemist that there was much to be learnt from visiting other lands and hunting out scientific developments that were happening elsewhere. With his overseer's approval, trips were organised to go to distant and uncharted lands, and the Sultan eagerly awaited the creation of the new ideas Bacbouck and his team had discovered on their travels. Much was promised but very little was actually produced. Vasilis began to sense that the travelling experience was more important to Bacbouck than developing any fresh ideas.

One of his initiatives was a regular trip out into the desert for the novice alchemists: this bonding session certainly had its merits, and the stories of team tasks and competitions all seemed to tie in with his wish to build a group who could work well together. The Vizier did express some surprise when he reported to Vasilis his concerns about the financing of such trips: the "Hunchback", as Bacbouck was known, showed little care over the recording of expenses, but what did filter through was that food was always "extraordinary" and not cheap! Steaks and wine were preferred to stews and fruit: the servants who accompanied such trips were extremely loyal to the Hunchback, but occasionally they let slip the odd account of Bacbouck telling ghost stories, followed by drunken hunts for the weaker members of the group, in a supposed attempt to toughen them up.

The Hunchback also considered himself to be a great entertainer: he would spend much of his spare time at the Grand Theatre, talking to the mime artists about how to create certain effects on stage. Eventually one could recognise his hand in the production of plays when explosions and the special effects became almost more important that the plot of the play itself. The Guardian of the Grand Theatre had welcomed Bacbouck's input, but often found it difficult to temper his enthusiasm, and many actors felt that his presence was detrimental to the sophistication of the plays. One production had so much smoke coming off the stage that it was impossible to see what the actors were supposed to be doing!

Vasilis found it difficult to decide whether Bacbouck's enthusiasm and passion was actually positive or negative within the Court: he could now appreciate the different views expressed by the Councillors. The Hunchback gave up so much of his time in order to give fresh opportunities and experiences to others. But was his commitment directed in the right direction? What did he actually produce that benefited the Sultanate? He was popular in the Academy of Alchemists, but the Sultan often wondered if he only heard the views of Bacbouck's supporters and not enough from the individuals who felt side-lined or ignored.

Gradually, reports of greater concern started filtering through to Vasilis. The Hunchback was often so carried away with his own enthusiasms that when someone challenged him his responses verged on rudeness. He was accused by some of sacrilegious language, even cursing in front of women. His drinking bouts with the Chief Alchemist and the Guardian of the Theatre – for this was his route to winning over both these two other lonely men – became more extreme and unpleasant. Complaints started coming in from families of some of his novices who were aggrieved that he had arranged some extra training sessions, and then had failed to arrive for them. In an attempt to win back hearts and minds, Bacbouck had thrown a party instead, to which it was rumoured that he had invited a number of courtesans as a distraction: unfortunately no-one was prepared to confirm this, and so Vasilis could take no action against him. The Hunchback appeared to relish notoriety, so much so that he sought to organise expeditions to extreme parts of the world. It was unlikely that these destinations would bear any alchemical fruit, and they were merely new places that he had not yet visited. On the other hand, Bacbouck had the reputation of trying to foster harmony within the Court – in order to raise funds for local orphans, the Hunchback was one of the first to volunteer to help organise an event and supervise activities for the younger members of the Court.

The Hunchback was so called because of his stature: he had had a stooped posture since birth, and he showed little concern for his appearance. He excused himself by saying he was an Alchemist, but a drinking habit had distorted his shape even more. This eventually had a major effect on his health. He had planned another of his trips with his novices: this time to a Tropical Island, famous for its primate wildlife. In an attempt to make the trip more appealing to the Council, he had sold the idea that the novices could use their alchemical skills during part of the trip to support the apparently primitive local communities. For example, Bacbouck suggested that the party could particularly assist in producing drinking water for this village at the edge of the ocean. To reach these villages the group would have to hike for a number of days through the jungle. In anticipation of this, Bacbouck had organised a number of training hikes out in the desert to ensure that the novices were fully prepared for the challenges ahead. Ironically it was on the first of these training marches that the Hunchback himself broke down physically. He was incapable of coping with the physical demands himself – too much weight in the arid heat revealed his lack of stamina. He had set targets for all his novices to match, and when he failed them himself he could not argue his way out of the problem. It was clear that he could not go as leader of this trip. Indeed he fell so ill that he was not seen in the Academy of Alchemists for many days. Rather than lose the opportunity to visit the tropical island and help the tribes-people there, Vasilis decided that it would be appropriate to replace Bacbouck on this trip himself. His own experience travelling was considerable, and while he was no alchemist, he was confident that he could supervise the work planned by Bacbouck.

As the time for departure drew near, Vasilis began to have doubts about the trip – how much alchemical work was really expected of the group? Would there be linguistic problems? Would the novices respond to his leadership over the water project? He had no doubts about his own fitness to cope with the physical challenges of the trip, but he wondered whether the trip had been properly planned, and he expected there to be a number of problems.

In reality there were indeed issues over the work carried out for the local tribesmen – not because they did not welcome the help, but because our novice alchemists had not been fully briefed on the skills needed. There were problems during the jungle hike which was far more challenging and dangerous than the Hunchback had ever anticipated, and there were problems over the health of some of novices who fell ill in the jungle and treatment was not easy to find. However, Vasilis' experience and calm approach enabled him to bring everybody back safely to the Sultanate – they had tales to tell, fortunately with happy endings, which he feared might not have been the case had Bacbouck been in charge.

At meetings of the Council Bacbouck remained a frequent topic of discussion, but there was rarely a consensus on how to deal with him. His supporters were very quick to point out how much time he gave up to support activities which would either not happen or not happen so successfully. The Vizier was less enthusiastic, indicating that the Bacbouck's attention to detail, particularly over the financing of his activities, was unreliable. From his point of view as Sultan Vasilis could see some positives but was worried that there were a number of moral dilemmas posed by the Hunchback. The influence he was beginning to assert on the younger members of the Academy of Alchemists was **the** major concern for the rest of the Council: "Are we storing up greater problems for the future?" they asked. It was eventually concluded that the Hunchback would 'hang himself if he was given enough rope'. However, no-one anticipated the way in which his fall from grace would finally be revealed.

It was customary for the Palace Guards to carry out impromptu checks on properties within the Palace grounds as well as those properties within close proximity as a matter of security. During one summer when Bacbouck was again away, this time on a trip with a troupe of travelling actors from the Grand Theatre, the Guards found that the door to his rooms near the Palace had been left unlocked. Out of courtesy they went in to inspect his rooms to check whether this was a result of a burglary. What they actually discovered shocked them in the extreme: Bacbouck had a large collection of sculpture, mostly made from bronze, but many in marble. They were all human statues in different sizes, and many of them seemed familiar even to the uneducated Guards; they could not understand why the Hunchback had such a collection. As they moved deeper into his rooms, they discovered even more sculptures which were weird and less familiar; the Guards became increasingly uncomfortable. Following a rapid investigation it appeared that many of these 'familiar' statues were actually famous works of art. It became clear that the Hunchback had used his trips as a means to steal these works of art, and by using his alchemical skills he had replaced them with copies.

When Vasilis learnt of this, he was very concerned that Bacbouck may have used his trainees on the trips to assist his thefts. Much to the Sultan's relief, all who were interviewed by the Guards talked about the Hunchback's significant absences during each trip – which was presumably when the artworks were being stolen and replaced - but they all confirmed that he had always gone off on his own. This had to be the predicted 'rope which hanged the Hunchback': he had used the trips when he was acting as an Official of the Sultanate to steal and defraud other nations which were allies.

The Sultan instructed Duban, the Chief of the Palace Guard, to arrest Bacbouck as soon as possible. Because he was travelling with the troupe of actors in a neighbouring country, there were potential risks over the Guards' activity in a foreign land. So to overcome this problem, Vasilis agreed to travel with the Guards in the appearance that he was there to encourage the Touring Actors Company: hopefully the distraction of the Sultan's presence would reduce the potential disruption that the arrest and removal of Bacbouck might have. All passed smoothly and although the actors were somewhat surprised to see the Sultan arrive unexpectedly and the Hunchback depart, any major international incident was avoided.

The Hunchback confessed to his guilt without the Guards resorting to any form of torture: he readily admitted that he had used his trips abroad to steal the artworks, and that he had spent much of his time in the Academy of Alchemists secretly making copies – hence his lack of progress on other matters. Vasilis found it difficult to believe that no-one else in the Academy of Alchemists was aware of his actions, particularly his drinking partners. But he steadfastly denied that anyone else was involved, and the Guards could find no evidence which pointed at any other guilty party. The Hunchback was escorted to the desert and buried alive within a cave, while his stolen art was returned as discretely as possible to their rightful owners.

After this disturbing revelation, and the unpleasant but traditional punishment of a criminal of this kind, what surprised Vasilis most was that all the roles which Bacbouck had carried out so effectively and enthusiastically were quickly grasped by other members of the Court. Any fears that certain activities would cease without him were proved totally wrong.

The Academy of Alchemists moved forward with many of the ideas that had remained stuck on the drawing-board; the Grand Theatre found that they could put on plays now without huge explosions as an integral part of the plot. There were always Courtiers, who were enthusiastic to take Ambassadorial Trips to foreign lands, but now it was accepted that genuine and clear purposes should be set before departure and they should be reviewed on return.

Vasilis worried that there were other stories linked to Bacbouck, the Hunchback, as yet undiscovered: he feared that someone in the Court would reveal other crimes by him. Many courtiers claimed to have suspected Bacbouck of criminal activity, and many admitted to have not liked him, but no-one seemed to have known what he had really been up to.

19 – A Tropical Adventure

I became more and more concerned about the management and supervision of trips organized by certain staff who seemed only to be interested in travelling to the more remote parts of the globe – I feared that the premise for some trips was just to visit somewhere new, with the parents of the children paying for a staff holiday: was that a valid reason for organising any school trip, and how reliable were those staff in supervising the children? There were many staff that I could trust onto most trips, but I remained unsure about one or two. One character, a bachelor with no family strings, in particular had organised a number of trips to exotic locations, and they had been completed successfully – but I sensed that this was probably more by sheer luck than anything. Luck played an important role when this member of staff suddenly became unavailable to lead his next planned trip – this time to Borneo. The apparent purpose for the trip was for some of the group to complete their Silver Duke of Edinburgh Award Expedition through the jungle on the slopes of Mount Kinabalu which would give everyone on the trip the opportunity to enjoy the unique wildlife of the rain-forest. Another challenge for everyone on the trip was to help some local tribesfolk with the construction of water towers to facilitate rainwater harvesting in their villages. The final attraction of Borneo was the chance to see Orang-Utans, either in the wild or, failing that, at a sanctuary which had rescued and nurtured large numbers of these amazing apes, under threat from the developing world. This trip was designed to take everyone out of their comfort zones, and the leaders had to be confident that they could handle the challenge. The thought of combining an adventure with some charitable activity appealed to me. What caused me some concerns was the fact that whoever took charge of the trip would have to pick up the organisation pretty quickly. At least the other leader for the trip, James, knew all the members of the party reasonably well and he had been involved in the planning before the trip. I therefore decided to fill the empty leader's place myself, and Maryta leapt at the idea of coming along too.

James and I agreed that first of all we both needed to get to know the party before we set off on this journey, and as the itinerary involved hiking in the tropical rain-forest on Borneo, we proposed a practice hike in the woods of the Kent Downs - I wanted to find out how fit the group actually were, since this would be the most difficult aspect of the whole trip. James enthusiastically agreed to organize the meeting point and to provide maps for all to follow. All seemed to go very well on the hike, albeit in Kent: the pupils, especially the six preparing for the Duke of Edinburgh Award Expedition, were more than capable of reading the maps and sustaining a healthy pace through the woods: we hiked for only six hours, but no-one showed any signs of fatigue. I wondered whether we should have organized an overnight camp to complement the hiking activity; we were all going to spend some nights under canvas in Borneo, and while it is one thing to be able to hike up and over hills for several hours, it is another to then spend the night cooking around a camp-fire and sleeping in make-shift tents as well. James was confident that the practice exercise had been useful and it certainly helped me get to know the rest of the party – except for the two who had never appeared at the start of the hike, and my sixth sense warned me that these two, Andrew and Joe, might be the two who would cause us some difficulties during the rainforest hike.

The other task to be done before we set off in October was to finish the fund-raising for the water-harvesting towers. Much of the fabric of the towers would be natural materials, and the Tour Agents proposed sourcing the plastic rainwater cisterns locally: so we still had to raise the funds to pay for these. Finding ways to raise the funds before setting out had been one of the objectives for the trip: the boys were keen on selling 'Kripsy Kreme Donuts' to the rest of the school during Break-time at a significant profit. This was all that had been achieved; so James and I persuaded the PTA to allow the boys to set up a stall at Autumn Fair just before we set off - a sale of bric-a-brac and other unwanted goods might just tip us towards our target. We expected the pupils to find goods for sale from their friends and families, and then it was their task to attract customers to the sale by spreading the word both verbally and by producing posters around the school. The pupils were generally good at supporting any form of charitable fund-raising, but they still needed to know about it.

On the morning of the sale, Maryta and I arrived at the Old Quad to discover that our fellow travellers had done really well: they had not only acquired a varied selection of interesting goods for sale, but from the sight of the queues outside the College Gates it was clear that many people were prepared to spend their cash to help others. I was amazed at the quality of some of the goods for sale, and James told me that the father of one of the pupils worked for a large Department Store - they had been prepared to donate a number of items, so that with a reasonable amount of bartering we should be able to make a handsome profit. And so it proved. The crowd that came to buy gifts for their families were also happy to pay that little bit more knowing that the profit was going to help others less fortunate than themselves. Maryta proved to be an expert at charming the customers – it was almost as if she had missed her vocation! I made a note to remember this talent of hers for the future. One never knew when one might need someone with the specific gift of raising money!

We reached our target to provide at least two water cisterns, and the group were ready to set out on our journey to Borneo. The island enjoys a truly tropical climate. As our plane began its descent, the afternoon storm over Kota Kinabalu (KK) was just abating. This happened almost like clockwork every day and the locals used to adjust their daily activities in accordance with this downpour. Our party was met by the local agents who informed us that the order of the itinerary would have to be changed to accommodate a festival which was being planned in the village where we hoped to complete their charitable work: it was hoped that we would complete our task in the village to coincide with the festival and that everyone would be then able to take part and enjoy the festive celebrations. As a result the hiking through the tropical forest had to take place first. We saw no problems with this change of plan. It would be good for the group to experience the local flora and fauna first, but the DEAS boys would need to purchase their food for the trek right away, (the rest of the group were going to have food provided and cooked for us by our local guides). So, shopping became the priority and having found a local market near to the hostel, we encouraged the DEAS boys to buy whatever they planned to cook straightaway – pasta, bread and some milk seemed to be their first choices: something to add flavours should have been on my list!

Our first night was spent in KK at a basic hostel close to the port, and after a light meal at one of the local restaurants, everyone was ready for a good night's sleep. We were all excited about travelling into the foothills of Mount Kinabalu where most of our trekking was going to take place: one potential sighting we might have was of the great mountain's primates, the Orang-Utans. These were suffering a decline in numbers, because farmers wanting a way to make real profit were being persuaded to replace the indigenous forests with palm-oil plantations. This farming was having a fatal impact on the usual food supply for the Orang-Utans. I had been told that the area we were entering was one where the tribes respected these amazing creatures. Hopefully this would mean the Orang-Utans would consider these foothills an area of sanctuary. If so, the possibility of sighting one or more was strong.

As is often the case in Third-World countries, travelling takes much more time than one might expect: our journey to the foothills of Mount Kinabalu took nearly seven hours in two minibuses. We arrived before the sun set at the village where our local guides lived, and just in time to enjoy the views out over the mountain. We unloaded our packs from the minibuses and were taken to a church hall where we were allocated into the various bunk-rooms for the night before starting the hike on the following morning. Another light supper of rice with scrambled eggs was provided, before some of the local children came to perform a charming set of songs and dances outside the hall to make us feel welcome in their home village. Almost everyone managed to get to sleep pretty quickly, even though the closeness of the mountain had again raised our expectations of the forthcoming hike.

Just after dawn on the following day, the group set off on the hike laden with heavy backpacks and guided by the locals who had agreed to help them find their way. The sky was clear overhead but the closer we got to the mountain the more the cloud cover increased. The children were in cheerful mood and when the rain began they kept their spirits up by singing their favourite songs. The guides were not so impressed and quickly the message came back to the group to stop singing – the Orang Utans would never been seen if the group continued to make this raucous noise. Maryta had also been upset by the singing – she had agreed to come on this trip primarily because of the hike and the chance to absorb the sounds and noises of the jungle. I had realised how upset she was soon after we reached the foothills and she had told him that she was going to drop back behind the group in order to get away from the noise. "That's fine as long as you keep us in sight!" "Don't worry" came her reply. "Even if I can't see you I shall be able to hear you!"

That was fine until the guides told the group to stop singing. I kept looking back to see if Maryta was still following, but as the path became more overgrown, I grew more and more concerned about Maryta's whereabouts. After an hour, our guides called for a rest, and I expected Maryta to appear from the jungle behind us. But despite a rest break of 15 minutes there was no sign of her. I shared my concerns with the guides. They remained fairly calm, since they maintained that there were no other paths for Maryta to follow. They were sure that once we reached the tarn half way up the mountainside Maryta would have caught up with the group. I was not so convinced and requested that one of the guides should retrace our steps with me: there was no sign of her on the path we had just followed. So I returned to the group while the guide went back to the nearest village where he could recruit other locals to help hunt for my missing wife. In the meantime the group carried on through the thicker jungle taking a muddy path; as we went the boys and I kept on calling out Maryta's name and then listening in turn for some reply. At various points along the path there were difficult crossings of fallen trees and streams; I could not believe that Maryta could have gone this way without help. After another hour the party arrived at the tarn – a small lake into which a number of streams flowed. As we put down our backpacks and helped each other clear our legs of leaches, no-one dared say what we were all thinking – Maryta had encountered some wild animal, and I had possibly lost my wife for ever.

Surprisingly quickly the guide who had gone back to the village appeared with many other helpers – they knew the route to the tarn very well and had no difficulty running along the route and making quick time. I explained what I thought had happened and they all began to divide the area of the jungle covered into sections for a more thorough search. The Head guide tried to reassure me that all would be well "Don't worry about her. She will be found. Perhaps the Orang-Utans will help her!" This was not what I had expected to hear, but I nodded and prepared to head off with some of the guides, leaving James with the rest of the party. Just at that point from the other side of the tarn, I heard a familiar voice calling in a loud whisper to him: "Paul! Come, look! It is feeding time for the Orang-Utans!" Maryta was sitting on a rock, partially hidden by the undergrowth, and pointing into the jungle forest. Confused and embarrassed, but also relieved, I led the group around the shore of the tarn. As we joined Maryta, she again pointed into the tees where we saw what must have been a family of Orang-Utans swinging from branches gathering fruit and leaves which they then ate with gusto. The primates seemed oblivious of our group and it was an extraordinary feeling to watch them completely relaxed. Our anxiety and tension was quickly replaced by smiles of relief; even the local guides seemed to have forgotten the worries of a few minutes ago. Everyone let themselves enjoy the acrobatic entertainment on offer: it was after all one of the reasons for coming here in the first place!

Eventually I crept closer to Maryta and asked where she had got to. "What do you mean?" she said. "I followed the path and once I got here at the tarn, I waited for you." "But how did you get past us? The guides say there is only one path; once you dropped back behind us, there was no way for you to overtake us." "I don't know" Maryta said, dismissing my concern, "but wasn't it good that I found the Orang-Utans for you?" I could not deny this, and while I tried to explain matters to the guides and all the extra helpers I really did not feel that my explanation was adequate. I hoped that I would be able to find a way to thank the villagers later in the trip. I remained unsure how Maryta had achieved what she had done. But the Head Guide crept up to me and reminded me "the Orang-Utans have looked after her!" Gradually the Orang-Utans disappeared into the jungle swinging like Olympic gymnasts on the vines and branches. Our party said farewell to the extra helpers who returned back to their village, and we set off trekking higher into the mountain's foothills. I had Maryta firmly in my sights right in front of me, and I was not going to let her go off on her own again.

The potential loss of Maryta had set our plans back somewhat, but the guides were confident that they could push on to our first night's campsite. Two river crossings later and, as the sun began to set, the rain started falling. The saving grace about the campsite was that it had a wooden shack as part of the facilities. The temperature was not cold but everyone was soaked through and few wanted to spend the rest of the evening trying to erect tents in the continuing rain. The DEAS boys were not allowed to use the shack so they set to erecting their tents and after lighting a fire in the lee of the shack, they were able to tuck into their pasta meal. The local guides had prepared some basic food for the rest of us and following a hot milky drink the rest of the party tried to find a dry space inside the shack: boots had to be taken off outside and coats were used as pillows as they all squeezed next to each other for what looked like being a cosy night. I spent a few hours outside the shack keeping watch on the DEAS boys, and staying quite close to the fire. Eventually I put up a small tent under a large tree and, since the rain had more or less stopped, I managed eventually to get more sleep than most inside the shack, where when one person turned so all the rest knew about it!

Breakfast on the following day was enlivened by the calls of Orang-Utans in the forest, and by the tales of whose feet had ended up whose nose during the night in the shack. Maryta kept quiet, perhaps because of her previous day's exploits, or perhaps because she was absorbing the positive energy from the rest of the group as they contemplated the next adventure. Our trek took us through more of the foothills, some of which were farmed by the locals with pineapples and rubber plants growing healthily in the damp tropical climate. On the previous day, river crossings had been easy since the water levels were not too high, but after the last night's rain the water had grown to be much more of a challenge. Ropes had to be suspended over the flowing torrents and back-packs had to be passed over separately in case anyone lost their footing and the weight of the packs would have pulled them under water, with potentially fatal consequences. The guides were keen to teach some of the boys about local skills and as everyone settled down at the second campsite, machetes and knives were used to cut branches of bamboo that eventually became mugs, pots, roofing materials for tents and ropes. Having stopped in time to anticipate the evening rain, hammocks were slung under trees and tents were erected close enough to the nearby stream, but in an area which was more sheltered from the rain. As it was, no rain came that night, and everyone had more problems sleeping with the humidity than the cold dampness of the previous night. The DEAS boys were beginning to realise that their food supplies lacked any sense of flavour – boiled pasta and buttered bread provides good carbohydrates but little taste! Mind you, I am not sure that the rest of us were faring any better with the guides' cooking.

As everyone emerged for the third day of hiking, one of the children, Andrew, failed to emerge from his tent. Maryta agreed to investigate, only for her to return quickly, her face full of concern. She reported that Andrew had slept very little, he had diarrhoea, and he was running a fever. I talked the problem over with the leading guide, who agreed to send me with our courier to the nearest town where there was a small hospital. I was not sure what they could do and whether this would solve the problem, but I had little option. Rather than take Maryta away from the safety of the group, I chose to go myself with Andrew and the courier, whilst entrusting James with the responsibility of getting the group and Maryta closer to their goal, the village where we were to help build the water towers.

Fortunately the sick boy and I did not have to hike too far before we reached a road where we could flag down a car to help. We were then driven for an hour along the mountainside roads until we eventually emerged at a town larger than I expected. Our courier was not terribly impressed by Andrew's illness and so it had been a very quiet day's journey! My conversations with Andrew suggested that he had just overdone it on the first two days hiking – I remembered we had not seen how fit he was on our training hike back in Kent – and I took this as a positive, since it suggested that Andrew had not contracted an unknown disease, or been bitten by a mosquito. When we reached the hospital, I hoped that Andrew's symptoms would be understood quickly and that a simple remedy might be on hand.

When the doctor arrived, I explained what I thought might be the problem, and then Andrew obliged by being sick at the man's feet! The doctor did not spend much time examining what Andrew's stomach had rejected, but asked a nurse to take a blood sample. While this was a good way to identify if Andrew had something like malaria, it was also a good way to delay any quick attempt to return to the group. After a couple of the most boring hours I can remember sitting waiting around the hospital for the blood test results, the doctor eventually returned to announce that Andrew had no dangerous disease. His recommendation was for the boy to get a good night's sleep and then meals with simple food. Therefore we found a taxi outside the hospital to get us back to the foothills of Mount Kinabalu. It was too late to make any attempt to catch up with the group, and so our courier gave directions to the taxi driver to take us to a small village. The courier negotiated with a family he knew for us to stay the night here before heading off early the next morning to catch up the rest of the group.

Andrew and I were shown to a small house where an old woman was boiling some sort of broth: I did not ask what was in the broth – I could not – but after insisting through sign-language on tasting the broth first, I agreed for the woman to pour a bowlful of it for Andrew. I was given the rest of the broth, and within a short while I sensed a drowsiness creeping over me. Andrew and I were shown a small room with one bed and a mattress on the floor. I opted for the floor mattress, hoping that Andrew would get a good night's sleep. Although I was not particularly sure that I should stay in the same room with Andrew, there did not seem to be much option: I was not sure how one might explain the principles of Child Protection to the old woman who did not speak English, and even if she did understand me, what were the alternatives. The courier had abandoned us for the night, so I decided that it was better for me to be somewhere where I was able to monitor the sick boy.

When I awoke, the first thing that I heard was the grunt of some sort of animal: it sounded very close to us, although I could not actually see it. As I shook off the last remnants of sleep, I became more aware of my surroundings. Andrew was still asleep on the wooden bed. The animal noises were coming from just outside the hut, and were now mixed in with a woman's voice. I quickly got up and emerged to be given a slice of brown bread and a hot drink by the old woman. What became more apparent as my senses kicked in properly was the fact that this was not such a small house as I had first believed: in fact, there were a number of other rooms, and the animal noises seemed now to be coming from one of these. It seemed that the old woman slept in a room with two goats, many chickens and a cow!

Andrew was now stirring and I was pleased to see that he was showing no signs of the sickness that had laid him low on the previous day. Whatever had been in the broth had been most effective. We were soon both standing outside the house and being greeted by our courier who had apparently stayed elsewhere in the village; he agreed that we should press on to catch up with the rest of the group. Before we departed, I went back into the hut to thank the woman for her kindness as best I could, despite our lack of a common language: I discovered her sitting amongst her animals collecting milk and eggs, and mixing them with some form of maize, for cooking over the open fire. I had not really looked at her properly until now – on the previous night I had been exhausted and more worried about Andrew. It was impossible to gauge how old the woman really was – her skin was weathered and she probably looked older than she actually was. She had dark hair tied in plaits, and was wearing a very bold multi-coloured skirt. I tried to show my appreciation and gratitude to her, but felt totally inadequate using my language which I doubt that she had ever heard before. She did not smile much, but nodded at my attempts to communicate with her: I think she understood.

The guide was keen to set off, and as soon as I emerged from the house, Andrew and I picked up our packs and set off following his lead into the forest. It again surprised me how quickly we seemed to cover the ground. Andrew had obviously recovered very well: in fact, I began to wonder whether he had actually been that sick at all. While I could not ignore the actual vomiting, I wondered if Andrew had just suffered from a heavy dose of homesickness, and the old woman's home cooking had cheered him up as much as driving off any hostile germs. Conversation between the three of us was again limited throughout the day, but I did discover that Andrew had never been away from home before, he was an only child who had been brought up alone by his mother after his father had mysteriously left. I was no longer surprised by Andrew's insecurities and tried to build on the positive experience we had both had with a good night's sleep.

Much to our surprise, shortly after mid-afternoon, the courier announced that we were only a few miles from the village where the rest of the group had gone. There was joy all round when we calmly strode into the village in time for the evening meal. I quickly found Maryta who had been billeted at the home of the Village Head Man. She was relieved to see us both, and after I had explained what had happened to us she agreed with my suspicion that Andrew's health had probably been more influenced by his mind than any genuine medical problem. Her own story about their day's hike before reaching the village focused on sightings of more primates – Orang-Utans, Proboscis and Vervet Monkeys. They had stopped on many occasions just to watch the monkey activity and the group had enjoyed these opportunities to relax. The only hiccup they had had was when one boy, Joe, had been reluctant to cross one of the rivers which was in full flood: when he had eventually been coaxed into going across with one of the guides, he had managed to leave his backpack on the other river bank! When he seemed to be getting out of breath on the uphill climbs, he had confessed earlier that he had failed to bring with him his asthma inhaler which would have helped him tackle such a strenuous hike. Maryta had convinced him that mind-over-matter would help him get to the top, and sure enough by taking it just a little bit more slowly, they had all made it. So the two boys, Andrew and Joe, who had failed to come on our training hike had now proved the point that staff need to have a complete picture about the children who go on such activities. Meanwhile the DEAS boys were delighted that their expertise in map-reading and 'leech-avoidance' had been so effective: their hike had been completed without too many problems. Everyone was looking forward to enjoying the rest of the trip.

Upon arriving in the village, the party had been divided into groups of about 3 or 4 and then billeted in the houses of different families. Maryta quickly explained that protocol dictated that the Head Man would host us: the downside was that the Head Man's wife was not so welcoming, and, from the previous night's experience, she was certainly not a star cook.

"Don't expect too much for the evening meal." Maryta warned me!

Sleeping on the floor, or not sleeping very much, had become the pattern for this trip, and after the 'mouth-watering' meal of strips of fried egg mixed in amongst some rice (again!), I hardly looked forward to a contented rest with a full stomach. At least the day's hiking had put my body in a state of needing sleep, and despite the grumbling of my stomach, I did manage to recharge my energy levels a little overnight.

The reason for coming to this particular village had been twofold: first of all, it was within what was called the Corridor of Life. Borneo's climate was considered ideal for growing palm trees with their rich oil-producing fruit. Many villagers had been induced to cut down the indigenous forest in order to create open land for palm-oil plantations for great profit. The disastrous impact on the Orang-Utans, whose natural source of food in the indigenous forest was disappearing, was obvious to all. The Corridor of Life was an area where villagers had agreed to resist the persuasion of the large palm-oil companies. Instead they had undertaken to maintain the rain-forest as it had always been as the ideal habitat for the Orang Utans. While this put financial pressure on the villagers, they hoped that having the Orang Utans nearby would attract many tourists who would pay to come and spend time looking for these apes. Perhaps we would be able to reinforce this philosophy during our time in the village.

The second point of the visit was to assist in the construction of the two water-towers which could harvest rainwater from the rooves of houses into cisterns. This was what our boys were looking forward to….. however, it soon became apparent that the skills needed to build a tower using basic materials were not their strengths. In fact, the simple skills of cutting wood with a saw, or mixing mortar to a suitable consistency was totally outside their experience. Fortunately, James and I both revealed that our fathers had made sure that their sons had learnt such simple but important skills early in our lives. Therefore we demonstrated how to use the skills necessary to complete the task in hand. Slowly but surely the towers began to grow next to the houses we had been told were in desperate need of help. Maryta also had the idea that the cisterns should be decorated to reflect the good works being carried out by our pupils. She asked for and quickly secured volunteers from the boys who wanted to help with this aspect of the challenge - probably they could see that some artistic input would suit them rather than the manual labour expected in the construction. The villagers were eager to help find some paints and, in a spirit of competition, our two groups tried to come up with their own designs and to complete their task in time for the erection of the cisterns on top of the towers. Progress was relatively slow, especially since the weather kept reminding us that we were on a tropical island with heavy downpours every now and then. During this time, our boys showed that they had more to offer the locals than building skills by playing football with them, even in the growing mud: it was not cold rain and the mud made it all the more amusing. It was clear that the village children enjoyed playing with our boys and it helped build closer friendships.

However, it was one of our boys who posed the most difficult question to me on the second afternoon:
"Why are we building these towers? I don't know why we are helping these villagers?"

The point he was trying to make was that the no-one from the village had helped in any way except in finding some paint for the cisterns. They had watched and some had even played games on their own **lap-tops**, but they had not come forward to help at any stage. In fact, there were also stories of some houses having **karaoke systems** in the main rooms. The provision of water from the cisterns would enable them to have showers and flushing-toilets, neither of which seemed to be their priority. During all of our time in the village, staying in the billets, none of the pupils could record evidence of water being used in a way we would have called 'civilised'. Washing was done by going into the river, which was also the place from where water was brought for cooking. The fact that crocodiles and snakes lived in and around the river did not seem to worry the villagers - they had grown up with this way of life. Going to the toilet was mainly achieved by crouching over drop-pits: water did not feature much in the process. I was worried that all the planning and effort that our party had put into the water-tower project was going to be futile. However, on the third day when the towers had been completed and the painted cisterns were ready to be raised into place, the whole village turned out to help. The cisterns looked splendid with their painted decoration – one showed famous buildings from London next to images of the village in relief, and the other had Eltham College's crest with the Latin motto "gloria filiorum patres" beneath it. These finishing touches seemed to please the locals more than anything, even if they made little sense to them. Although I remained sceptical that our good intentions would be scorned after our departure, I did feel that something positive had come out of our efforts.

Completion of the water-tower project coincided with the village's festival – the one which had led to the adjustment of our itinerary. The village threw themselves into their celebrations, even to the extent of a bull being slaughtered, and the meat being shared out amongst the whole village to be cooked in time for a feast that evening. Then we discovered that our party were expected to dress up wearing local costumes for the dancing and feasting that evening. This helped explain some of the apparent inactivity of the villagers and their preoccupation with music and the decoration of clothes. All of our children were given colourful outfits by their hosts, a bit like pyjamas, and there was much amusement at everyone else having to wear local costumes and floral hats, including Maryta and me. Everyone gathered at the village hall and music was played out of one of those impressive sound systems.

Soon everyone was dancing and there was a great feeling of harmony. Even the teenager boys in our party, who tend to have the most inhibitions - and were not known for their dancing abilities - were encouraged to join in by their hosts, and soon they were dancing with surprising enthusiasm; the dance of simple patterns became more and more intricate as the night wore on. Meanwhile as a climax to the evening's festivities, while the villagers were feasting on the roast meat, fireworks were lit and filled the night sky with intermittent loud explosions. It took some time for everyone to calm down from the night's excitement and an even longer time before we managed to get any sleep, since the fireworks seemed to continue being set off every five minutes right through the night!

On the following morning I had given instructions that our party should be ready to depart as soon as possible after breakfast. I was not surprised to find that very few of our party were ready at that time; and so while we were waiting for the last stragglers, I took one last stroll around the village: I wanted to take away with me a clear and positive image of what had been achieved over the past few days. After examining the two towers, I found myself wandering into a section of the village which I had not visited before. Behind a row of houses I saw some cultivated fields. As I moved closer I was horrified to discover what was being grown in the fields – palm trees with a ripening crop of fruit nearly ready for harvesting and turning into palm oil. I rushed back to the centre of the village where the rest of the party had now gathered. I found our guide and dragged him away from the crowd.

"Who owns these fields?" I demanded.

"The Head Man owns all the fields around the village" came the response – "he wants all the money he can get from the palm oil, like so many others."

"So much for the Corridor of Life!" I cried.

I was furious, and if Maryta had not stopped me, I would have confronted the Head Man, then and there. I was even tempted to pull down the two towers we had built, but our kids would have been disappointed that their efforts were being destroyed. But I hoped that some on the villagers might still benefit. In fact, the boys had been welcomed most warmly by their host families, and for them the visit had been a tremendous success. So it was with heavy hearts (but for different reasons) that we left the village.

The final day of our trip required us to hike back towards the main road which is where we were to be picked up by a bus and driven back to Kota Kinabalu. The only problem was that the hike was not straight forward – we had to go back through part of the Mount Kinabalu foothills, and the path was both slippery and very steep. We were given an excellent reminder of what we had faced during the early part of the trip – at least one of the boys was persuaded that he should not "adopt" a leech, which he had decided to call "Moriarty, and bring it home with him! Most of us had had enough of the leeches trying to get under our socks or trousers to suck out our blood. Our guides again proved their worth and skill, particularly for Fraser who was a prop forward in the 1st XV – he slipped on the muddy slope and was not able to grab any of the spikey tree trunks to help keep his balance: one of the local guides dived forward and caught Fraser's ankle just as he was about to topple over a thirty foot drop – it was an amazing show of speed and strength. The other guides quickly moved in and together they helped pull Fraser back to safety.

The final stretch seemed to be a climb up the side of an almost vertical valley wall. As we all emerged at the top we were greeted by some of the locals who had cut the pineapples growing at the top of the hill and chopped them up for us all to enjoy as a reward for our climb. The image I shall remember most was that of Maryta sitting flat on the ground, looking completely exhausted, having refused the help of any of the youngsters or the guides, yet determined to prove that even in her sixties she could do everything just as well as the teenagers!

Once back in KK we had an argument with the Hostel about mud (apparently from our boys' boots) blocking the drains. No matter where you are in the world, one can expect something to upset hoteliers and for your children to be blamed! That evening the Director of the Tour Company visited us to check on how the trip had gone. I challenged him on the Risk Assessment grades applied to some of the hikes we had faced: to describe them in their literature all as Low Risk seemed nonsensical – the tropical climate created considerable problems with the muddy narrow paths through the jungle and on one occasion one of our guides had to dive full length to save a boy from tripping and falling down a sheer drop of 40 feet. One could also say that the river crossings all carried moderate risk, but this was mitigated by the care taken by our guides. I was also particularly mindful of Fraser's potential fall on our final climb out of the jungle, which had only been prevented by the prompt and skilful action of one of the guides. I believed that we had experienced activities which had High to Moderate Risk, but that the guides had taken great care to ensure that we survived these challenges. I put it to the Agency Director that his Risk Assessment was misleading, and had been published in a way to calm the nerves of anxious parents back in the UK. The reality was that there were many risks associated with this trip, particularly on the hike through the jungle. What made the trip possible for all of us was the way his staff handled those risks in a very professional way. I suggested that it was important for the children to face risks and challenges:

"We should not wrap our children up in cotton-wool, and your company showed how one could mitigate the risks by being prepared and ready for all eventualities".

I went on to urge him to be more honest in his assessment of the risks, but show how the care provided by his company could alleviate any concerns anyone might have in advance of a similar trip. While he agreed to consider this, I was not sure that he would change any of his paperwork.

On the last day of the trip we enjoyed a morning on one of the small islands just out of Kota Kinabalu, which were popular with locals and tourists alike. We encountered large monitor lizards – and I mean large, over eight foot long with equally impressive tongues which they kept on flicking out – and whilst snorkelling a number of the boys were nipped by some of the colourful fish. Maryta also found time to make friends with a group of Muslim young women students from one of the Sabah universities who were also enjoying a day relaxing by the sea. As the clock moved round we saw the daily tropical rain cloud coming in, and on our boat ride back to the mainland we experienced the fresh shower when it hit KK.

Unfortunately as we got back to our Hotel, I slipped on the steps to the Reception area which had become drenched from the rain downpour: I crashed down onto my side and felt a crack. I quickly got up, but it was clear that I had done something to my chest – every time I coughed or laughed I received a stabbing pain across my ribs. I went to the Receptionist and asked for some pain-killers: I explained what had happened, and his reaction was to burst out laughing. I was not too impressed by that, and even less so when he just suggested going to a pharmacy around the corner in response to my request for some painkillers. I demanded to see the Hotel Owner, who was equally unhelpful – she still seemed to have a bee in her bonnet about mud blocking drains. Meanwhile Maryta had found some Ibuprofen and I returned to our room, not best pleased.

That evening we were all taken to a popular tourist restaurant where we enjoyed a final Chinese-style meal – although a visit to the kitchens was not to be recommended! I can't claim to have slept very well that night, nor during the return flight – my ribs were still very uncomfortable. Notwithstanding that, it gave me plenty of time to reflect on the trip: I was confused with a mixture of encouragement and dismay. I wondered whether our rain-harvesting project in the village would have a positive outcome. It had seemed like a good idea, but I was not convinced that all the villagers saw it in the same way. Even our boys had questioned what the priorities were for the villagers – karaoke or flushing toilets? Should the Head Man be able to go so blatantly against the principles of the Corridor of Life, by growing the forbidden palm-oil crop? And if so, what was the future for the Orang-Utans? It had certainly been an eye-opener for me and the rest of the party. I had been very impressed by the majority of our boys throughout the trip: even those who had experienced, or caused, problems had eventually survived all the challenges thrown at them, and emerged with credit. We all came away with our memories full of amazing experiences, but there were also more questions than answers.

Post eventum

Upon returning to South-East London I visited my GP who immediately sent me to have an x-ray of my chest – I had indeed cracked three ribs and enjoyed many uncomfortable nights until they managed to knit back together again. Ironically, after all our experiences in the jungle, I don't think there was a risk assessment for such a fall!

Lessons learnt

One's wife can display an amazing capacity for survival, whether she is trying to find some Orang-Utans in the quiet of the jungle, or whether she is hiking up the muddy slopes of a rain-forest.

Use TripAdvisor to get your own back on unsympathetic hoteliers!

Power corrupts and absolute power corrupts absolutely...... even in Borneo villages within the Corridor of Life!

James and his team with one of the completed water towers.

Maryta after the last hill climb!

20 - *The Poisoned Dwarf*

To keep the state running forward effectively, Vasilis recognised that it was important to maintain a high quality of advisers within the Court. He was constantly on the look-out for talented new members of the Court, who were not stuck in the ways of the past, but were capable of bringing new ideas and a fresh approach to familiar issues.

However, sometimes new advisers did not necessarily prove as successful as he hoped: indeed one particular appointment led to more headaches than Vasilis felt he deserved. Feeling the need for more financial advice, he sought out the successful merchants who identified for him a number of their 'bright young things'. The person who impressed him the most was unexpected – he was a young man, who had risen quickly within a family of cloth-traders, and was now looking to broaden his experience. Apart from his rapport with the courtiers working in the Treasury and his passion for numbers, he was most memorable for his height – or lack of it! He did not seem to mind being called "The Dwarf" seeing it as a term of affection. Vasilis saw no reason why this should be an impediment to him joining the Treasury.

Encouraged by his advisers to bring him on board, Vasilis made the appointment which seemed to thrill everyone including the young man (Zumurrud). Everyone was surprised when he announced only two days after accepting the role, that he was suffering from an acute illness and he would not be able to start his training in the post for the next three months. At first Vasilis was disappointed, but he soon began to question the story – no-ne had sensed that Zumurrud was ill and there were no obvious signs of what the illness was. Zumurrud had announced that he was very infectious and no-one should be allowed to visit his at home. Vasilis became very annoyed and instructed the Vizier to look for someone else to fill the role. However, the Vizier struggled to find anyone as suitable for the role. He suggested to Vasilis that perhaps the post could be left vacant until Zumurrud recovered from his "illness", since everyone had agreed that he had looked the ideal candidate.

"Let us be patient, my Lord. Perhaps the illness will leave Zumurrud as quickly as it arrived?" Jafar said.

In fact, the "illness" lasted nearly five months! Then, almost out of the blue, the Dwarf appeared at the Palace, looking full of health, and announced that he was ready to start work.

Vasilis should have known that this was only the beginning of his troubles with this diminutive creature! Zumurrud did work hard and gained a reputation for being prepared to go out of his way for the good of the other staff. Vasilis hoped that he would put his false-start, so to speak, behind him, and from the start of his time in the Treasury he seemed to be very committed to his work in the Palace. Indeed, Vasilis learnt that he was regularly present at almost every Palace Event, wearing a bright but seemingly forced smile all the time.

Almost because of his size, the Dwarf found ways of making sure that he was noticed around the Palace – wearing very brightly coloured clothes made from silk and speaking with a loud and affected voice as well as smiling constantly. Most bizarrely he decided on more than one occasion to wear high-heeled shoes, which were to compensate for his lack of height. Vasilis was worried that he was drawing too much attention to himself and asked some members of the Council to have a quiet word with him. The Dwarf needed to accept what he was and to concentrate on his job, rather than find ways to stand out, figuratively if not literally. Eventually Vasilis had to summon him and tried to point out the folly of his ways: "This pretension you adopt with your clothes is a poor joke you are playing on yourself. Snap out of it! Recognise your strengths, work on your weaknesses. Real achievement is liking what you see in the mirror every morning." He was not sure that Zumurrud got the point.

Vasilis grew more concerned about the Dwarf's interests when it was reported to him that he was a regular supporter of the Vizier's drinking sessions with the Pride of Lions, and that he was frequently found drunk wandering the streets near the Palace after these sessions. Was there a danger that he was getting involved in the wrong crowd? Was he prone to making the wrong friends? In contrast to this, it was discovered that Zumurrud had a particular passion for falconry, and he gave up a lot of his spare time to train new falcons and the young courtiers who showed an interest. He organised special events for falconry when not at the Treasury, and some of the Palace slaves questioned whether he ever went home. Vasilis found it difficult to judge whether Zumurrud was likely to be a valuable member of the Court or a liability. At least he had not had any more "illnesses" since he had joined the Treasury!

Eventually the Sultan's wife, Princess Shirin, came to him with a very disturbing story. One of Vasilis' young nieces, Adelpha, who was pretty but kept herself to herself at Court, had begun to spend much of her time away from the Palace out in the country. Princess Shirin had asked the Palace Guard to follow her discretely to find out what she was up to. It transpired that she had fallen under the spell of the Dwarf, and was particularly happy learning the art of falconry from him. He was spending many hours apparently explaining how to train the birds and how to develop a relationship between the birds and handler. Adelpha was apparently a diligent student, even though she had never shown any enthusiasm for any sport before.

Vasilis was not sure how to react to this turn of events, but shortly afterwards he was informed that Zumurrud had told Jafar that he would be unable to attend an important Treasury meeting, because he was accompanying a group of young courtiers going on a falconry trip to the southern desert. The Vizier was not impressed by Zumurrud's lack of commitment and he informed Vasilis about the Dwarf's departure.

"What is he playing at? Why has he given priority to a falconry trip, ahead of an important Treasury meeting? He must realise that I would not be pleased." complained Jafar.

No-one could understand what was behind Zumurrud's behaviour, but Vasilis was beginning to suspect he knew. So he asked Yunan, another courtier on the trip, to keep an especially close eye on Zumurrud. Meanwhile, he advised Princess Shirin's sister to refuse to let Adelpha go on the trip – she was to make up some excuse about her being needed for a State Occasion: as a result, Adelpha spent the whole of the week moping around the Palace.

Yunan came to see the Sultan as soon as the falconry trip returned: he was most concerned about Zumurrud's behaviour. Adelpha's late withdrawal from the trip had clearly thrown Zumurrud and he spent most of the first part of the trip sullenly going through the motions with everyone else there. Of most concern was his behaviour on the last night when the falcons had all been housed for the night, and the traditional end of expedition feast was held. The Dwarf threw himself into the party, eating and drinking to excess. Yunan reported that he had had to stop Zumurrud wandering off aimlessly into the desert and had escorted him to his own tent that night. He had been so intoxicated and kept repeating comments like "It's all going wrong! It was not supposed to be like this!" Yunan could not explain what Zumurrud had meant, but Vasilis was very grateful to his courtier for taking the steps he had and reporting back to him so promptly.

Naturally as Sultan, Vasilis felt that he had to put an end to this sort of behaviour and summoned Zumurrud again to the throne room. Zumurrud initially appeared most contrite and full of apologies for getting drunk: his ever-present smile had disappeared. Vasilis asked him to explain himself but he made little or no comment, avoiding eye contact with the Sultan. Vasilis then challenged him about his friendship with Adelpha, but he denied that he had done anything wrong. He acknowledged that he was pleased that Adelpha had developed her interest in falconry, which he saw as one of the noblest sports. Vasilis made it clear what he expected of Zumurrud in future and that he would not tolerate any inappropriate behaviour towards any member of his family.

"I will not give you any further chances." said Vasilis, drawing the interview to a close.

But the Dwarf wanted to have the last word:

"I may have over-indulged on the falconry trip, but I have nothing to be ashamed of, and I don't see what Adelpha has got to do with anything!"

With that he turned and left the Sultan with much to think about. Vasilis had decided that it was time to investigate more about Zumurrud's background and to find out what Adelpha's role was in his present antics. So he asked to see Duban, the Chief of the Palace Guard.

Meanwhile, it looked as though there had been a cooling in the relationship between Zumurrud and Adelpha. His work in the Treasury was reported as being more focussed, and she avoided any events organised for the falconry group. So all seemed to be progressing in a better direction....

Several days later Duban sought an audience with the Sultan: he had conducted a comprehensive investigation into Zumurrud's background and he had further information about the Dwarf's involvement with the Sultan's niece. Little could be found out about Zumurrud before he had started working for the cloth merchant, but during the Dwarf's time working there one of the slave-girls had mysteriously disappeared: no-one could explain what had happened to her, but there were suspicions that the Dwarf had had something to do with it. He had frequently been heard to comment how attractive the slave-girl was. When it came to investigating Zumurrud's "illness" before starting to work at the Treasury, Duban had been forced to resort to torture to get the truth out of the Dwarf's landlady: she eventually confessed that Zumurrud had never shown any signs of being ill during that time.

"He did spent much of the day alone in his room, but he regularly left her house under the cover of darkness, only returning before day dawned. I have no idea where he went and what he did but he told me to keep silent about his comings and goings. He may have smiled a lot but he had a very nasty side to him." she confessed.

Vasilis and Duban began to realise that this young man's sinister side may have been the cause of danger for other young women: what else was he doing during the nights when he was supposedly ill? They agreed that it was essential to keep a very close eye on him from now on. In a further worrying twist to his investigation, Duban reported that Adelpha had turned her attention away from falcons but was now focussing on another 'noble sport', that of horseback archery. And it came as no surprise to anyone that Zumurrud frequently met the group, when they went out riding into the woods and across the open plains beyond the Palace grounds.

After hearing Duban's report, Vasilis began to fear the worst. Indeed, matters came to a head when Adelpha failed to return from one of these outings, and the Palace Guard led by Duban were called out to track her down. After many hours, Adelpha and Zumurrud were discovered at an oasis: Adelpha had her hands and feet tied up with silk inside a tent, and the Dwarf was preparing to kill her with a knife he was sharpening by the fire. Fortunately, since Vasilis and Duban had suspected Zumurrud's motives, one of his soldiers had been instructed to track Adelpha's movements and was able to lead the search party to this spot. Under Duban's instructions the Guards creapt up on Zumurrud's encampment before he was aware, and so saved Adelpha from her planned execution.

The Guards brought them back in the early hours of the morning. Adelpha was horrified at what had nearly happened to her and confused by Zumurrud's treatment of her. Zumurrud just appeared smug at all the attention he had attracted: but he seemed unaware of the punishment about to be meted out upon him. Vasilis interviewed this 'poisoned dwarf' for the last time: Vasilis had begun to suspect that Zumurrud had led a secret life of collecting attractive young women and when he grew tired of them he tortured them to death.

"How many women have you collected and killed?" Vasilis demanded.

"I wondered how long it would take you work that out" replied the Dwarf, still wearing his horrific smile. "You know, I think I've almost lost count – there must be at least five. I lose interest when they are gone."

"What have you done with their bodies?" pressed the Sultan.

"Aha! That's for me to know and for you to find out!" Zumurrud answered defiantly.

The Sultan handed the Dwarf over to Duban to see if he could extract the information by any means. But even Duban's methods drew a blank: In the end Vasilis ordered that Zumurrud should be executed. Further enquiries throughout the Sultanate confirmed that a number of attractive young women had gone missing, but no-one had made any connection with the small smiling young man who stayed for a while before moving on. Vasilis could not believe that someone with such an evil mind had successfully deceived so many people, including members of his Court and himself. He did not take the decision lightly, but only the death penalty was appropriate for such a criminal. However, Vasilis was haunted for many months by the smile that was found still on Zumurrud's decapitated head.

And every time Vasilis saw Adelpha he was reminded of the poisoned dwarf. It took many more months for his niece to return to a calm state of mind – however, she was never really comfortable in the company of men after this experience, and Vasilis feared that she was destined to have a lonely life as a spinster within the apparent safety of the Palace. The whole episode shocked the normally peaceful nation to the core, and it was some time before the feeling of confidence and security returned to the Sultanate. Vasilis hoped that he would never have to deal with anything similar ever again.

21 - A Celebratory Year

Twelve years after I became Headmaster at Eltham College we were able to celebrate one hundred years of the school's residence in Mottingham, having moved there from Blackheath in 1912. The Senior Management Team agreed that we should organise a number of events which reminded the Elthamian community what had been achieved over these years. Our aim throughout the year was to highlight the achievements and successes of the school. So festivals in music, drama and sport were devised and organised.

Given the foundation of the school by Christian Missionaries, it was agreed that the first event should be a Service held in the College Chapel. As the school had now grown to over 800 pupils we had to organise three repeat services for the different age groups in the school (ie the Junior School, then Years 7 – 9, and finally Years 10 – U6) throughout the morning of the first school day in January. The Chaplain, Rev'd Peter, an Old Elthamian himself, was delighted that this event should start the year of celebrations, and he made every effort to devise a Service which reminded everyone of the school's Christian heritage, reflected the Christian ethos and promoted the strong sense of community that describes Eltham so well. At the end of the Services, every pupil was presented with a Centenary tie: the Centenary emblem on the ties was the school Cross projected inside the outline of the great Plane Tree. My explanation of this symbol attempted to link the Missionary background with the new growth in the body of the school (ie the tree), which was in turn nourished by its former pupils – I am not sure that the Old Elthamians' Association appreciated being compared to compost! However, I think that all the pupils, including the

Sixth Form girls who received a scarf instead of a tie, were extremely surprised and delighted to receive their Centenary Tie as this memorable year commenced.

In the evening of the first day, a Centenary Dinner was held in King George's Hall for as many Heads of School, and present and former staff, that we had been able to contact, as well as key members of the Old Elthamians' Association. The College caterers produced food of the highest quality and the atmosphere was quite special: a specially-commissioned cake, created by the company run by the Chair of the PTA and her husband, also appeared with images of the school including a marzipan model of me on the top! As our Guest of Honour I had invited Lord David Puttnam, who had of course been the Producer of the film "Chariots of Fire", relating the story of the Paris Olympics where Eric Liddell had made his mark. We were all honoured that Lord Puttnam had agreed to address the assembled company. As the most famous son of the School for the Sons of Missionaries (ie Eltham College), Eric Liddell was a most popular subject for a talk, and Lord Puttnam's message was both uplifting and challenging: he reminded everyone of why Eric was so admired, and then urged everyone present to aspire to the philosophy of "helping our fellow men as if they were our brothers": he challenged us all to follow Eric's philosophy, christening it "Liddellism". As the guests departed the Hall, I saw Maryta engaged in deep conversation with both Lord Puttnam and Lord Knight, an OE and recent Minister of State for Schools, on the subject of Eric's philosophy: it was a wonderful image that I personally shall remember with pride. I thought that all the events throughout the day had been a real success, and everyone who had been present would remember them for a long time.

The SMT and I had decided it was important to mark the actual relocation of the school from Blackheath to Mottingham in a partial re-enactment of the pupils' journey. The Big Run from Blackheath was organised in March for pupils, staff and parents, any who wanted to take part – for the two years previously we had had dry "runs" of this event, the biggest challenge being how to cross the A2 and the South Circular with over 200 runners. By running on a Sunday morning – *pace* Eric – we were able to avoid the largest flows of traffic, and by manning a couple of pelican crossings with staff, everyone's safety was more or less guaranteed. Every participant raised funds for charity by taking part, and upon crossing the finish line they were given a medal struck with the year on it. In 2012 we opened the run to former pupils as well – one gentleman aged 80 even took part, while Maryta ran with our dog Murphy! Although the mass start for these races was in the middle of the heath in Blackheath, in 2012 we began with a ceremony at the building which had been the old school, now a Private Hospital where three of the doctors were parents of current pupils. They had kindly sponsored a plaque to be hung in their Main Reception identifying the building as the former School for the Sons of Missionaries. So, in the presence of the Chairman of Governors, the plaque was unveiled and the Head of School carried a flaming torch about half a mile through the village to the start of the race on the heath: this was the signal for everyone to set off, recreating the event of 100 years ago when the whole school, including a certain Eric Liddell, set off from Blackheath , apparently all carrying a school chair each "across the meadows to Mottingham" to the site of their new school (previously the Royal Naval School). At this point the SSM became Eltham College. Chairs were not included in the 2012 event!

By the time we reached the height of summer, a Centenary Sports Day was organised: it had two themes running through it, one to recall and recreate the type of races that had happened 100 years ago, and the other to display how strong the intramural House Competition was now. I was absolutely delighted when I received a message from Eric Liddell's eldest daughter, Patricia, agreeing to attend. Although she lived in Canada, the fact that the Olympic Games were being held in London in 2012 had stimulated great interest in Eric's story. Many television companies were interested in recalling his story, and Patricia had been invited to a number of events before the Olympics began. I had decided to ask her to attend our Sports Day as Guest of Honour, and give out the prizes at the end of the event. Then she could officially open the College Meadow Pavilion which featured an Honours Board similar to those I had seen in China, recalling and celebrating Eric's story. Just to add to the relevance of this event, College Meadow had been chosen as a suitable training ground for the Olympic football competition, and the pitch immediately outside the College Meadow Pavilion was about to be used by eight different countries' (men and women) soccer teams. Patricia had readily accepted this invitation to come to Eltham - she is a most charming lady and is always ready to support the school. She appreciated that this was not just an opportunity for the school to celebrate, but it was also a chance for her to remind everyone about her father's Christian faith.

I had been contacted by BBC Scotland earlier in the year about their proposed programme on Eric's life after the Olympics, and they became very excited when I told them that Patricia was due to attend our Sports Day; they booked themselves to attend in the hope of getting an interview with her, as well as some shots of the school. BBC Songs of Praise had also contacted us in March and our trebles had featured in a recording filmed at Greenwich in May, but to be broadcast just before the Olympics began in July. When they heard that Patricia was coming to London, they also requested the chance to interview her at Eltham. A third TV company had also been to the school to record a programme entitled "The Real Chariots of Fire" featuring Nigel Havers on a visit to the school; the pupils were recorded singing "Jerusalem" (from which the words Chariots of Fire come) in the College Chapel, some boys were filmed running 400 metres around the school race track, and the Chaplain was interviewed by Nigel Havers about Eric Liddell and his faith. The school's centenary coinciding with the Olympic Games in London just seemed rather serendipitous!

So when Patricia arrived in early July at Eltham College with her husband, she was much in demand. It was a real indication of the respect still felt by the majority of people towards Eric Liddell who knew his story; and Patricia, despite being a lady of mature years, rejoiced in the opportunity she was being given to tell her father's story to a new audience.

When our Sports Day commenced, several of the competitions were designed to mirror those events that took place one hundred years ago; for example, in one race the runners took part in the Businessman's Race, which involved them putting on suitable clothing for a businessman throughout the race. The prizes in those competitions were equally linked to the past, for example they were a box of paints or a kite, reflecting the simple nature of competition at a boarding school in the past. These races were run alongside the modern athletics competition which was as usual hotly contested between the four Houses. I was particularly pleased with the way the school responded to having a film crew (from BBC Scotland) present throughout the event. They took many shots of the races and I was even interviewed while standing amongst the crowds – I am afraid that most of what I said was eventually cut from the final programme about Eric, but perhaps that was because I did not take a very Scottish line on his life – he was born in China, sent to boarding school in South-East London from the age of six, and only really went to Scotland when he attended Edinburgh University: I even suggested that he might not have had a very strong Scottish accent! Fortunately Patricia's interview was just what the Director wanted with plenty of comments about Eric wanting to help his fellow men, being inspired by God, and stressing that although he did not want to run on a Sunday, he never said others should not – that was Eric's manner.

Rather unexpectedly, a bizarre occurrence took place at the end of the Games. Traditionally there is an Open Race for anyone who had not taken part in the House Competition thus far, to gain points for their House just by completing the course. On this occasion lots of visitors were invited to take part: even Maryta decided to run again with our family dog, Murphy. The principle was, in line with the Olympics, that taking part was more important than winning. One of the other participants, a latecomer to the race, was Patricia's husband, Mervyn. It did not seem right to advise him against taking part, but it became clear that Mervyn did not accept just taking part was for him – he wanted to win, which he was unlikely to do given his advanced years. It was therefore no surprise that very quickly after the start of the race the medical team was required to look after Mervyn who had collapsed through too much effort too soon: he had torn a tendon in his leg. Patricia was obviously worried about his health, but she was also most reassuring to me about Mervyn's folly. He recovered well and within a week, he and Patricia flew back to Canada: this was possibly too early for someone with his leg in plaster, and he spent much of the journey complaining about the treatment he had received by the NHS. I understand that Patricia let him grumble away until they reached their home; she then made Mervyn understand how he alone was responsible for his injuries and that some humility was in order. Mervyn was put in his place!

While the Sports Centenary events had been a great success, there had been less enthusiasm for any Drama to recall the past 100 years. In the end one of our academic staff, Andrew, put together an evening's entertainment to be performed in the Central Hall: the first half was full of scenes from dramas dating from a century ago, while the second half had glimpses of plays written during the rest of the years. When I saw what had been planned, I was very impressed by the clever way in which the scenes had been fitted together, to make the first half almost feel like a whole play telling the story of the school. The second half was less successful in having the same sense of wholeness, but it did provide some good opportunities for the pupil actors to perform some challenging scenes. In advance of the evening's performance, I had been informed that the actors were very anxious that their entertainment would not be appreciated. In the end, and thanks to some extra work promoting the evening through social media, a large crowd gathered for the show and loud applause greeted every scene and performer, so that the whole evening passed with a feeling of good cheer and appreciation.

In advance of the Centenary Year the College Archivist, Mark, approached me with the idea of creating an official record of the past century – a "coffee-table" book, with plenty of photos, so that it did not just fall into that category of a dry history of the school (which already existed!). I was delighted with the idea, as long as Mark could find sufficient photos and images from the early years. He set about the task with a real determination: he divided the books into topics and at the same time aimed to balance the number of photos from every decade evenly. It was clear that this was the type of task that Mark relished. When it came to putting all the material together, Mark was less confident about the presentation style and design, so I asked Maryta, who had spent the last 30 years of her life working on the lay-out and design of major newspapers, to work alongside Mark and the printers to produce the final publication. The end result, entitled "Our Century", was stunning and I was very impressed by their combined efforts. I was also rather proud of my contribution to the finished volume – the cover was a combination of pictures from the book arranged in such a way to give an overall image of the school crest, all laid out on a pure white background. Everyone who bought a copy could see how hard Mark in particular had worked to dig up interesting stories to be included, and there was something for everyone to enjoy.

The publication of the book was ready by Christmas 2011. Parents of current pupils bought copies, especially as we had included an annex with photographs of every pupil and member of staff at the school in 2012. We then created a separate Newsletter at the end of the year which detailed all the celebratory events of that year. It was popular with former pupils, as it complemented the previous publications on the history of the school, presenting stories from a different angle. Perhaps it also reflected the way society had moved to a more superficial world where you can just dip in and out of any story as you wanted. I hope that it has a more lasting value, however.

Music was a major element in the education of children at Eltham College, and during my Headship I had introduced the idea that every child in the Junior School should be given at least one term's free tuition on an instrument; this eventually became two instruments over two years. I had always felt that playing an instrument in a band or orchestra, or singing in a choir was just as thrilling as playing behind the scrum in rugby or performing on stage in a play. Making music together teaches young people to be aware of each other and they develop a greater empathy and awareness for each other through these activities. Therefore a number of musical events were high on my agenda to mark our Centenary Year.

The first event was the Centenary Concert performed at the Queen Elizabeth Hall on the South Bank. Although our usual venues for concerts, the Blackheath Halls and St Alfege's Church in Blackheath, were good acoustically, I felt that we should aim for a major London concert hall so that as many as possible (700+) could attend. This concert had over 120 pupils performing; from the first drum beats of Copland's Fanfare for the Common Man, through to the last chords of Parry's Blest Pair of Sirens, there was a genuine feeling of joy and celebration at the quality of music being performed. The Jazz Orchestra, the Consort Choir, and the percussion ensemble Stick Attack, all were accommodated. It was a particular joy for me to welcome back in the audience Tim, my first appointment as Director of Music, who had been particularly responsible for the advances in the quality of music we enjoyed on that evening. What a stroke of luck his appointment had been. It is often said that the two most important things a Headmaster does are attract the right pupils to their school, and make wise teaching appointments: and of course, the latter helps the former!

The other musical event I had been eagerly anticipating was the open-air ECCO Pops Concert in the College grounds. The **E**ltham **C**ollege **C**ommunity **O**rchestra had always been that, ie full of members of the Eltham Community, and this concert was no exception: their summer concert had been a regular fixture for the past 30 years, usually held inside the marquee set up for Speech Day. We had celebrated ECCO's 25th Anniversary by going outside the marquee, and it seemed the right thing to repeat the exercise as part of our Centenary Celebrations. I had discussed the music for the concert with the Director of Music, Alastair, and we devised a programme which included some of old favourites – film-score music alongside some opera choruses and bits of Orff's Carmina Burana. A highlight for me was being asked to play the anvil in Verdi's Chorus from Il Trovatore: I was supposed to play along with our guest presenter from Classic FM, but he revealed in the afternoon rehearsal that he had no sense of timing and could not read music – fairly typical of Classic FM! So I ended up playing solo. Another special piece was the National Anthem, arranged by three younger pupils, and the concert was supposed to finish with audience participation, consisting of waving flags and singing *Jerusalem* and *Land of Hope and Glory* – but as a surprise encore, the orchestra played the main theme from Star Wars complemented with a fireworks display lighting up the sky. The Bursar was worried (again!) about the cost of arranging such a concert – the cost of an outdoor stage along with sound and lighting system are always more expensive than you think - but I persuaded the Chairman of Governors to 'sponsor' the fireworks. The Director of Music had insisted that not only there should be a large choir for some of the pieces, but he wanted the Junior School choir to perform as well – having as many of the children taking part certainly ensured parental support for the event, and nearly 2000 people brought their picnics and enjoyed the show on the College grounds. The finale was truly inspiring with everyone singing heartily, the fireworks almost competing with the moon and stars as they lit up the night-sky, and the whole concert bowl was again full of an amazing feeling of celebration. The crowds who had turned up for the event had clearly enjoyed themselves: many had dressed up for the occasion and brought large picnic hampers full of food and wine to add to the evening's festivities. Even the Bursar had a smile on his face when he left, although this may have been more because of the wine he had enjoyed throughout the night, than because of the music! I left the event filled with a true sense of satisfaction that this was something which everyone had enjoyed.

If there is one problem that all Headmasters face, it is finding a suitable Guest of Honour for their school's annual Speech Day. My failed attempt to secure the services of Mike Brearley, one of my cricketing heroes, who declined on the grounds that he did not like to single some children at the exclusion of others: I saw his point, but our awards for "Good

Eggs" and other Improver Prizes had always aimed to overcome this problem. Anyway, since this was a special year I had asked the Chairman of Governors for help in securing the services of someone famous. In a previous year he had generously helped by "winning" Mo Mowlam in an Auction at the Hackney Empire. She was memorable for two reasons: she arrived in a wheelchair, which we were not expecting, and she squealed with delight on being lifted onto the Speaker's platform by members of the 1st XV. Secondly, although her speech was quite dull, being slowly delivered from some note cards, the question and answer session that followed was full of life and bite – she even challenged me for planting questions around the marquee! She was a very impressive lady, but tragically she died only one month later.

Anyway for the Centenary Speech Day, I was hopeful that the Chairman might again come up trumps. Sure enough, he told me quite early in the year that his friend, the TV personality, Griff Rhys Jones, had agreed to talk to the school – Chairman David was sure that Griff would fit the bill for our Centenary Speech Day. Unfortunately, as we approached April, I was sent a message by Griff's Personal Assistant letting me know that Griff's new television programme about 'saving old buildings' was proving unpredictable, and he was not sure where he would be at the beginning of July (when our Speech Day was planned). I was therefore left with the problem of what to do if he did not turn up. The only answer was to find someone else to fill the slot, and even give a second speech if Griff did turn up. As luck would have it, I had managed to get to know the Head of Harrow School quite well, and he, Barnaby, was an Old Elthamian! I explained my predicament, while also emphasising the importance of having someone of the highest quality to deliver the main speech. Since Barnaby knew exactly where I was coming from, it did not take much to persuade him to fill the possible 'second' slot. And that was why our Centenary Year Speech Day had two Guests of Honour (Griff was able to attend, with Barnaby also doing his turn) as well as having the daughter of Eric Liddell sitting in the front row of the audience: one could not have bettered the cast list. I also think it is worth recording that I thought that Barnaby's speech was far more memorable than Griff's, but they were a good double act!

One important element in the Year's activities related to the Old Elthamians. I had asked their Association committee how they would like to recognise the year, and their response focussed on the school's foundation by Christian Missionaries. Our discussions quickly moved away from Eltham and into areas of the world where disadvantaged children needed help. My thoughts then turned to Tanzania and Elaine working on her own in Dodoma. While Elaine had agreed to spending two years in Dodoma working at the Kisasa High School, it seemed obvious that she would benefit from any available help. Therefore with the Old Elthamian Association support, an advert was published within our community for any Old Elthamian who could offer some relevant skills to spend time with Elaine. The OEA would pay for their travel expenses out to Tanzania and provide some financial support for board and lodging over the period of six months. Two young women and a young man, all recent Leavers, stepped forward and stayed with Elaine at different times over the next two years, helping with Drama, English and Science, as well as Sport at the school. There is no doubt that Elaine was very pleased to have some familiar faces, as well as allies against Tanzanian issues like corporal punishment: the introduction of positive rewards (ie commendations) went some way to reduce the amount of pupil degradation, but having another teacher who disapproved of the use of the cane helped her sanity!

In the Junior School, a project was proposed by the Master, Edmund: the pupils worked with an artist to create the design for an outdoor mosaic commemorating the past 100 years. The image they produced was tied together by the River Thames running through the middle of the overall story. At various points along the way there were images of famous London sites as well as personalities linked to Eltham, like WG Grace (who died in the house opposite the Junior School), and three OEs, Eric Liddell (of course!), George Band (part of the team to first climb Everest), and Mervyn Peake (author of Gormenghast). In addition there were symbols which were specific to an education at the Junior School (sports, music, chess and fencing). As it was a work of modern art, we invited Gerald Moore OE to unveil the mosaic; during his speech, his false teeth began to fall out, much to everyone's amusement, especially to those of us who knew that he made his fortune out of being a specialist dentist in Harley Street!

One other event in 2012 took place which had very little to do with our Centenary, but nevertheless was extraordinary in the history of the school. As I mentioned earlier, College Meadow had been selected by the London Organising Committee to be a Training venue for some of the Olympic Football teams. I pass over the fact that LOCOG did not think that the pitch was flat enough, and so a new grass pitch was sown in March to be ready for use in July after the ground had been levelled using lasers to get it perfectly flat! I shall also pass over the fact that the school did not benefit in any way from this privilege, financially or in any other way – I had assumed that we might be able to secure tickets for the pupils to watch some of the football games, but the only tickets offered were for matches in Manchester! I shall also pass over the fact that no-one from the school, except myself and the Bursar, was allowed to visit the training ground when teams were there – security was so tight, even more so when the USA Women's team arrived with the FBI! I did manage to take one or two still photos of the Mexican and Brazilian Men's teams in training, but only after the video I had taken for our Archives had been confiscated and erased by the LOCOG organisers! The one "perk" that the school received fell to me, I am afraid. I was invited, on the Wednesday before the Olympic Games actually commenced, to a meal at the Olympic Park with other providers of facilities. At my table were Jonathan Edwards and a couple of important GB Hockey players. After a very pleasant meal we were then all ushered into the main Athletics Stadium, and we became the audience for a Dress Rehearsal of the Opening Ceremony. On that night, I can only say that I felt so proud to be British and to have contributed in a small way in supporting the Olympics. Danny Boyle, the Director of the Ceremony, asked us all to keep what we had witnessed as a secret: I sent a message to Maryta who was working that evening at The Times, to tell her how brilliant the experience had been, but I could not give any more away. We did not have any inkling that the Queen was going to be involved as well – that was the real secret! All of us who were there that night knew how special the whole event was going to be. I was equally delighted when the school was then able to secure tickets for some of our pupils to attend the Paralympics later in September.

As the calendar year moved to its completion, we arranged the final anniversary event to balance the very first event held in the College Chapel. Instead of our annual Christmas Carols by Candlelight Service in the Chapel, I asked the Chaplain and the Director of Music to plan our final religious service of the year at Southwark Cathedral. Members of our community of all ages and backgrounds were invited to take part with readings and musical performances, and I hoped that as many people as possible would be able to attend – in fact, we decided that there should be two Services, one held in the afternoon primarily for members of the current school community, and another in the evening so that former pupils and parents who would be working during the day could attend. The setting may have lacked the intimacy of the College Chapel, and there is no doubt that using only candles to light that smaller building has always helped create a special atmosphere; but to fill the magnificent setting of the Cathedral with such joyful singing will be a memory to last for a long time for all who attended the services. One new carol had been specially commissioned from Tarik O'Regan, and the brass accompaniments to the descants of *O Come All Ye Faithful* and *Hark the Herald Angels*, were most uplifting. All the sleepless nights, caused by the logistics of getting the children to and from Southwark safely, were certainly all worth it.

When the end of the year arrived, in the final assembly, it was important to highlight the year's memories. I wanted to remind the pupils that we had not only celebrated the past 100 years, but also had acknowledged our achievements in the life of the current school.

"Everyone has some talents, whether it is as a mathematician, a historian, as a singer or an athlete. What I hope that you can all feel with confidence is that as a pupil of Eltham College you have been encouraged to push yourself with that talent and to go as far as you are able. You should be proud of what you can achieve. We are all members of a community which looks out for each other – we celebrate what each of us can do and together we can achieve even more. I look forward to the future when ideas, as yet undreamed of, can be nurtured and can flourish in such a way to encourage others to admire and want to be part of our success."

I found it difficult to sleep well that night, for I was still wrapped up in the positive emotions of the day, with the singing from our Chapel Service still ringing in my ears and the blood still racing around my body remembering such a positive celebratory year.

A Lady with two Lords (Knight and Puttnam).

Patricia, Eric Liddell's daughter, presenting prizes at Sports Day while being filmed by BBC Scotland.

22 - *The Hobbit - who just wanted to be remembered*

Vasilis had always wanted people to remember his reign for its promotion of culture: he wanted the Sultanate to be known as a seat of learning. So when he was approached by his Minister of Culture, Elithorn, he was eager to respond positively to his suggestion:

"We have nowhere that shows how we promote learning, my Lord. I hope that you will soon want to create a Library or a Museum"

"I should be very happy for this to happen, Elithorn. I am not sure we can create such an impressive Museum as the one at Alexandria, but if somewhere like Pergamum can create a Library known over the educated world, then I don't see why we can't emulate them. Perhaps we can start by offering my collection of ancient manuscripts for scholars to use in research." was Vasilis' immediate reply.

"That would be very generous, my Lord, and it will give us a tremendous start. But this will enable only a select few to benefit from your generosity – I wonder how we can find a way to encourage more ordinary people to discover the joys of learning and to celebrate their own culture."

Vasilis remained enthusiastic about the Minister's ideas, but he knew that he was in no position to finance such a project. Despite this he felt that it would be worth finding out how much would be needed to build a suitable library building, and so he asked Elithorn to find an architect who might be able to design a building. Although he did not want to discourage the Minister too much, he anticipated that anything presented to him would be far too expensive and he would then have to put the plans in 'moth balls'.

Sure enough, the first set of plans was truly magnificent and included halls for the storage of manuscripts, rooms for lectures, and even outdoor areas for the presentation of plays. However, Vizier Jafar had been swift in dismissing the proposal as being far too expensive. Vasilis urged Elithorn to try to reduce the scale of the project to a less expensive size. When the next proposals were presented again they met the same response – "We just cannot afford such a project at present."

Meanwhile Elithorn had suffered several nights of sleep filled with strange dreams. All he could remember clearly from these dreams was a small human-like creature reading a series of adventures to him.

Although Elithorn knew that Vasilis appeared supportive of the whole project, he appreciated that, unless the money could be found from somewhere or someone else, it was never going to happen. His dreams had given him an idea about who might help pay for the building.

Elithorn went to the Keeper of Records and asked him to search through his records to see if there was anyone in the Sultanate who was famous for writing books. After only a few days, the Keeper of Records presented Elithorn with his list: it was not very encouraging.

"I cannot find any record of a successful author living in the Sultanate. The only reference I can find to anyone of that inclination is to a young Hobbit, whose family had been told to leave the Sultanate a few years ago because his father owed the State lots of money; the story is that this Hobbit joined some adventurers on a quest to a distant land, and then recorded his adventures in a series of books."

"Where is he now?" asked Elithorn.

"He returned to the Sultanate and became a successful alchemist, living in a small town some distance from the city." replied the Keeper of Records. "It seems that the Hobbit always considered himself a great author, but I have never read his books."

Elithorn became excited. "I must seek him out. Perhaps he will be the answer to my plans."

No sooner had the Keeper of Records provided Elithorn with the relevant information, than the Minister presented his plan to Vasilis. The Sultan was intrigued and allowed Elithorn to travel with some of the Palace Guards to seek out the Hobbit, whose name was Merry. It was over a month before he returned. Much to Vasilis' surprise he returned not with the Hobbit, but with three large manuscripts.

"These are a gift from the Hobbit, and an indication that he wants to help with our Library." explained Elithorn. "The Hobbit is a prolific writer and has much work which he wants to put into a Library. Although these three manuscripts are not by him, they were given to him by a relative who was grateful for Merry's help in his adventures. The Hobbit's own books are not as readable, or as well-written, as these manuscripts, but I think we can strike a bargain whereby he will help pay for the Library, if we agree to accept some of his work. He seems to have a lot of gold!"

Vasilis accepted the manuscripts and decided to read them as quickly as possible: they told the adventures of a small party who set out on a quest to find some lost treasure; they faced a number of challenges along the way (which is why there were three manuscripts) and returned triumphant and much wiser than they had been at the start of the adventure. Vasilis enjoyed the tale and felt encouraged by the quality of the writing. However, he remained unsure about Elithorn's proposal.

"What does this Merry fellow want from us?" asked Vasilis.

"He wants the Library to house all his written work, as well as having his name on the outside of the building." replied Elithorn.

"And what will we get out of this?" "A Library......" "So, what are his books like?"

"Those I have read so far are pretty difficult, full of horror and empty of happiness; I suppose it reflects much of Merry's own unhappy life." Elithorn admitted.

Vasilis was not encouraged by this assessment but he agreed to accompany Elithorn, along with Princess Shirin, on a visit to see the Hobbit, to get a better idea of how serious the Hobbit was about paying for the Library. He lived in a very rural part of the Sultanate, with his house tucked into a hillside. The first thing Vasilis and the Princess saw was the garden, full of flowers and birds singing. Merry emerged from his home to greet them and ushered them into his house for a welcoming drink. Everyone, except the Hobbit, had to stoop as they stepped over the threshold – the Hobbit was no more than four feet tall, and therefore high ceilings were not a major requirement. Immediately Princess Shirin felt as though she had stepped into the Grand Bazaar – there were countless curios on the walls and shelves: there were many striking paintings of unrecognisable animals, as well as leather-bound books and manuscripts.

The afternoon was spent sitting beside a fire listening to Merry giving an account of his life – his unexpected exile with his penniless father, as well as his quest to find hoards of gold with the troupe of adventurers. He had eventually decided to take his life seriously and trained himself in alchemy; he had rented rooms in an important part of the foreign city where he hoped to work, and made many friends with those who lived around him. This included many authors who had encouraged him to keep writing his tales as a means of clearing his mind of some of the unpleasant experiences he had had as a child and a young man. As a result his books, whose genre he described as "grotesque", featured innocent children struggling to survive in a harsh world dominated by cruel adults, wild animals fighting to establish supremacy in a human world and many other tales with suffering at their heart. Vasilis was secretly worried that this collection of books was not going to be appropriate in his centre of learning. However, the Hobbit had a definite charm and Vasilis hoped that there would be a more positive side to his books as yet undiscovered.

Merry then went on to explain how he had become a particular friend of a wise old man who lived in the house next to him. It turned out that this old man suffered from a terrible disease, which Merry had tried very hard to cure through his alchemy. When he could not save him, Merry did his best to make what was left of his life more comfortable. It was inevitable that he would die, but on his death bed he had told Merry of a pile of gold concealed within a cave. This cave was home to a large dragon who had over the years hoarded the gold: the old man had explained how to get into the cave and how to distract the dragon while removing some of the gold. This was obviously the key to Merry's wealth and so Vasilis and the Princess were eager to learn more. Not surprisingly Merry refused to reveal many details about this adventure, only referring to his friends who had helped find the cave and distract the dragon. It was obviously an extraordinary adventure and Vasilis expressed the hope that Merry would eventually write it down as one of his stories; but the Hobbit admitted that he did not want to tell too many people of the source of his wealth for fear that others would find the cave and the gold for themselves. Moving on from this, Merry confessed that as a result of his new-found wealth, he no longer needed to work at his alchemy, and to add to his luck, he shortly afterwards had married his wife, Belladonna.

Vasilis and Shirin were intrigued by this small creature and the stories he told. It was hard to know what to believe and what not to. Merry clearly had a level of charm that quickly won people over but Vasilis was not sure how genuine he was about building the Library. He pressed Merry about financing the Library project. Merry's response was clear:

"All I really want is for the Library to have my name on it – The Merry Library!"

The irony of this name was not lost on Vasilis given the very un-merry nature of the Hobbit's books!

"I also want you to have all my books on the shelves at all times." insisted Merry.

Vasilis continued to have grave reservations about this demand, but he felt sure that it could be managed somehow without it being a risk to the reputation of the Library.

"I shall find an architect: he will design a building which you can have built and I will pay for everything in that design." promised the Hobbit.

"Surely this sounds too good to be true?" thought the Sultan.

Sure enough it was too good to be true. It soon became apparent that Merry had a limited amount of funds that he had set aside for this project, and so whenever he found an architect in the city who drew up plans for a gallery, the projection of costs was always too high. Clearly Merry did have considerable wealth, but he wanted to keep a large part of it in case he died before his wife - he was many years older than Belladonna and he was determined to ensure that she was looked after once he died. Secondly, Elithorn and Vasilis were determined that the Library should house as many manuscripts and books as possible: these were a greater priority than Merry's own work, and so time and money had to be dedicated to their acquisition. Meanwhile many journeys to visit Merry and Belladonna were required to convince him that if the

Library was to be a success, it was important to have a wide range of work in it:

"If this is going to be a genuine centre of learning to rival the other great Libraries known to man" explained Vasilis, "it is essential to have as wide a range of authors as possible." Belladonna, who always had a very positive outlook on these matters, was Vasilis' chief ally in convincing Merry to think of a building housing more books than just his own. She could see that Vasilis and the Minister were working to help create something of which Merry would be proud, and she kept reassuring him that it would be worth it in the long run.

However, the building was never going to be built until an architect was found who could design a building to match Merry's financial commitment. A number of years passed and a number of raised hopes were dashed, so that everyone was beginning to despair about the project ever happening:

Belladonna remained the most positive, and it was she who found an architect who agreed to design a building of which Merry would approve and to do so within Merry's budget – Vasilis always wondered how Belladonna had persuaded the architect to accept the commission! Whatever the story was, Merry was indeed happy with the simple design produced by an architect. It had two storeys with large spaces in which to store books. Merry had hoped to have a building which made an artistic statement as a building, but he was convinced that this simple design would work, especially when he saw that his name would feature in large letters over the entrance.

The Vizier secured the services of a local set of workmen and work started eight years after the initial idea had been mooted. Vasilis was relieved to see the footings being dug and he hoped that the people would be happy with the eventual outcome. Building projects never seemed to run to plan: the first problem was when they discovered an old well which had been under the site of the building, and an intricate form of foundations had to be created to ensure that the building would not sink – a sort of stone raft!

Vasilis tried to keep Merry away from the problems which beset every construction project because he did not want him to be upset, and possibly withdraw his money. Meanwhile the Minister of Culture had appointed an official to be in charge of the Library: unfortunately, this only added to the problems, as this official wanted to change a great number of things during the construction period. Both the official and Elithorn saw the Library as a building which would stimulate great minds to think, so they were keen to have spaces set aside for just that, thinking. Vasilis could not deny that this was a good idea, but while they all talked about "space to think", no-one fully appreciated the financial impact that these changes would have on the building design. Vasilis hoped to convince Merry to contribute more to the overall cost because of the increased reputation the Library might enjoy.

Notwithstanding these construction issues, the most difficult problem that arose during the construction period was the newly-appointed official's hostility to Merry's writing, saying that he would not even put his manuscripts on the shelves. Then there were rumours that the Librarian was distantly related to Jafar, the Vizier – these were false as it turned out, but it was a sign that he did not have the support of those working on the project - Vasilis soon decided that this official would have to go. Vasilis had to act quickly before Merry became aware of this problem, and so he persuaded Elithorn to accept the role of overseeing the Library for its first two years. He had been part of the whole scheme from the start, and had established a good relationship with both Merry and Belladonna. Vasilis was sure that this would be the only way to give the Library a positive start to its life.

The final issue was to resolve the cost of the building: when the builders had finished, the Vizier was surprised that the cost had increased by nearly a third from the initial figure quoted. Elithorn explained the modifications during the construction would have a significant effect on the reputation of the Sultanate, attracting great thinkers and scientists to the city. Merry paid what he had initially agreed, but refused to give any more. Much to Vasilis' relief the Vizier went away, and found a way to fund the remaining costs: he emptied the State coffers of any surplus that he had set aside for a "rainy day". Vasilis just hoped that this decision was not going to haunt him in the future.

The Grand Opening of the Merry Library took place ten years after it had initially been proposed. Merry had his name on the outside of the building in large green letters, and his own manuscripts were to be found on shelves next to the stories of other great adventurers. Merry himself found another hobbit, Pippin, whose reputation as a writer was also apparently significant, to come and cut the ribbon – although Vasilis had never heard of him, and this "author-friend of Merry" seemed more interested in the wine during the Opening Reception. Everyone who came was impressed by the building and Elithorn was able to talk confidently about plans to expand the collection of books every year so that as many people would have the chance to read all the most famous authors. Intriguingly, and much to everyone's surprise, Merry's own tales proved rather popular, which only goes to show how difficult it is to judge what appeals to the man in the street.

Vasilis was extremely relieved that the project had been completed and hoped that he would now be able to enjoy more sleep, confident in the knowledge that Merry was happy and that the Library would enhance the Sultanate's reputation for being a centre for learning.

But life can never be predicted and almost as if it had been taken from one of Merry's tales tragedy fell shortly after the opening of the Library. Belladonna became very ill and she died most unexpectedly within two months. No-one had anticipated this, least of all Merry who was at least twenty years older than her. In fact, there had been much discussion about how Belladonna had hoped to help in the running of the Library when Merry died: her positive outlook on life would have been a welcome addition to the librarians. In her final weeks, she confessed to Vasilis that when she had found the architect she knew that he had had no experience in designing such a building before – his work until that point had been on small houses – but with her typically generous spirit she had believed that he would be able to design something that worked in the end. Vasilis was unsure how to take this information!

Vasilis and Princess Shirin were upset for Merry as he faced his final years alone in his house under the hill. He may have achieved what he had always wanted, but the latter part of his life had been together with Belladonna, and they feared that he would be lost without her. They promised to visit him often in an attempt to keep the dark lonely nights at bay!

The Vizier had readily agreed to using the State funds for the completion of the Library, especially as he did not feel that he had been responsible for the increased cost. However, he made it clear that the consequences of depleting the Treasury in this way were far reaching: the Sultan would not be in a position to initiate any other developments within the Sultanate until he, Jafar, had created the means whereby the funds might be recovered. Vasilis felt uncomfortable at being so reliant on the Vizier's good offices!

23 - Large enough to excel, small enough to.....

Schools used to be full of teachers, and one of the Head's most important tasks was to appoint good new teachers, full of ideas and fresh from different experiences. Of course, it was important to maintain the ethos of the school by keeping a critical mass of experienced teaching staff as well; and the Bursar looked after the appointment of cleaners and caterers, maintenance staff and ground staff. But the focus of every school was teaching and learning.

Not now. In the age of competition and parental choice, all schools need to show how well they perform compared with their rivals; they need to 'market' the school through websites and social media, and they need to attract 'customers' through a 'Unique Selling Point' – USP. The world of Marketing and Public Relations is big business and you risk being left behind if you don't buy into it. Very few Headteachers have any experience in this world and while common sense can enable you to keep your head above water, it won't let you swim out in front of your competitors. And then you realise that you need to enlist the help of your Alumni, either as general supporters of the school, or more likely as financial supporters of the school. So the world of Alumni Relations and fund-raising opens its doors, and it is clear that the school's records or Archives need to be kept more up to scratch than they had been. The result is the appointment of more staff who have nothing to do with teaching!

Inevitably the Governors and I had ambitions for the school: to extend the academic reputation of the school we needed to offer scholarships and bursaries to attract strong candidates and not lose them to our rivals; at the same time, some of the facilities were extremely tired (the Chapel) or too small (the dining-hall), not to mention the lack of facilities for music. All these proposals cost money, and the school did not have any fund which could be ring-fenced for such developments. It did not take too much time to realise that we needed to establish a fund-raising office, which could appeal to former pupils and their parents (ie friends of the school) to donate money for various projects. I hoped that those pupils who had attended the school free of charge during its Direct Grant days might consider donating funds for bursaries, the equivalent financial help in today's terms. At the same time it was hoped that existing parents might contribute to smaller projects to improve some of the physical aspects of the school during their son's (or daughter's) time.

The appointment of our first Development Officer was not a huge success, I must confess. First of all, the field of applicants was not large: lots of educational institutions were aiming at the fund-raising market, and schools more famous than ours as well as universities had commanded the market, although I am not convinced that they all achieved much success. John's background was from working in the private Higher Education sector, and his experience looked as though he knew his way around the whole fund-raising experience. In truth, he talked a good game, but he found that we had little of the basic building blocks in place for him to work with – records of our alumni were adequate without being full of information, and our school Archivist (a retired member of staff) was most interested in the records of the school over 100 years ago.

John did subscribe to the philosophy that "friend-raising" needed to take place before any successful fund-raising could be introduced, and parents were invited to events aimed at promoting the Development Office work – but hardly anyone turned up, presumably fearing that they were going to be asked to cough up money. Similarly former pupils did not know who this man was, inviting them to "drinks" up in town, and only a few stragglers appeared when they were told that some current members of staff, whom they might know, were going to be present. After a reasonably successful 'auction of promises' event was held, the second attempt to raise funds was a huge embarrassment: parents and friends of the school were invited to a "Night at the Dogs" at a local greyhound stadium. Not all Governors were happy that the school founded by Christian Missionaries was relying on a gambling event to raise funds. Notwithstanding this objection, tickets were sold on a 'sponsor a race and you get a table to yourself in the smarter end of the stand' basis. John spent a considerable amount of time seeking sponsors and eventually all ten races were covered. However, not everyone appreciated that if you had not become a sponsor you were relegated to watching the races with the "hoi polloi"! On the night there were many disgruntled parents and some governors who left feeling like second-class citizens. It was not a success, and it was not long before John was applying for jobs elsewhere.

Trying to learn from this, and after listening to other Heads' experience, I turned back to the existing staff at Eltham College. Simon had been Head of Physics, Head of Science, a rugby and cricket coach, and was currently Director of Studies, designing the timetable. His personable and outgoing nature combined with his length of service at the school were good indicators that he would be able to manage the "friend-raising" really well, and I was fairly sure he would be able to learn the fund-raising aspect, particularly with the help of one of our governors (who had some experience of it within the University of London), and from other professionals. While I was not sure that he really wanted to give up his teaching role, he was happy to step back from the timetable, but insisted that he could continue initially coaching the 2nd XV. I have to say that it was one of my best appointments during my time at Eltham: Simon was a natural at rebuilding the bridges which had been damaged in our first clumsy attempts to woo donors, and he established a number of regular alumni events, both formal and informal which attracted former pupils to attend and enjoy themselves reminiscing about their time at the school. He eventually introduced 'Breakfast Meetings with the Senior Team' for existing parents as we moved forward to explain our grand plans for further development of the site: hardly anyone turned down the invitation to attend!

Shortly after establishing himself in the role of Development Director, Simon introduced an annual Telethon Campaign to interest alumni in donating towards bursaries and specific school projects. He recruited recent leavers from the school to be trained in calling OEs to talk about what had been going on at the school and then to try to get donations however small from them. All those who were contacted had received a letter warning them and inviting them to indicate if they did not want to be bothered by us; I did not want to be accused of just cold-calling OEs. Simon's team were trained by a professional company who had much experience in this approach, and quickly a healthy annual fund was established through these sessions.

In order to assist Simon's task to identify suitable supporters of the school, it was necessary to work through the lists of former pupils and to establish what they were now doing. Again we used a company to improve the data we had on our alumni, but what this emphasised was that the role of Archivist could be far more significant in helping our relations with the alumni. So, shortly after Simon was established in post as Development Director, the then Archivist decided to step down from the role, and I was required to recruit. After finding someone who we thought would manage the role, I was approached by a former member of staff who had left Eltham to work as a Civil Servant. He had been a very positive Head of German whilst at Eltham, and he had recently returned to the German Department as their part-time Language Assistant. Simon quickly encouraged me to reconsider my appointment as Archivist. As luck would have it the gentleman to whom I had offered the job had an illness which meant that he was not prepared to work the amount of time we had hoped. It was one of those moments of pure luck and serendipity: Mark was just the right man for the job – he knew the school, was fascinated by history and detail, and was also keen on first class cricket! We got on really well, and he became an essential part of the Alumni Relations Team, supporting Simon with historical details for OE events and identifying important OEs who might support us. When we celebrated our Centenary at Mottingham, his contribution was to put together the wonderful historical review in the book "Our Century".

Meanwhile, the SMT and I decided that at Eltham we needed to appoint someone to help us with marketing the school. Fortunately we discovered that a parent of a boy in the Junior School was a Marketing Consultant, and she agreed to conduct some research through a number of 'focus groups' to help identify our USP. I suspect we would all have accurately identified how important academic results and discipline were to prospective parents. Pastoral care and the wide range of extra-curricular activities at a successful level were also seen as important. The fact that we were mainly a boys-only school mattered to most, although a certain number of those questioned liked the fact that we introduced girls into the Sixth Form – there was no desire for a complete co-educational school. What did come over strongly from the research was the importance of our size – we were not too large, and parents felt that their children were therefore able to thrive as individuals and not get lost in the crowd. Similarly parents liked the image of a local school, with children coming from a limited distance radiating from Mottingham. As a result of this research, our consultant suggested that we should adopt a 'strap-line' for all our publications: "Large enough to excel, small enough to care". Although it sounded rather cheesy (and one Governor really did not like it) it was felt that it was a fair definition of our USP, and we included it on our website and other forms of communication. Ironically, I subsequently found an Undertakers' firm using the same catchphrase!

The internet has become the first point of contact for most prospective parents, and the creation of a new short film to introduce the school was commissioned. The company we recruited were keen to get into the Independent School market and they tried very hard to respond to the emphasis we wanted. We eventually agreed to a film that travelled up through the different stages of school life. Every clip was accompanied by a voice-over from a member of staff or preferably a pupil. But the most striking element of the whole film was the linkage between the five or six different clips – a ball being kicked into the air became a chemical ball falling into a saucer as part of an experiment; an umpire's finger giving a cricketer out became the finger of a conductor in front of a choir; a Sixth Former writing notes in the Library became me as Headmaster writing a pupil's report. Everything flowed smoothly and with a touch of charm. We decided to show a slightly longer version at our Open Mornings, just to remind those parents who had come to visit the school how clever we were!

Open Mornings are seen as the most important opportunity to influence both children and parents before they decide to which school they are going to apply. I had spent a lot of time watching one of my mentors, Andrew, as he spoke to the assembled groups who had booked tours around St Albans School over six different days during the academic year. I quickly decided that although Eltham was in just as competitive an area as North London, six Open Mornings were too many - something I am sure the teachers were relieved to hear. After I had been appointed to Eltham I was able to come to an Open Morning before taking up office. It certainly helped me get a feel for the place and some of the staff, one of whom did not impress me - I walked into his room and found him sitting with his feet up on the desk. Needless to say, he moved to another school shortly after I arrived in South London!

The Marketing Consultant's research indicated that parents liked my personal touch of greeting the children on the foot of the school steps as they arrived, and this helped confirm the idea that we were interested in the children first. I visited one Prep School where the Head said that he was interested only in interviewing the mothers of prospective pupils – I presumed he felt that he would discover how supportive they would be, but that seemed to give the wrong emphasis to me. Before my first Open Morning I had performed my speech to the SMT to gauge their reaction – their silence was deafening! As a result, I decided to suggest that I was improvising by tearing up this speech and reminding the audience that I had been a parent and tell them about those things I had thought important when choosing a school. Over the years, I decided to involve pupils more and more – they had been there initially but I gave them more opportunity to perform. I even threw balls and other significant items (chess pieces, CDs, camping equipment) for them to catch to show how wide an extra-curricular programme we ran, while emphasising that we aimed to stretch everyone – the throws became more challenging and varied! Yes, it was a gimmick, but the feedback we received was that it was both convincing and, what was most important, most memorable!

In truth, the real successes of our Open Mornings were the pupils who acted as guides and the staff who ran stimulating sessions in their subjects for our visitors. Anyone who visited Eltham should have left feeling engaged and would have had an opportunity to have talked to children, teachers and the Senior Management. The presence of the School Nurse reinforced our image of being a caring institution, and she was indeed an important member of the Pastoral Team. Our new Marketing staff were able to show that we had a high rate of transfer from a visit to a registration. The idea of emphasising the personal touch was replicated in our Sixth Form Open Evening where we tried very hard to allocate guides who were already studying the A levels that a prospective candidate wanted to consider – who better to consult about what the courses and teachers were like?

The final recommendation that our Consultant put forward was that I should enter the world of Twitter. I was initially shocked at the idea that I would have anything of value to say once a week never mind once a day. I know that Twitter has become the method of communication of choice for many now, but in 2007 it seemed radical. It should have been no surprise as to how easy it was to find something positive to say about the school, and by the end I was sending out more than one tweet a day. The other surprise was that our consultant left us when her son was attracted to a rival independent school: I wondered how soon some the ideas she had suggested to us would appear over in Croydon!

Before she departed from our scene, I enlisted our consultant's help in appointing a full-time Marketing and PR Manager. Rachel seemed ready for the challenge of Eltham College, although whether we were ready for her was another matter. I did not expect that the first area to receive her attention was the fonts used in all our correspondence. I suspect that it is an easy target when any new Marketing Manager moves in: not so easy on the budget when you have to change all the letterheads, and ensure that the school crest used throughout the school literature and signage all conform to the corporate style. Anyway once we had moved on past this,

Rachel wanted us to look very carefully at the images we used in advertising. And she was absolutely right. Given that we had now adopted the "Large enough to excel...." strapline, the question was how could we incorporate that into the images promoting the school in the local press? The short answer was we could not. However, what we could do was show how we expected our children to have a go at everything. Therefore, images of a hockey goalkeeper playing the saxophone, a timpanist performing whilst in his rugby gear, an actor dressed as Henry V conducting a chemistry experiment, and others in similar vein were professionally produced to great effect. Suddenly our message to an enquiring public looked innovative and intriguing. So perhaps this marketing idea was worth it.

Of course, the cost of all these additional support staff was not insignificant. The Governors wanted the role of Development Director to pay for itself through the funds raised, but one Governor appreciated that it would take time to establish the whole fund-raising process and agreed to underwrite the costs of the Development Director for the first two years. It was still a few more years before the whole Development Office (this included two assistants/secretaries as well as Simon and Mark) could claim to be covering its own costs, especially once bequests from OE wills began to be provided. As for the Marketing and PR Office, Rachel and her assistant worked tirelessly on Open Mornings, Newsletters, Press Releases, Social Media and the website, as well as helping Departments like Art to promote the Gallery once it was built. We did receive more applications as a result of the increased awareness prospective parents had about the school, but I cannot confirm whether more parents accepted places at the school because of the marketing of the school, or because it was just the right fit for their child.

Lessons learnt

Schools no longer just employ teachers and ancillary staff (like cleaners and technicians), but as a business they need to have staff to help support the teachers and the whole community.

If you keep the idea of the community to the fore, then everyone will want to support it.

Hockey goalkeeper playing the saxophone.

24 - *The Genie: are there always three wishes?*

Many rival Sultans observed with admiration what Vasilis had achieved over the years of his reign: his people were creative in music, songs, and plays which reflected how happy they were in their lives. In turn, Vasilis looked enviously at his various neighbours' wealth enabling them to build impressive Palaces and Temples. He was sure that their names would be remembered in history for the marble used in such buildings. Princess Shirin tried to reassure her husband:

"Your name will be remembered for our people's creativity and happiness, as well as by all those who enjoyed the benefits of a prosperous and peaceful life under your leadership."

Vasilis accepted the fact that his country was not a rich land: it grew enough crops to feed its population and merchants were always able to sell their goods in the markets and bazaars of the towns and the city. Many visitors visited the land to enjoy the festivals and admire cultural life of its people. However, as the Vizier never failed to remind him the Treasury was never going to be able to afford major construction projects.

"What we need is a genie to find us some gold!" joked Vasilis, always hoping that such a miracle might be just around the corner.

On the borders of the Sultanate, next to the Sun Temple Precinct and Meadow, was a second enclave of land which was under the control of the Hospitallers of Pan, the God of the countryside. For many years, the Sultanate had enjoyed a very close relationship with the Hospitallers: there were no barriers between the two lands and many visitors to the Sultanate even believed that the Hospitallers' land was ruled by Vasilis as well. The Hospitallers' Creed was to offer opportunities to young people to experience the countryside without any barriers or controls put in their way. However, there was little evidence of any activity on this land. It was clear to close observers that very few took the opportunity to embrace this Hospitallers' laudable goal, and as such the land itself was beginning to appear abandoned and neglected. Therefore, it was no surprise to Vasilis when Vizier Jafar came to him with further news, this time about the Hospitallers:

"They want to offer their land to someone with sympathy towards their beliefs, and they are encouraging us to consider this proposal."

Adding this second enclave to the Sultanate would further increase the prestige of his land, but this time it was Vasilis who was anxious about over-extending the limited coffers of his Treasury: "I cannot see that we could accept the land without the Hospitallers expecting some financial arrangement, and we just do not have the funds available."

"I do not think that we could even recover any of our money once the Hospitallers are satisfied. We will have to spend a lot of gold just to create something that would give us anything in return." agreed the Vizier, always with an eye on future profit. With these doubts hanging over them, neither Vasilis nor Jafar felt comfortable about accepting any deal with the Hospitallers. However, they both remained anxious that some rival Sultan might step in and make an arrangement with the Hospitallers, causing long term difficulties for Vasilis.

Much to their surprise, Vasilis eventually learnt that the land had been acquired by a consortium of merchants, and he experienced a number of sleepless nights worrying about what they intended to do with the land. Despite what the Hospitallers had hoped, it soon became apparent that the merchants' plans centred entirely on making money, and this would mean the destruction of the peace and calm associated with the

Hospitallers' Creed. However, the merchants could not agree amongst each other – some wanted to build large sheds where animals could be stored for food, and others wanted to flatten the land to grow crops, whilst another group wanted to build many caravanserais, or hostels, all over the land for visitors to use. Although Vasilis was relieved that a rival Sultan had not acquired the land, he remained sceptical that the merchants would ever agree on how to make money from the land. For the next few months Vasilis' scouts were ever present on the border keeping an eye out for developments. Apart from the clearing of a small area near to the border, there seemed to be no obvious activity on the land: this area was apparently designated for one of the caravanserais, but the tentative activity came to a rapid halt once the Hospitallers discovered that their land was being developed beyond the terms of their agreement. Vasilis and the Vizier often met to observe the lack of progress on this land, and they both remained confused as to why the Hospitallers had agreed to let the merchants have use of their land.

Vasilis could not believe the news when the Vizier met him for their regular meeting: the Vizier, wearing a smile wider than usual, announced "The Hospitallers have just told me that they are recovering their land from the consortium of merchants. It seems that the merchants have not agreed amongst themselves on how to develop the land, and the Hospitallers now realise that the merchants are only interested in using the land for personal gain."

"I don't suppose the Hospitallers are very pleased." Vasilis said.

"They are definitely not pleased, and they would like us to consider accepting responsibility for their land."

"I don't know why they didn't ask us in the first place! It is a great chance to make sure no-one else can get their hands on this land, but what do they want in return?"

"The Hospitallers will be happy if the land is just cared for: they want someone to maintain and preserve its beauty and natural charm."

Vasilis was lost for words. He suspected that the Vizier had some scheme to make profit from this proposal, but he was delighted that he was being given the chance to secure another buffer on his land's borders. At the same time, he appreciated the Hospitallers' desire to honour Pan's countryside in an appropriate way.

"I assume that you do not need to wait for my answer." Vasilis finally said to the Vizier, who was already heading out of Vasilis's throne room to draw up the documents to confirm this arrangement. He was still wearing a very broad smile!

Of course, after acquiring the Hospitallers' land, Vasilis and the Vizier were quick to realise the challenges facing them. The land needed care and attention; it was not good agricultural land, and that was clearly not a route the Hospitallers wanted pursued. The only buildings anywhere on the land were two stable-blocks for use by those who wanted to explore the countryside on horseback. This had never been a popular activity, and so the buildings had gradually fallen into disuse. Vasilis was determined to keep the land as the Hospitallers had hoped, and he decided that he needed something else to make a visit to this land more attractive. His first thought was to turn the stable block area into a really welcoming caravanserai, so that visitors could have somewhere comfortable to stay and rest before or after enjoying their visits to the wild countryside. He was sure the Hospitallers would approve of that. But where was he to find the money to transform these stables?

Princess Shirin was delighted with the Hospitallers' land. As she spent hours walking over its hills and through its valleys, she learnt to enjoy its beauty, and she encouraged Vasilis and other members of the Court to visit it regularly. She was enraptured by the rolling hills, punctured by jagged escarpments; she would happily sit on the shore of its lake, listening to the silence broken only by the chirruping of the birds and the wind in the trees. There was nothing that she enjoyed more than walking by the streams which trickled along the valleys down to the shoreline, accompanied by her dog, Argus. Argus would cover many miles, sniffing out rodents and rabbits, but always staying within sight of the Princess. Unfortunately, Argus was no longer a young dog and the trips on the Hospitallers' land gradually took its toll. On one excursion by the lake, Argus did not come back when the Princess called him: she eventually found him lying at the foot of an escarpment, exhausted from a chase of some small deer. Princess Shirin had to fetch some Guards to help her carry Argus back to the Palace. He never recovered and passed away a few days later. His death cast a shadow over the whole Palace, and the Princess felt that she had lost one of her closest friends. Such was her grief that she found it difficult to go back to the Hospitallers' land.

Vasilis shared his wife's grief and decided that he should try to find a way of remembering Argus, beyond a simple burial within the Palace grounds. He hit upon the idea of building a Mausoleum in memory of the dog, on the Hospitallers' land, close to where Argus had been found on that fateful day. He asked the High Architect to design something appropriate and he talked to Jafar about how he would pay for this mausoleum. Vasilis knew that Jafar intended to use the money, collected from the Pride of Lions for their use of the Sun Temple Meadow, for the caravanserai on the Hospitallers' land. But he wondered if there was any other money stored away "for a rainy day".

Like Vasilis, Jafar had been relieved with the acquisition of the Hospitallers' land. However, he was not able to help the Sultan with his request. The Treasury was just not able to fund the construction of any other buildings; if a mausoleum was to be built, he suggested that the money would have to come from Vasilis' own funds. But Vasilis did not have the funds to build anything that matched his vision.

Some years previously, Alibaba had arrived in the City, and his success as a merchant was legendary amongst the Court; although it remained a mystery how Baba, as he was more commonly known, actually had made so much money - one day he was just an ordinary silk-trader and the next he had become one of the wealthiest men in the City. Jafar had instructed his agents to find out as much as possible about Baba: where had he come from? What was the source of his wealth? Very little could be discovered: he had come from a distant land and was well-known for making long journeys which lasted for at least six months. As to his wealth, all that anyone could say was that he arrived with modest success as a merchant, and then almost over-night he had begun to flaunt great wealth. Jafar feared that he may have been a thief in his former life, but could find no evidence to support this theory. The Vizier was wary of getting involved with Baba, but Vasilis took a more positive view: he had met the merchant on a number of occasions and Baba had made it clear to the Sultan that he would be happy to help his newly-adopted country in some way or other, and so, when the topic of the mausoleum for Argus came up, Baba readily offered his support.

"My Lord, if I can help you in any way - you only have to wish it, and it shall be so. The whole City has been touched by the loss of the Princess' dog and I should be more than happy to assist you in finding a way to help her remember Argus. I understand that you have instructed the Architect to design a mausoleum for Argus."

"Yes, but I wish I could find the money to build something which will be truly memorable. Any building on the Hospitallers' land must also be worthy of the God Pan." As soon as Baba heard the wish expressed, he immediately replied with the words "Your wish is my command!"

Everything then seemed to happen overnight. The Vizier, Architect and Baba rapidly reached an agreement on the design and cost for a magnificent Mausoleum, and the building was built within the blinking of an eye. No-one had ever seen such an impressive building, which consisted of a formal Pavilion providing an entrance into a courtyard with a central altar to Pan in front of an ornate marble mausoleum, housing a bronze statue of the dog Argus. The Princess was overwhelmed by the whole project: she even gave up her reluctance to visit the Hospitallers' land. Vasilis insisted that she should be the first visitor to the complex. Shirin sat alone next to a statue of Argus, looking out over the lake behind the Pavilion. Vasilis felt that he had done something worthwhile for his wife. Every evening, before the sun set, she would ride out to visit the Mausoleum and offer a prayer to Pan asking him to keep watch over the spirit of her faithful dog Argus.

What the Sultan and Baba had not anticipated was that they had created an attraction for many visitors to come to the Hospitallers' land, and crowds came to stay at the new caravanserai, with its underfloor heating, shiny tiles in the hamam (bathing areas), and spacious bedrooms for visitors. The visitors were then able to go to enjoy a visit to Argus' Mausoleum and make an offering to Pan. Vasilis was delighted that almost by accident he had found a way that this land acquired for the Sultanate had a real purpose. He realised that none of this would have been possible without the help of Alibaba, and he made sure that the silk-trader knew of his gratitude. However, Baba had asked to be kept in the background on this project – he was just pleased to have been of some assistance to the Sultan's family.

Jafar remained sceptical of Baba's motives in helping the Sultan: why did the merchant want his help on the Mausoleum to be secret? What were his motives – was he just trying to get closer to the Sultan and what was his ultimate goal? Therefore he decided to keep a close watch on his activities in and around the Palace.

In contrast, Vasilis felt that his faith in Baba had increased following his help with the construction of the Mausoleum, and dismissed his Vizier's concerns as unwarranted. Instead Vasilis had many more meetings with Baba after this. Baba's links with the Army Veterans Sports Corp soon became apparent: this group attracted many young men to play sport, and this became a most successful route for recruitment into the Army itself. Baba regularly praised the Veterans' role in training the younger members of the Corp, and he often expressed a view that they deserved better facilities in recognition of the role that they carried out for the Sultanate. Vasilis understood Baba's comments: he readily acknowledged the importance of keeping the Corp as a thriving unit; and he was forced to admit that the Corp used a decrepit old building for their training activities. However, despite the poor condition of their facilities, the Veterans were still very successful in recruiting youngsters into their Corp: hundreds of youngsters had joined up in the last year alone. In fact, they had now outgrown their home - there was insufficient space for them to occupy all those youngsters.

Vasilis (and his Vizier) soon realised that Baba was trying to persuade him to allow the Veterans Corp to move from their inadequate quarters with the new opportunities available on some of the recently acquired plots of land. The Sultan would not consider the idea of the Veterans Corp taking over any of the Hospitallers' land (now renamed the Argive Fields, after his wife's dog). However, Vasilis had always been uncomfortable with the association with the Pride of Lions, and he wondered whether moving the Veterans Corp to the Sun Temple Meadows might be more suitable. He was not surprised that Jafar was against this plan – the Vizier reminded the Sultan of the money which the Pride paid into the Treasury's coffers for the privilege of using the Temple's Meadows. But Vasilis suspected that his Vizier's close association with the Pride was more of an issue; if the Pride were to leave this land, Vasilis hoped that he would be able to get the Veterans' Corp to pay a similar sum. However, he had some concerns that the Veterans would have a very similar culture to the Pride of Lions, and moving them out of the city, particularly at a distance from the Palace, seemed a good idea. The Sultan's problem was, as always, money: would the Veterans Corp need a new range of buildings, and if so, where would the money come from to pay for that? Baba acknowledged that some of the Meadows area would need more building work to enable the Veterans Corp to train and carry out their sport more effectively. At a meeting to discuss the plans Vasilis blurted out, before he realised what he was saying, "I wish I could find the money to develop the Meadows in a way that everyone would find acceptable."

With the blink of an eye, Baba replied "Your wish is my command!"

It soon became apparent how grand Baba's plans for the Meadows were. He had obviously given it much thought already: he had great ambitions for the Veterans Corp, providing them with facilities which could be used all the year round, and he intended to create many more buildings for sports, which would be grander anything that had been seen in the Sultanate previously. Vasilis soon became worried that Baba even had his eyes on the Temple Precinct itself. The Vizier seemed more concerned about how Baba was to pay for all this, as well as what would happen to his friends, the Pride of Lions. So the Sultan and Vizier agreed that a close eye needed to be kept on Baba's proposals. As before, construction seemed to take no time at all: within weeks Vasilis could not recognise the Meadows – open meadow land had been turned into clearly defined fields with buildings to match. The Veterans quickly started their training for youngsters and the Meadows became a hive of activity. What really surprised Vasilis and Jafar was that Baba had struck a deal with the Pride of Lions, who he had allowed to stay on the Meadows in return for a fee - was this how Baba found the money to pay for the rest of the work, Jafar wondered? Rather than getting rid of the Pride of Lions, the Sultan now found that he had the Pride and the Veterans using the Meadows as partners. He was not convinced that this would be a harmonious arrangement for long!

Everyone speculated on the source of Baba's wealth; rumours even circulated that he must be a genie! If Baba was indeed a genie, then Vasilis concluded that he would only be granted three wishes in total – which meant there was only one wish left.

Vasilis and Vizier Jafar spent a lot of time debating whether to ask Baba for more money, and if so, on what to spend it? Vasilis had always wanted to improve the condition of the poor in his city, b ut to do so would require a lot of money. The Vizier was more interested in opportunities to increase the money kept in the Treasury, to cover any future lean years. They eventually agreed that they proposed to remove the slum area in the southern portion of the city and replace it with new housing and an indoor bazaar. Vasilis hoped to sell the project to Baba, the silk merchant, by emphasising the potential profit of the second element; however, if Baba was a genie, then he would be honour bound to grant Vasilis's third wish.

Vasilis decided not to take any risks and asked his wife to lay on a special banquet for Baba in recognition of all he had done for the Sultan. It seemed like a shrewd move: after a hearty meal accompanied by entertainment from the musicians and dancers of the Palace, Vasilis praised Baba and expressed his gratitude for Baba's generosity. Baba seemed happy to be the centre of attention for once:

"I have always wanted to give back to the land which has given me personal success in the past. My contribution to the development of the Veterans Corps fields has given me as much pleasure as it has benefitted our country. Furthermore who could have refused to help in honouring the memory of the Princess' faithful companion on the Argive Fields? These have been but two small gestures of my gratitude to the prosperity of the land under your rule, O my Sultan."

After this exchange of flattery from both sides, Vasilis thought the time was right for him to put forward his next proposal. Baba, the merchant, quickly grasped the possibilities a bazaar might bring, but he did not dwell too much on the slum clearance. Vasilis did not press the matter, but he was eager to announce his wish ...."I wish I had the gold to help transform this part of the city for the poor!" ....but before he could get the words out, Baba rose and announced that he was going on a long journey. "I shall be away from your land for some time – when I return we shall see if I can help you in this." - not quite what Vasilis was expecting, nor what he had hoped to hear.

No-one could give them any information about Alibaba's journey: both Vasilis and the Vizier had been surprised by Baba's announcement, and when they attempted through their various sources of information to find out more, they drew a blank. They both suspected that Baba was running short of money, especially after the amount he has showered on the Veterans Corp, but neither of them knew how he was likely to solve this problem. They both doubted that his business selling silk would bring in large profits, and they both wondered what other activity might produce the type of money that Baba seemed to have. As the days became months, speculation grew about Baba's absence: perhaps he had been captured by pirates? Perhaps he was a pirate himself and had been taken prisoner by another power? Vasilis did not mention his idea that Baba was a genie: that was pure fantasy, surely.

To add fuel to this speculation, a number of unaccounted events took place. Some large oil jars (40, to be precise) had gone missing from one of the other merchant's warehouses just about the time that Alibaba had gone on his travels. There was no obvious connection to him, but rumours began to spread. His shop stopped selling silk and began to "diversify" by selling cheaper cloth and even local pottery. Then Alibaba's wife was reported to be unwell; soon she left the city as well, apparently in an attempt to find medical help from a "wise man", she had visited in another country previously. Even the Veterans Corp did not know where Baba had gone, and without his support they were beginning to question whether they could maintain the standards he had set. After three months, Duban, the Chief of the Palace Guard, reported to Vasilis his concerns about a young man who was frequently getting himself into trouble. Aladdin was his name, and upon further investigation it was revealed that he was Alibaba's son. Like his father, Aladdin displayed great confidence, bordering on arrogance: he was heavily involved in the Veterans Corp, and that was where much of the trouble associated with him had occurred. He wanted to have his own way and was not tolerant of others who stood in his way, especially women. He was handsome and obviously talented in many activities; but he assumed too much in his dealings with others, and, because of his father, no-one was prepared to challenge him when he stepped out of line.

At last, Duban had evidence which he felt confident to use against Aladdin. It transpired that Aladdin had written a letter to a young lady in the Palace suggesting a moonlit dalliance, offering many inducements for her to attend. Either Aladdin was incredibly arrogant about his choice of lady – she was a one of Duban's cousin's daughters – or he was just stupid. The letter was passed to Duban, who instructed the young lady to respond positively, and then he set a trap for Aladdin. Before he executed the plan, however, he advised Vasilis of the situation. Not surprisingly Vasilis was horrified at Aladdin's audacity – he had heard Baba frequently talk about his son's talents, but Vasilis had never met him in person – and so he supported Duban's plan. Was Aladdin more arrogant now that his father was absent from the city? At the same time, Vasilis wondered how Baba would respond to his son's behaviour, when and if he ever returned from his travels.

Aladdin had arranged to meet the lady in the gardens of the Palace. That night there was a full moon, but Duban had disguised one of his guards to take the place of the lady. Aladdin clearly did not expect any subterfuge and was completely astonished when the guard revealed himself not to be the lady expected! Aladdin did not even try to escape, and he was arrested as soon as the meeting took place. - many other guards had been stationed at the potential escape routes, just in case he had tried to make a run for it. He confessed that he had written the letter, but asserted that he had not intended to harm the lady. Vasilis was furious that Aladdin had proposed to take advantage of one the Ladies of the Court, and felt strongly that his audacity should be punished. Not surprisingly Duban felt even more irate at the insult to one of his relatives. They agreed that Aladdin should be punished publicly to make an example of him. He was required to work at a laundry next to the slums, using his time for the good of others, and that he would only be released from such demands when it was apparent that he had learnt his lesson.

It was not long after this incident that Alibaba reappeared in the city. His wealth did not seem to be as apparent, and there was no sign of his wife: a generous view of his lack-lustre demeanour explained that he was worried for her continued poor health which was not responding to treatment. Others suggested that Baba's travels had not produced the expected increase in funds, by whatever means, and he was seriously concerned about his future. Notwithstanding this, Vasilis decided that he needed to talk to Baba about Aladdin's behaviour, and how they had decided to punish him. Baba's reaction fitted in with his overall image of stoicism:

"In many ways, I think my son has been treated too lightly: he must not be allowed to think that he can get away with any sort of misbehaviour, just because he is my son. This arrogance is intolerable! I shall impose further sanctions on his time in my home. I thank you, Sultan, for telling me personally and being honest with me about this matter."

Baba left the Palace without making any further comments about his wife or his travels. Vasilis was anxious to establish how Baba's finances stood, since he still had hopes to replace the city slums with fresh clean homes as soon as possible.

Jafar was surprised that his informants could not get to the bottom of Alibaba's activities: surely someone would know where he had been for the last months? Surely someone could be either bribed or tortured into revealing where Baba had gone and what he had done? As soon as Baba had settled back in the city, his shop began to function more successfully and the Veterans Corp regained their confidence. But it was not clear whether Baba was just a moderately successful silk merchant, or whether his fortunes had been restored to their previously high level. What seemed clear to Vasilis now was that Alibaba was certainly not a genie with three wishes to grant.

At this point in the tale, the book "One thousand and one sleepless nights" finished – a number of pages had been removed towards the end. To add to my frustration, I was never able to find another copy which might have explained what had happened to the Sultan's plans with his "Genie".

Needless to say, I never found any of these tales calming or helpful towards my insomnia: in truth, the tales seemed to have so many similarities with my own 'reign' with familiar characters and circumstances.

25 – Epilogue: The Black Hole

And so, the final year came and went. As if we were heading towards a Black Hole, everything seemed to speed up and we were no longer in control of what was happening. My successor had been appointed (with, as is the custom, almost no input from me, even though I had come across him when I was a Governor at Reigate). The plans for the development of a replacement teaching block and Sixth Form Centre were taken out of my hands and were totally redrawn by a new team. The Bursar and his wife retired to Yorkshire, and the Governors appointed his successor from the Navy.

"West Side Story" was the latest Musical to be performed to great acclaim: this was something I had encouraged as soon as I found someone (Ben) keen enough and good enough to direct them. Bernstein's music is notoriously difficult and in many ways it is as much a ballet as it is a musical, but the youngsters all rose to the challenge and brought it off brilliantly. As in previous years, the musical showed what young people can achieve by working hard together: it was one of those things that fell in line with my philosophy of an all-round education – to have members of the 1st XV rugby team singing and dancing in the chorus of an Oscar winning musical was a real triumph. And how the kids loved it – "That's the best thing I have ever done!" was commonly heard after the final curtain.

Then it was time for the final concert, ECCO Pops (this time both inside and outside the Marquee!): I had not too subtly suggested a number of my favourite pieces which Laura, the Director of Music, had graciously agreed to perform. As Laura was eight months pregnant when the concert arrived I did have a number of sleepless nights, but I had asked Geoff, a close friend and former Director of Music at a number of schools, to attend and be ready to take over the baton in case the conductor's waters broke! Fortunately his services were not needed. I was asked to repeat my performance on the anvil – well, two steel pipes – during Verdi's famous Chorus from Il Trovatore. Then we all moved outside for the finale with fireworks accompanying the orchestra's selection of John Williams' film music inside the Marquee: it was spectacular, and a lot cheaper than hiring a special outdoor stage for the whole show!

The last week arrived before I knew it: a portrait of me was unveiled in the Dining Hall, painted by a young man, Andrew, who had been a pupil during my time at Eltham and who had gone on to make his way creating artworks in various media. The whole school surprised me on the last Tuesday by turning up wearing bow ties! John (Deputy Head) and the Secretaries had done a great job keeping me unaware of this plan and I was lost for words as everyone gathered in the Chapel wearing some form of bow tie to match my own Tuesday eccentricity, which had lasted over 30 years! Two days later it was the final Assembly of the 'Henderson era': House Cups were awarded and the Chaplain referred to the school's Christian heritage, before turning to me, thanking me for my years of service and wishing me well in my retirement. I confess that as I walked out of the Chapel with the pupils all rising to applaud me I had a tear in my eye, just like Mr Chips – a teacher who in real life, W.H.Balgarnie, had begun his teaching career at the School for the Sons of Missionaries at Blackheath; he then made such an impact at my alma mater, The Leys, that a pupil (James Hilton) wrote his well-known story *Goodbye Mr Chips!* using this teacher as his inspiration for Chipping, or Mr Chips..

What next? Was retirement the right thing? I suppose you do run out of ideas after a period of time? Change is a necessary evil, but for whom? Can you anticipate how you will feel when you no longer matter? It is easy to consider that what you need is a rest and that stepping back from decision-making is a good thing. Once that decision is taken, it is right to move out of the way and allow your successor to have their way.

One thing that was clear: I did not want any more sleepless nights over the 11+ acceptances in early March. Despite the interviews with all the children and then my follow-up interviews with the parents of the boys who had done well in our Entrance Exams, the number of offers always had to exceed the number of places available. With so many candidates taking Tests to Grammar Schools as well as other Independent Schools, it was always difficult to know who would finally accept a place and who was going to go elsewhere. We would learn on the 1st March about the Grammar School offers, and although we expected replies from everyone by the end of that week, the whole process could easily drag on beyond Easter, especially with Appeals that parents would place at State Schools. As well as making a number of offers, I would have a waiting list, so that if I had ended up short of the numbers required to fill the Year Group, I would have a few candidates in reserve. Parents were anxious to get the best for their children, but I felt that some often behaved quite unreasonably withdrawing late in the day from the offer of a place, and then were surprised when I required fees in lieu of withdrawal, especially after we had set our budgets based on their acceptances.

Offers at 11+, 13+ and 16+ included Scholarships and Bursaries, and I was never totally happy with either of these. Scholarships were a reward for exceptionally talented children, but they were also a way of enticing parents to choose your school over others: every year I would be confronted by parents who wanted to barter with me over the size of the scholarship, because another school had offered more! As for

Bursaries, one could see this as an engine for social mobility, but the biggest problem was how to assess the worthiness of such an award. HMC had a formula which our Bursar's Department applied to calculate the level of such an award: it was basically Income and Assets against Expenditure. Quite frequently I found worthy candidates excluded because their parents lived in a modest South-East London house, the value of which totally undermined their qualification. I eventually tried to counter this problem by offering Community Bursaries (without the asset of a house being used in the calculation) to children who went to local school within a mile and a half radius from the school – this numbered 20 Primary State Schools! I then found that large numbers might apply, many parents of whom did not understand the system or even had to use an interpreter to conduct any interview – then, I was never sure who was telling the whole story. I would have preferred using a Home Visit with the Bursar to assess the suitability for Bursary qualification – but I never achieved this. A further issue was how the money for Bursaries was found: as a school founded by Missionaries we had no generous 'founding benefactor' and very few former pupils who were either wealthy or inclined to give money back to their school. So essentially the Bursary money came from the school's income, which meant primarily from fees paid by other parents. I was lucky that few parents questioned this – I suppose that being a Missionary school allowed us to promote the principle of this act of charity, when "charity begins at home".

The other thing that would no longer cause me sleepless nights relates to the employment of staff, particularly part-timers. Knowing whether staff can be employed for the following year is always determined by the numbers of pupils at the school and then more specifically the numbers of pupils choosing to study individual subjects; inevitably the part-time teachers are more vulnerable than full-time employees. Being able to give accurate information at an early date about the school's needs for the next academic year was not always easy; and I know that I tended to err on the side of keeping staff rather than lose them. This did not always help the school's finances, but a good part-timer can often be a greater asset than is apparent from a simple contract. However, there were a couple of occasions when I know that I was not able to make the decision in good time which caused difficulties for those staff, and I regret this. In retirement, not having to spend nights worrying about one's responsibilities to others should be a bonus.

I suspect many thought that I would have had many sleepless nights before and during the Independent Schools Inspection processes. In truth, I always viewed Inspections in a positive light – having some fellow professionals spend time in your school and then comment constructively on the pluses and minuses of the institution seemed a very good thing to me. I remained confident that the education we provided at the core of our school was admirable, but having someone else give an objective view on the school had to be a good thing. However, I will confess to being annoyed on two different occasions when the Lead Inspector decided to criticise the school for matters which would not lead to any changes; and on one of these occasions the Inspector agreed with what we had done and that she would have done the same, but she defined it as a matter of non-compliance under the ISI regulations! It made no difference to the way we managed the school, but it did appear as a blemish on an otherwise excellent report.

I cannot remember the actual moment I decided to retire, but I knew that Maryta and I had agreed that the time was right. She wanted us to enjoy more time together, and perhaps I would then be able to sleep better! The decision to retreat into the hinterland of Norfolk had made sense to us both – I had joked that I had become pretty reactionary in my old age and so

Norfolk would be a good place to go; but in reality, Norwich was familiar from our earlier time there, and we had a number of good friends who might help cushion the change of life-style for us both - but neither of us had realised how difficult it was going to be.

How do you fill your day when you don't have Senior Managers to meet, assemblies to lead, sport to cheer on and concerts to applaud? When you have spent most of your life fully engaged in a structured world, how do you create a new structure, especially with someone with whom you have not spent enough time? What I missed most was the sense of belonging, as well as, I confess, feeling important: I had not realised how important the morning greeting with the College gardeners or the College kitchen staff had been, until it was not there. I did not expect to be treated as the boss – the whole point of retreating to the country was to avoid such expectation and demands – but I missed being someone within the community.

Ironically I learnt that Norwich School needed some cover for a maternity leave in the Classics Department, and I offered my services for Junior Latin. Maryta was convinced that this would be a good bridge for me to gradually get used to life beyond school. The discovery of what it is like to be a part-timer teacher was eye-opening and I realised how many staff I had appointed might have felt – very much on the periphery! Going back to a school I thought I knew well had the added dimension of intrigue: to discover staff who had been juniors when I had left now being important senior staff 20 years on, for example! But the real shock was to learn how I felt like a nobody instead of a somebody: yes, it was obvious, but that did not make it any easier. It struck home most when I went to plays and Carol Services where previously I would have been playing a significant role: now I was hardly an extra, in whom nobody was interested. I enjoyed the teaching, and having some structure to my week. I also offered to my services to umpire school cricket matches (where I had been Master in Charge of Cricket 20 years previously), as a means of becoming more part of the community: but I never got the phone call! I even lost 15lbs in weight, probably by walking in and out of the city three times a week, and not eating school lunches! But it might have been something to do with the feeling of not being an accepted part of the community. I was not sorry I took on this work, but ironically it highlighted my change of life rather more than I had expected.

Sometime after returning to Norfolk, Dot, a close friend, suggested that I offer my experience to the Diocesan Board of Education: they were looking to recruit more ex-Heads as mentors for the 115 Diocesan Schools around the county. This seemed like a good use of my experience and time: the big attraction was that I would just be a visitor to the school with no hidden agenda - I was not an Inspector, not a Governor, nor did I come from the Local Authority. My role was just to listen to the Heads as they went through the ups and downs of their daily life at school. So instead, I became a Diocesan School Support Officer for 13 schools in South Norfolk. Two visits per year to each school plus the odd extra visit and meeting, gave me the opportunity to give something back to education as well as keeping me intellectually stimulated.

Maryta found it even more difficult. She felt totally cut off from the world she knew, and she found everything she tried to pick up frustrating and hollow. She had expected to be able to get a few nights' work at her old newspaper in Norwich, the Eastern Daily Press, where she had been the highest ranking woman in her time. However, they hardly used sub-editors to produce the paper – and it showed! She applied for an editing job at the UEA, but it probably was a formality of an advert, with someone already lined up. She kept in touch with some of her friends in London, but there was always a feeling that we had moved away. Regular riding of horses at a small local stables got her out of the house, and she became a regular visitor to an old lady in a Care Home nearby, playing Scrabble with her once a week: I am not sure who was more grumpy after those sessions, Maryta or the old lady!

A friend who was a retired GP compared coming to terms with retirement rather like going through bereavement. I think after what Maryta and I have experienced we understand this. We both found some solace in travelling to distant lands – enjoying the natural world, while trying to keep the political world at arms' length. Voyages had been so much a part of our early lives that it was only natural that we would find comfort in this together. However, this is probably just a distraction from the main issue. I had foreseen the Black Hole that lay ahead of us before the retirement, but neither of us had anticipated how hard it would be to escape from it.

Lessons learnt

After spending most of my life within school communities, the feeling of not belonging has been the hardest aspect of retirement to deal with. Not fully understanding one's strengths and weaknesses is something most of us have to face at some stage. I realise now how much I have needed to be part of a team or community – I know some would say that I only wanted to be in charge of that team, but now it comes home to me how much just having that sense of belonging has mattered throughout my life. The sentiment that 'one's school days are the happiest days of one's life' is probably even truer for me than was initially meant. And I still find it difficult to sleep.....

ULTIMA SCRIPTA

Out of the blue I received an email from the Head of Classics at the Norwich High School for Girls: she had discovered that I had done some Latin Cover Teaching for a Maternity Leave at Norwich School (her husband worked there). She was looking for some Cover during her won Maternity Leave, and wondered if I knew of anyone interested and available! Initially I was not too sure whether to offer myself, but once I met the Department and agreed with the powers that be what I would teach, I was welcomed into the world of the Girls Day School Trust.

I quickly realised that I had thrown out all my notes on Classical Civilisation, and while it was great to be asked to teach Ancient Greek, it was twenty years since I had actually performed in a classroom in that language. So I had quite a lot of refreshing of my own memory before work started in September. However, I soon found that I genuinely looked forward to discussing the depths of Virgil's Aeneid, analysing the grammar and syntax of A level Latin translations, as well as trying to get the girls learning GCSE Greek to focus on the complexities of Herodotus and Socrates. I quickly felt a sense of belonging within the community, working with colleagues in the Department, but also joining the Choral Society, and just sitting down for everyday chats in the Staff Room. The Head also invited me to assist in the first round of interviews for a new Director of Finance and Operations, which took me back to my former world of decision-making. But I found that it was the joy of working back in the classroom which made the biggest difference: that was what I had chosen to do over forty years before, and I rediscovered that feeling of helping young and eager minds to discover more. Coming back full circle to where I started worked for me, and I hope that I was able to make a difference for individual pupils once again.

Chronology II

2000 - 2014   **Eltham College**: Headmaster

        Choir tour to Rome - 2001
        Cricket tour to Grenada and Tobago - 2003
        Hockey tour to Greece - 2004
        French Exchange (25th) to Laval – 2006
        Choir tour to USA East Coast – 2006
        Eric Liddell Pilgrimage in China – 2009
        Choir tour to Venice and Verona, Italy – 2010
        School improvement trip to Kisasa, Tanzania – 2011
        Choir tour to Malta - 2011

Centenary Year of Eltham College at Mottingham 2012
        DEAS charitable trip to Borneo - 2012
        Follow-up visit to Kisasa School, Tanzania – 2013
        Spanish trip to Mexico – 2013
        Choir tour to New York – 2013
        Geology trip to Iceland - 2014

2014   **Retirement** in Norfolk:
        Diocesan School Support Officer

2014/5   Part-time Latin teacher at Norwich School

2016/7   Part-time Latin, Classical Civilisation and Ancient Greek teacher at Norwich High School for Girls

Printed in Great Britain
by Amazon